Kevin R Atkinson

Gliding
in
Lift & G-SINK

Gliding
in
Lift & G-SINK

Essential advanced techniques
for competent soaring and
confident cross-country
gliding

Kevin Atkinson

Published by KA Publications
First edition, September 2015
Printed in the United Kingdom

NOTE:

Whilst every effort has been made to ensure that the content of this book is as technically accurate and as sound as possible, the author cannot accept responsibility for any injury or loss sustained as a result of the use of this manual. If the reader is in any doubt regarding aspects of the advice contained herein he or she should discuss the issue with their instructor.

Contents

Introduction

Gliding is a unique sport because there are so many rewarding qualities within it that can give an individual a strong sense of personal achievement and success. To take part there are no age limitations and you may be anybody, young or old—even any early motion sickness can be overcome. You don't have to develop special physical strengths or follow rigorous training regimes. To stay in form you don't have to do it every day or even every week. You can fly a club glider, share in a syndicate for a few hundred pounds or you can buy an outstanding machine for a lot more. The price is essentially performance based.

Vintage gliders can give fun in equal measure and local soaring opportunities are just as rewarding. Regardless of how much you spend on your glider, the competition handicap system is extremely fair. A better glider only gives more opportunities but it won't give you a free advantage. Unlike vintage cars, vintage gliders are just as reliable as new ones and both the running costs and parts are considerably cheaper than modern machines.

You don't have to wait for the best days either. Some of the most memorable flights are flown when the weather is particularly challenging. Despite the difficulties, or perhaps because of them, you never conquer the sport, you can only strive to get better at it. Winning is not everything. You may come last on a competition day yet because it was your longest cross-country or the average speed was a personal best, the flight would be one to be celebrated. You can fly alone, with someone in a two-seater or fly as a gaggle of single-seat machines.

Then there is the view: better than any mountain climber's and a lot less stressful. There are many people, quite normal people just like you, doing quite amazing things in all types of gliders and it is why we all do it. It is truly awesome!

About the author

I recognize that I have been very privileged to fly professionally and in so many expensive bits of hardware, accumulating more than 7,500 military flying hours. During this time I have flown in a wide range of aircraft, from the Tiger Moth to the Typhoon. For the vast majority of this time I was instructing.

My flying career started in the RAF, in 1972 at the age of 20, and continued until 1993, when I retired as a squadron commander of Central Flying School, RAF Scampton, commanding a squadron of up to 45 pilots. During my latter years in the RAF I was also the CFI of the Humber Gliding club and I can assure you the latter was the more challenging job! With the anticipated prospect of working in London, flying a desk, I left the RAF and, employed by BAe Systems, trained pilots on the Pilatus PC-9 (single-engine turboprop) for the Royal Saudi Air Force.

After nine years in Riyadh I returned to the UK and, after a short sabbatical, I rejoined BAe Systems as a flying instructor at their factory at Warton, primarily teaching Qualified Flying Instructors how to fly the PC-9. This was yet another really interesting job, which I enjoyed for seven years. However, despite what may be considered by many to have been a fantastic career, if I were to reflect on what my top 50 flights have been, I can tell you that they have nearly all been glider flights!

Why I wrote this book

Primarily I want to give something back to the sport that I love! As a glider pilot with more than 40 years of experience, I spend as much time as possible in regional and national competitions as a competitor and teacher, regularly completing flights of more than five hours from a winch launch on a flat site. I have over 4,000 hours gliding including competing in standard national, open national and regional competitions since 1987 (*K21, Duo Discus, ASH 25*), teaching cross-country and competition techniques to P2s both at clubs and in competitions.

If you ask yourself how much of gliding is soaring and cross-country, you would probably suggest at least 50%. You might then be surprised

about my driving! His first piece of advice was to never aim too low in life. The second was that although the CFI had plans to send me cross country in the club's hot-ship, a *Skylark 2b*, and he would probably suggest that I do the *5 hours* at the same time (because the glider would most likely be gone for the day), I should fail! His reasoning was that once I had achieved both of these Silver legs I wouldn't get the glider for

Photo 1.1 The author's *ASH 25*, G-SINK.

that the BGA gliding instructor manual devotes less than 1% of its content to this subject. Yet for realistic progress to be made, advanced flying has to be taught.

You might also ask yourself, is gliding a team sport or an individual sport? Certainly we need fellow members to help with the finance of a glider and the gliding site, along with the various coordinated tasks that have to be achieved to get us off the ground, but once airborne we usually find that we are largely on our own.

I went first solo in a glider on my 16th birthday and cross-country shortly after my 17th. Just prior to this I had a couple of life-skill lessons. As a 16-year-old I was driving a glider pilot's car from the hangar to the launch point, when he said he would tell me two things. I expected a comment

more than 30 minutes and I wouldn't go cross-country again.

As it was, setting off quite literally with lots of enthusiasm and little more than a wing and a prayer, I failed at my first attempt through total incompetence. I was flying with a basic compass and a quarter-mil map, with no effective training. So, four years later when I joined the RAF, I had two cross-countries to my name. I vowed to be more proactive towards anything that I really wanted to do and despite being an *experienced* glider pilot I quickly realised that I had been taught very little and indeed, knew very little about flying.

Sadly it would appear that 45 years later, advanced gliding instruction has hardly changed. In fact, with the progressive development of the average private machine being quite a hot-ship compared to club trainers, the opportunity to learn and progress has probably become more difficult. In an effort to help clubs I volunteered to take on Club Coach Lead for the BGA *Aim Higher Initiative*. Some clubs are on board but whilst articles in S&G will seep out information, it would take many years to accumulate the knowledge required to make the transition from a safe solo pilot, to become a safe, competent, confident, cross-country club pilot.

Task weeks are brilliant as long as we get some good weather but it would take me until the age of 70 to cover all clubs and of course some of these only operate at weekends. Gliding is my passion and it really is the best way of flying. There is an opportunity for most glider pilots to do amazing things but first they have to be shown the way.

As a result I feel compelled and motivated to present to you this book, based on my lecture notes *Lift and G-SINK*. I have tried to avoid the geeky bits so that the information will help you progress more quickly and save you 200 aero-tows into the bargain!

The aim of this book

"When pondering all aspects that can influence success in gliding, good flying skills and technique emerge as the basis. If basic training is well organised, 80% of the trained population can achieve the level of proficiency necessary to win any competition."

The above is a quote from Sebastian Kawa, the most decorated glider pilot of all time. Nine times World Champion, twice vice World Champion, and three times European Champion during the years 1999–2012. Frequently ranked world number one, a world record breaker.

The scope of this book is essentially limited to thermal flying and techniques, which are beneficial to speedy cross-country gliding used in competitions. I have not included either ridge or wave flying. Both of these types of useful lift are well-documented elsewhere and are relatively easy to understand and use. I have also not covered many of the peripheral subjects, quite simply because this book would become too big, and

also because these subjects are adequately covered in other publications.

The bulk of cross-country flying is done using thermals for which there is an inadequate level of research and understanding. Thermal soaring, however, is arguably the most mystifying and difficult skill to teach and learn, and yet it is a skill which is fundamental to our cross-country tasks in the UK. Understanding thermalling is the glider pilot's most important tool for success. To me this is so important that much of the content of this book is focussed specifically to this area of need.

Perhaps you have done a short course to achieve solo or simply only ever followed a ridge and therefore had little opportunity to be taught thermalling techniques before going solo. All is not lost as this book has been written to help with the aim of providing pilots with some clarity on what is happening in the air around them. This includes the underlying physics of thermals so that those glider pilots who aspire to excellence

Photo 1.2 The author, after a successful field landing.

in cross-country flying can improve their soaring skills. The air motions, which we are trying to understand, are simply driven by the laws of physics and this book explains how to read the sky for gliding purposes and how you may operate your glider efficiently, whilst encouraging you to have confidence and fun whilst doing so.

What follows has been mainly sourced from a series of presentations that I have used over a number of years teaching advanced training and competition glider racing and concentrates on the structure of the air as a result of thermal activity. It was put together to clarify, in the simplest way I could, the otherwise bewildering confusion of what really happens in the atmosphere and it contains information and explanations that you will not find anywhere else.

I have used a number of analogies throughout the book but bear in mind that these are simply tools to enable you to try to get a picture of what is going on. For example, the phrase 'women are from Venus' will give you a picture but any emphasis on a direct comparison should not be made. Likewise, the analogies in this book are there to give you a picture, but the actual physics is unlikely to be the same.

The simple computer binary language of ones and zeroes produces an extraordinarily complex world in technological capability today, yet a

Photo 1.3 The *Duo* that the author (KEV) uses to teach competitive gliding.

simple error generates an utterly failed program. In a similar way gliding is the simple moving of the stick forwards and backwards or from side to side in a timely manner, which results in a successful 500km task or alternatively, in a brief circuit due to one simple error of judgement. The information contained within this book is here to help you know when, by how much and in what direction you should move the stick to increase your chance of success!

1
The need

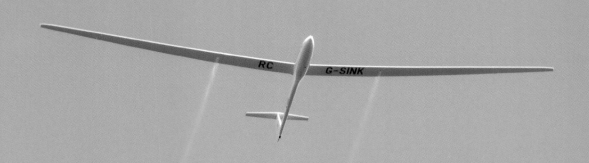

- ▶ Getting a better understanding
- ▶ Progression after solo
- ▶ Four key aspects for progression
- ▶ Where gliding is today

It can be fun. I was flying a *Capstan*, a lovely side-by-side glider. After the climb I was explaining to someone, a professional pilot who should have known better, that if you lean over hard to one side the glider will ever so slowly roll to the same side. I demonstrated this, hands off, by leaning over to him. To reinforce the point that the glider was not bent I got him to lean towards me as far as he could, specifically until he was nearly suffering cramps and pain. At this point I showed him how little rudder you need to cause roll!

Gliding is fundamentally all about having fun in gliders! The basic mechanics of launching and flying a safe circuit in the various weather conditions is simply a necessary procedure to master before we progress on to the real delights of gliding—soaring and beyond. Each soaring flight and cross-country is a real and different challenge, even when we fly the same route several times.

Getting a better understanding

The weather doesn't just allow us to be successful but makes a huge difference to the difficulty of any task. It is not just the big tasks or the highest climbs which give us a feeling of satisfaction but the 30-minute flight in February when we never expected it, or the slow task, sometimes getting a bit low in unexpected poor weather somewhere along the way, which all contribute to our memorable moments and personal satisfaction. As an example, during an early February morning during 2010 there was a severe inversion at about 300ft. The ground temperature was freezing with 5kts of wind but at 500ft the wind was 240/28kts. On the first flight of the day I flew a wide turn onto final and instead of losing 150ft, climbed some 10ft. Turning around to fly the reciprocal a further 20ft was achieved. Patience produced an eventual climb to 2,000ft and everyone who launched connected and most of the club gliders achieved significant soaring, for most of the day. All this was achieved whilst flying from a flat site (Cranwell). Also, I unexpectedly had a five-hour cross-country flight in thermals in mid February 2012. Overall, 2012 was a terrible year yet I achieved a little over 7,000km of cross-country instructional tasks!

For me flying long distances as fast as possible is why I go gliding, preferably with others in a competition to identify sometimes just how slow I can be! For the majority perhaps, having fun in gliders probably means being able to identify and climb in whatever type of lift is available just to stay airborne within a few kilometres of their site and enjoy the delights. But whichever soaring you choose to do, a better understanding will help you do more.

Progression after solo

We all know that many of our pilots and new friends drift away from gliding after solo. We also know from a previous membership study that more experienced pilots give up the sport for lots of good reasons, but notably because they just don't get enough satisfaction from taking part, including making effective use of their own gliders. That's an important point. Unlike a performance car, we can legally use every aspect of a glider's performance. The thing that makes the difference with the glider is that you do need to know *how* to use it. Too many pilots don't stay airborne or cannot complete cross-countries simply because the required knowledge and skills have passed them by and their confidence is not as high as it might otherwise be.

You probably still remember the delight of your first solo and then your progression to your first single-seat glider and completion of the Bronze Badge. For many that's where progress seems to stop. The lucky ones are edged towards the Silver Badge. It is rare to find a pilot who has their Silver Distance and has done a previous dual cross-country soaring flight in a glider. Most take a lot of time to pluck up the courage to cut the string and face a number of challenging firsts: leaving the local area; navigating over places that they have never seen before; staying as high as possible and landing somewhere other than home base. Landing safely anywhere is more of a relief than a delight and puts many off doing anything similar again. It is all rather a leap of faith. We seem to readily accept sending pilots cross-country for the first time, anticipating only something like a 50% success rate.

Photo 1.1 With a glider you can legally use every bit of performance.

Perhaps we should not be surprised that quite a few pilots don't perceive this stage of gliding as fun. After all it is a steep learning curve with relatively little guidance. First flight to Silver Badge does seem quite a challenge and will invariably take a couple of years or so, especially if a club only operates at weekends. Most of this flying instruction is achieved through very short local flights in a basic two-seat glider. The full Silver Badge is an excellent indicator of basic soaring skills, demonstrates that the holder is an internationally recognised true soaring pilot and opens the door to a potentially exciting and rewarding set of opportunities. It is such a pity that more pilots don't stick at gliding long enough to discover these opportunities. Whether our motivation is hanging onto members or simply getting the best out of people, the challenge for all of our clubs is probably in helping people to progress through and beyond the Bronze and Silver Badges and to open their eyes to the endless possibilities and the enormous amount of fun to be had within our sport.

Four key aspects for progression

There are four main things to consider in order to provide effective support to pilots who need some help to progress in gliding:

The weather
Historically in the UK, out of 104 weekend days plus bank holidays per year, weather limitations mean that advanced gliding using thermals to go on bigger tasks may only be feasible on some 20 days. On those 20 days, it's very easy to overlook the long-term value that can be extracted by ensuring that those pilots who need and want help with their soaring skills are provided for at your club. The longer-term member is as important as that new student or trial lesson—perhaps more so.

The reality of life is that the weather, a glider, a suitable P1 and the P2 who is the focus of the activity all come together at very short notice. Of course much greater value can be added to any airborne training with some good preparatory work. Spending time sat on the ground under a sky dotted with Cu working through the theory isn't an effective use of anyone's time. Remember 84 of those weekend days may not be suitable for thermal cross-country soaring, but may be an opportunity to chat through the theory, as well as to practise other skills.

Sadly there has been a huge reduction in the number of local Met observers and forecasters, being replaced by automatic sensors, and despite huge sums of money being invested in the Met Office computers it is fair to say that the forecasting for gliding is not becoming noticeably more accurate. Lorenz, the inventor of chaos theory, was a Met-man who applied physics and mathematical logic to guess what would happen. So despite the term chaos, his theory simply suggests that chaos might be predictable. He soon discovered that tiny changes in the start criteria were enough to yield very different results and that it would be impossible to forecast more than two weeks hence. Well, nothing has changed then! There are many reasons for this drift towards mathematical prediction of the weather. The Met Office is a commercial organization primarily for (and financed for) advising military flying operations, commercial flying, shipping operations and supermarkets regarding stocking up for hot summers etc. Meteorology is simply the physics of the atmosphere, i.e. mathematics. If they can get a big enough computer to do the sums then they believe that they can give a more accurate forecast.

For gliding, however, the finer detail that we want is lost in the big numbers and not likely to become readily available. It is for this reason that there are some organisations and people working towards better gliding forecasting, e.g. RASP.

Both the butterfly and domino effects can affect the real weather. An example of the first is when a few hundred farmers decide to cut their fields one particular morning. This makes a difference to the thermal development and structure as the ground will heat more quickly and generate more hot air in different areas. So the *fiddle-factor* of an adjustment away from a statistical average, which might have worked for yesterday's forecast, fails today. Clouds form and the associated shadows cause a complex shuffle of thermal triggers. Equally, whilst the Met Office will predict the height for the formation of contrails (contrails contribute to the reduced amount of sunlight reaching the earth's surface, known as global dimming), they are unable to predict how these will impact on any specific area for cooling and the generation of our thermals. A domino effect can be generated by the cloud street, which often forms downwind of a power station on an otherwise blue day. Again this development is useful to us but it is too small for the Met-man to include in his predictions.

If you've read *The Hitchhiker's Guide to the Galaxy* you will know that the answer to the meaning of life is 42! To me this is substantiated by the fact that the Met Office admits that they are correct 42% of the time. If they only considered the forecasting of sun, wind, cloud, rain and pressure, we might consider this not too bad. When you include sunrise, sunset, tide tables and the moon crescents, when their forecasts should be 100% accurate, then an overall 42% is not too good. But do not lose heart, as I will show you in simple terms how you can easily do your own forecasting and get a confident local forecast a couple of days in advance. You can update your forecast using the same methods to get a more accurate feel on the day you wish to fly.

Access to a glider

For as long as I can remember gliding clubs have insisted on prioritising their two-seat machines for basic instruction on how to fly and for passenger flying, introducing new members to the sport. Generally the performance of the basic gliders was poor by today's standard and you could only learn advanced flying skills and techniques the hard way, by reading books and by discussion with others, then going flying—learning by trial and error. Often, this was a disheartening way to learn something so complex.

Today there is an increasing number of appropriately performing two-seat gliders out there, but the training policy has not changed; yet I believe it needs to. In my view, where these old policies go wrong is that they fail to support the existing membership in the skills of advanced flying. I have even heard of clubs selling passenger flights on soaring days in their *premier passenger flying machine*, a glider that cost over £100,000, instead of allowing the members to fly it. To me this makes no sense. For example, would you really take someone out in a Ferrari to experience driving before they have even been in a car—let alone driven one—and then suggest that you will teach them in a 20-year-old Ford Fiesta. The opportunity in the UK for good weather, an appropriate glider, skilled P1 and P2 to come together must be a priority but we do actually get this chance more often than we think—during basic training. After all, for most advanced gliding techniques, the handling skills required by the student is only to fly in trim at a speed and turn. Why not teach proficient thermalling before first solo?

But even if a club is limited by access to a *K13* or a similar two-seat glider, opportunities still exist. The possibilities and limitations need thinking through. You may belong to a small and busy club that has a two-seat fleet flying passengers, but once again it is worth considering that long-term members need looking after; there's a need to consider the club's priorities on those few suitable days available each year.

Then there is the 30-minute limit. A winch launch to 1,200ft and 6kt thermal to 3,000ft with a flat glide takes 30 minutes. So somehow a 3-minute climb means thermalling has been taught. Whenever soaring weather is available I would suggest task or mission accomplishment should determine the termination of the flight. For some years now this has become the normal procedure on good days at my own club, and has included taking the *Duo* on instructional 300km tasks. Meanwhile the other three two-seat gliders will be used to teach thermalling techniques or flown solo for those pilots chasing early soaring qualifications. The *Duo* is also used in two competitions each year for the specific task of teaching competition flying to Bronze C and higher qualified pilots. The *K21* and *Acro* are both used in competitions to teach club members the skills required. At my own club all two-seaters are used for advanced gliding instruction.

A suitable P1

The best cross-country pilot in the club might not be the best individual to do this type of flying with another person. What's needed is a suitably experienced P1 who understands the P2's needs and is capable of clearly demonstrating appropriate preflight preparation and explaining what is going on during the flight, including for example, reading the sky, considering the terrain and making the most of the soaring conditions. There will also occasionally be a need for instructor mutual flying to enhance further the in-depth knowledge and practical application of techniques.

Any insurance requirement, or not, for the P1 to hold an instructor rating when flying with another club member depends on the circumstances. It would seem logical though that any improvement of successful cross-countries is a financial benefit to the club and the insurance company.

Guidance material and theory resource

This is where this book can help. It is written specifically for the glider pilot who simply wants to go farther but, for whatever reason, has access to a glider but not the knowledge/instruction at the club where such opportunities are limited or considered unavailable.

Where gliding is today

It is important to note why we are where we are. During the First World War pilots were trained to fly solo and learn about warfare in battle. The result was what was termed by BBC TV's *Black Adder* as the *20-Minuters*. Actually that was takeoff to ill fate and the survival rate was more like two weeks after joining the front line, but the similarity is there. If we are only going to teach circuits as quickly and as cheaply as possible then we are teaching gliding in a similar manner to which flying was taught a century ago. As a result learning anything beyond flying the circuit is going to be slow progress.

Also, 40 years ago the performance differences between dual and single-seat gliders was, in reality, not that far apart and the techniques for flying cross-country were very similar. Sure, the better gliders went a little farther from the same height and did it a little faster, but nothing like the differences of today's machines. It is not just in pure performance that there is a big difference, but also in the instrumentation.

In the past, a ¼ mil map and a simple compass was the order of the day. Certainly a *K13* did not go far and even short distances were achieved at a slow speed, but the essential need to get high, stay high and use mostly the next thermal that you would hit, were sensible suggestions which minimised the decision process to make progress and increased the chance of finishing any task. Equally the simple task of using hill-lift or wave remains the same and today the techniques are essentially the same in whatever glider you are manning at the time. Better gliders and more complex instruments don't make us better glider pilots and they don't teach us anything new, they just give us greater opportunities with whatever ability we might have.

Thermal flying techniques, using the primary source of lift used for racing and achieving truly big tasks has, however, changed significantly and you cannot teach racing techniques, required for today's modern machines with their newfangled instrumentation, using a *K13* instrumented for basic circuit tuition. Of course the vast majority of cross-country techniques have been learnt in privately owned gliders at regional competitions where one rarely finds a club glider entered, so the opportunity for the average club member to progress is strictly limited.

For clubs making the decision to support and encourage up-and-coming pilots, there are two ways forward that I recommend considering. However, in both cases it is essential for there to be an advanced syllabus within any club, which can be applied.

The ideal, most efficient (but expensive) option would involve the club having its own high performance two-seat glider suitably equipped with some modern instruments and a team of instructors who are dedicated to teaching advanced gliding. The club as a whole must also recognize that this is what the machine is for and not as a premier passenger-flying glider. On the other hand there will be many clubs, which, for a number of reasons, cannot afford or operate such a large, heavy machine (finance, club membership too low, insufficient hangar space, small airfield, narrow strip, weak winch or no aero-tow to launch with water). Despite these club limitations there will still be a need for those members who buy their own glider to aspire to achieve more. This leads us then to the second option.

The essential ability of a student to learn advanced gliding is to be able to fly straight, in trim, and turn as directed. So throughout any basic flying lesson we already have the glider, P1 and P2

and so, in order to provide the additional training for exploiting thermals, we only need the weather. A supplementary syllabus including lectures, instructional packages and video facilitated by an appointed lead advanced instructor or coach would be invaluable. This way, solo and pre-solo pilots could, with sensibly controlled supervision, learn and practise the various techniques. They would gain both competence and confidence such that they will be prepared for the future to fly in their own high performance single-seat gliders. The appointed lead coach or senior instructor would ideally have considerable experience in (competition) cross-country flying and a wide knowledge of the various instruments and how they could be used to good effect. Gaps and holes can only be filled if this individual is prepared to go and learn these techniques and for that matter understand them. You will see within this book that there are many techniques which can still be practised in flat weather and indeed, some of the exercises will best be carried out in a stable environment.

The whole point is to train for success in soaring, the fundamental skill required for all advanced gliding, achieving a steady productive rate of progress within the student's capability in the glider they are flying and not to train for a safe soaring failure!

2
Improving your skills

► **Preparation**
► **Going faster and farther**
► **Three key aspects for cross-country flying**

This book is intended for the Bronze C pilot and beyond and will give you the knowledge and guidance on techniques which will be useful for your solo flying. It will improve your soaring skills and understanding of the sky around you so that your cross-country success rate is improved. Apart from the process of getting airborne and being taught the fundamentals of how to fly, once you have gone solo gliding tends to be very much an individual sport and it can be extremely difficult to gather such knowledge. Strange as it may seem, some of the techniques that are described will mean that you will need to learn to fly in a completely different way. A comment made to me by a former student was that the only similarity between club flying that he had been taught and flying fast around a task was to fly safely!

Preparation

Gradually, you should learn all of the potential conditions which you might encounter and have a full tool box to respond correctly. With the limited learning opportunities available, to be competent in all conditions a building block approach is the only way to effectively progress. Preparation to fly any task should be thorough and well planned in advance so that there is no rush, concern, stress or uncertainty about any aspect just prior to your launch. I have some 20 pre-planned routes to fly so that once the weather obliges me, I am able to pick an appropriate task, or perhaps task my syndicate partner with it.

More often than not great days are preceded by good days and so you can anticipate that the weather of today may be similar tomorrow. Note the minimum and maximum temperatures and cloud base, including the cut-off time and what the sky looks like as it dies. If we only fly

at weekends then the opportunities to develop better skills in a season are potentially few. In just the same way that there are local hotspots, there are regular hotspots (and cold spots) as you wander around the country so remember not just the location but the reason why such hotspots exist so that you may recognize them again whilst flying over new territory.

Many competitors invariably find that they have so little opportunity to fly cross-country from their own club that they double the number of cross-countries they do in a year by entering a competition. Please don't be daunted by regional competition flying, even go with the club two-seater and share the experience as hors concours. Go to a large flat site regional competition and treat it as a gliding holiday where you are about to have some of the most rewarding lessons and cross-country flying that you will ever get.

If you want to be competitive, you will need more than knowledge of the competition rules but you must recognize that you are flying in a race, and some people will be racing. At the end of the day most people there (not just the winner) will happily tell you why they did or did not do something and having been on the same task at about the same time then you will both easily relate about a certain situation. With the technology of today you can directly compare your performance with gliders that were around you at the time, which leads to the entertaining *maggot racing shows*.

What do you need to progress beyond successful local soaring? Firstly you do need to practise the techniques and develop your flying skills. The glider must simply become an extension of your sense of the air motions around you and your responses to manoeuvre, as you desire, should require almost no thought or distractions, rather like we ride a bike.

You do need the knowledge of being able to read the air picture ahead and recognize the many different weather patterns of the sky as they change, and to respond with correct timely decisions. As a result you have to regularly look up, across and down track, identifying the various cloud patterns and then anticipating how they will change over the next 5–15 minutes and how they will be once you reach them.

You do need to learn the skills to go beyond local soaring with more than a 50% chance of making it around a 150–500km task and to understand the instrument and string indications, your map, the navigation aids and all of their shortcomings. In addition, you will need to be able to maintain your concentration, comfort and confidence for more than three hours over areas and in airspace that you have never visited before.

There is a lot of benefit from flying cross-country with an instructor, especially one who is or has been a keen competition pilot. It is not about the flying but about looking out and understanding what you see, along with making decisions. For example, my syndicate partner and I will usually set each other a specific task rather than fly aimlessly about for a few hours. If you are setting a task it should be very specific and one which develops your skills rather than just getting airborne and pottering around. One such task into a strong westerly wind is an out and return, Cranwell to Chesterfield. On paper it seems like a simple and under-set task for the weather—and it is until we reach Mansfield. From there, however, we have to penetrate the strong downdraft driving into Chesterfield caused by its position being in the lee of the hills, and this downdraft generates turbulence caused by wave and rotor. Sometimes we just don't like the look of the sky and run home rather than take the risk the inevitable field landing. On one occasion we connected with wave and eventually climbed to 7,000ft and ran to Camphill as the new TP. The point is that the weather cannot guarantee one technique being successful so to have experience of different conditions over the same area is a useful lesson at reading the sky and coping with it. It is the weather that is the challenge, not the location!

Challenges should realistically stretch you with the intention of teaching yourself a little something new which you might need to use in the future, away from home, but always remember neither skill nor experience will magically improve the real weather or defy basic aerodynamics. It is better to slightly over-task and run home early. The Met-man can be over-optimistic just as much as he can be pessimistic. Equally there is no point flying a 100km task on a 300km day. The point is how to learn the skills and techniques to fly farther, faster. Here is a list of things you need to be familiar with:

► Field landings and what to do after a successful landing.
► Navigation, map reading and airspace plus NOTAMS.
► All electronic equipment and navigation aids.
► Logging equipment, radio, FLARM® & EFIS.
► Altimeter settings and what they mean.
► How to join and achieve the best rate of climb in a thermal.
► Different types and structures of thermals.

The weather en route may change significantly so you must be able to recognize and handle the following:

► Flying with water.
► Priorities leading to a work load cycle.
► Decision making.
► Good days.
► Low cloud base days.
► Sea breezes.
► Streeting days.
► Windy days.
► Wave days.
► Band flying.
► Blue days.
► Speed to fly.
► Block speeds.
► Spread-out days.
► Managing showers and thunderstorms.
► Hilly terrain.
► Survival days.
► Turning point needs for badge claims.
► Turning at TPs efficiently.

None of this can be learned in a couple of 10-minute circuits but could be achieved in 20 dual and 20 solo flights of a couple of hours each. We are talking here of 40 hours of instruction and 40 hours of practice, which is far more than you needed to go solo. Hence to progress we must fly on every good day with the intention of improving some particular aspect of our gliding techniques, but there are also many other aspects which can be practised or exercised on flat days. Consider some of the building blocks that you can utilize to progress to flying long distance cross-country as indicated in *Fig 2.1*. The required level of knowledge is significantly more than needed to simply achieve first solo.

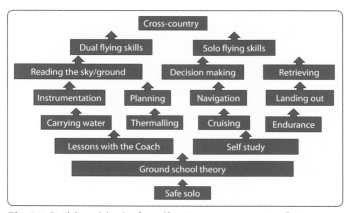

Fig 2.1 Building blocks for effective cross-country flying.

Going faster and farther

To develop the skills for flying faster and farther it is not a question of being lucky or chasing after everyone else in a competition (a leech, although this can be useful in your first competition) but reading the good air, avoiding the bad air and making timely efficient decisions. In other words the thermal sky is purely physics and you have to understand how it works if you are to be able to make sense out of it. Participation in the club ladder is a good guide to your personal performance and improvement, but if you are not improving and not at the top you clearly must be doing something wrong. In competitions each pilot will be busy making his own decisions depending on many things and trying to be the fastest with the energy lines (or the lack of) available.

Consider how important the following questions are—just how many of them do you feel confident in being able to answer thoroughly?

► How much practical cross-country training have you already had?
► How do you determine if a day is going to be good?
► How does the Met-man know how high cloud base will be?

► How does the Met-man know how strong thermals will be?
► Can you explain clearly thermal structure(s)?
► Exactly what is a trigger point/action?
► How often have you seen the *birth* of a thermal cloud?
► How do you find a good thermal?
► When would you bounce a five knot thermal for a three knot thermal?
► Explain why, as cloud base moves up, thermals are farther apart?
► Is the relative humidity of the air significant?
► What determines the vertical structure (movement) of the air?
► Can you explain the formation of sink and is it important?
► What is the yaw string used for?
► Do thermals rotate?

Three key aspects for cross-country flying

In most books on gliding there is a huge array of different subjects written as guidance for aspiring cross-country pilots. These subjects are certainly important but most are not the subject of this book. If we break down the individual aspects which contribute to the average speed around any cross-country flight they are the speed to fly, efficient routing and effective climbing.

Speed to fly

It should be clear that there will be an optimum block speed from the top of each thermal to the bottom of the next climb. Inspection of the polar curve will indicate this theoretical best speed to fly. Modern vario instruments and the MacCready speed ring can also be used to give you this information.

All this is, however, theoretical and is dependent on your accuracy on predicting what the next thermal strength will be. Further examination of the polar curve shows us that flying a little slower or a little faster during the cruise will mean that your *average* cross-country speed (climbs and cruises) will always be slower than the optimum. Fortunately, you only incur a small *average speed loss* of around 5% if you cruise within 5kts of the optimum speed.

> **KEY POINT** Speed errors of about 5kts cause a small loss (around 5%), and there is no possibility of a gain in performance.

Flying at a slower speed gives less height loss so some of the time lost by cruising slowly is actually gained by climbing for less time to reach the top of the next thermal. Conversely, the time gained by cruising faster is partly lost by the fact that you have to climb for longer. Of course, some of these losses may be reduced by adjusting the speed during a glide as you pass through favourable or bad air. As the instrumentation is always a little behind what is required and cannot predict the air ahead, try to anticipate the short term small gentle adjustments of speed during the cruise. This requires finesse and is only learned through handling experience, and this skill will really only have a significance in winning races.

The important aspect is that whatever speed you choose to fly there is no opportunity to increase on your average speed around a task but you will almost certainly incur a small loss as a result of accumulated speed errors.

Whilst you are gaining experience in cross-country flying it will probably pay to fly a slightly slower block speed (perhaps 5–10kts slower) as other decisions will be more critical than your speed. This slower speed will give you a little more time to read the sky and the opportunity to search further. As your ability in these other more important aspects improve, you can refine your cruise speeds.

> **KEY POINT** Consider flying a slightly slower block speed until you gain experience.

Efficient routing

If you track a direct line from the top of each thermal to the bottom of the next climb, flying through lift or sink will have a significant effect on how high you arrive at your next climb. The average structure of the sky means that if we fly a fixed straight course through a thermic sky then we will pass through longer lines of sink than lift. Statistically, flying in this way and regardless of the supposed perfect speed we cruise at, we will lose more than we might gain. This loss can easily be as much as 15%. You will arrive lower at the next climb than you might otherwise have anticipated. On the plus side, however, if you route with minor deviation via areas of lift which give you a net gain on the cruise descent, you can achieve a gain in efficiency of more than 10%. If you have to make a significant detour off track to achieve this then the net gain will be reduced. So reading the sky and routing efficiently is more important to cut losses or make gains than the actual speed we cruise at.

During any long cruise you may achieve a good link of energy lines on which you gain on the glide, resulting in less time climbing. Of course, you might also lose on the glide if you route via poor lines, which will mean that a greater amount of time will need to be spent climbing. As a result, it is quite common to make gains of 10% or even losses of up to 15% on your average speed around a task due to routing.

Flying slightly away from the perfect speed might cost you a 5% loss in average speed. So, on a 300m task at 100kph (180 minutes) this would equate to 95kph and an extra 9 minutes of time. On the other hand you may gain 18 minutes or lose 27 minutes due to routing!

> **KEY POINT** We can gain more than 10% or lose more than 15% by routing.

Effective climbing

The faster we climb the less time we spend climbing. This alone can make a huge difference to our task average time. Climbing more quickly means that we can cruise at higher speeds which makes our performance more impressive. If we required 10,000ft to achieve a particular task, climbing at 5kts (500ft/min) would take 20 minutes, whilst climbing at 1kt (100ft/min) would take 100 minutes!

Also, if we take one turn (which takes 20 seconds) with no gain to establish a 5kt thermal to climb 500ft (3 turns in 1 minute) the net effect is that we climbed 500ft in four turns (1 minute 20 seconds) so the actual achieved rate of climb is 3.75kts. A staggering 33% loss. Even if we climb a more realistic 1,250ft, it is eight turns (2 minutes 30 seconds) plus the wasteful turn (2 minutes 50 seconds), so the achieved rate of climb reduces to 4.4kts. A 10% loss. It does not matter if the wasteful turns are done searching for a core that we subsequently connect with, or any additional turns throughout the flight coupled with slowing down which are not beneficial, it means that we have been going nowhere for no gain. Even a 2kt safety climb of 1,000ft in lieu of a 4kt climb is a 2 minute 30 second loss on a single short climb. So we can lose about 30% by poor thermalling techniques! Therefore it is important for you to concentrate significantly on your skills to achieve high climb rates and to thermal efficiently as this is far more important than efficient routing and also flying an accurate cruise speed, which comes well and truly last in the priorities! Effective climbing must be your first priority. That includes every aspect of it, reading the sky, feeling the air, centring efficiently on thermals and climbing at the maximum rate you are able to and climbing in the strongest thermals with no delay. Additionally,

as explained later, it is important to understand the task efficiency of into-wind and downwind thermal strengths.

An aspect which is important when reading the sky is to recognise the two key aspects of thermal generation. One is the effects of the sun heating the ground and the other is the natural instability of the air mass itself.

Photo 2.1 was taken at 09:35 during a demonstration 50km out and return cross-country flight and the close-up photograph is the same photograph, zoomed in on a power station. The winch launch was at 09:30 and the landing

Photo 2.1 Reading the sky.

back home was just 30 minutes later (100kph). Careful examination of the cloud structure shows a very active sky. The power station some miles away, shown in the close-up, displays the fact that the early morning inversion has not broken. There is no ground thermal generation. You can see in the close-up picture that the steam and smoke is struggling to climb as it streams back downwind showing the lowest levels to be quite stable. Perhaps this is not what you might have expected to see! Reading the sky and recognising whether the thermals are ground based or from mass instability is a fundamental part of successful gliding.

3
Self Met-briefing

- ▶ **Considerations for self met-briefing**
- ▶ **When to launch?**
- ▶ **Effects of humidity on air density**
- ▶ **Finding thermals**

Only follow a two-seater in a competition with caution! On one occasion we went down track 10km so that P2 could practise a start and for the first time thermalling fully loaded with water away from the massing start line gaggle, which was far too distracting. Having established the centre for just a short time, sadly, a number of gliders immediately followed us. At this point my P2's attention on maintaining the thermal was abandoned and he proceeded to lead the 6 or 7 competition gliders out of the thermal, all of us losing 500ft in the process!

We need to develop our Met-briefing skills so that we can analyse the sky and understand what it is telling us, in order that we will get the best results when flying. The Met-man will only give us part of the story, and that part can often be out of date or incorrect. For example, if a cold front has passed through overnight the air will be unstable over a large area producing a consistent structure to the sky. The wind direction will have some north in it, usually from the north west so that the Pennines and Welsh hills will protect the eastern side of the country. A NNW wind would be very nice. So, let us consider some of the critical aspects for self met-briefing.

Considerations for self met-briefing

Air mass
Our daily weather is mostly dependent on where the huge block of air, which is with us today, has come from. In the UK, if the block comes from the north then the cold air (relatively dry because it can carry only a relatively small amount of water vapour) is warmed during the day by the ground from the bottom up and we end up with a really unstable band to operate our gliders in. If the air is from the south it will be humid and as the ground is cooler than the air, very little unstable air is generated leading to a poor day. Of course the average wind in the UK is westerly.

Consider that the air above us today, with a 2,000ft wind of 20kts, was 480 miles away 24 hours ago. A change of 5kts therefore puts the weather window 120 miles either way forwards or backwards. A 10° change in wind direction means the weather is shoved about 80 miles to one side

or the other. So the Met-man is always correct, but just wrong in either his timing or location.

> **KEY POINT** The 1 in 60 rule is a great guide for navigation assistance, or for working out problems such as the one above, as long as the angles are small. It states that a 1° heading change over 60 miles will give a displacement of 1 mile.

The complex topography and the fact that the UK is an island means that these small changes in wind speed and direction can have a large impact on the actual weather, come the day. This situation will not get better so it is up to us to recognize what conditions might give us a good day and interpret the picture in front of us as we fly.

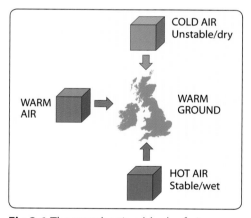

Fig 3.1 The weather is a block of air.

Thermal development
Not all thermals are generated from the *hot* ground so thermal development is influenced by the interaction of the following:

- ▶ Instability or potential instability of the atmosphere.
- ▶ Humidity and relative humidity.
- ▶ Convergence.
- ▶ Troughs.
- ▶ Sun.
- ▶ Angle of the sun to the ground surface.
- ▶ Ground ability to absorb and heat the air.
- ▶ Thermal contrast of adjoining areas.
- ▶ Wind.
- ▶ Cloud shadow including amount.
- ▶ Rate of cloud evaporation.

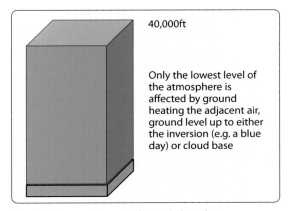

Fig 3.2 Normal band of instability that we use.

Furthermore, we only use thermals in the lowest level of our atmosphere, as indicated in *Fig 3.2* above.

Visibility

In previous times visibility was important as navigation was achieved by looking out of the window and referring to a map. The burning of stubble fields presented a double-edged sword. Late thermals could be *seen* and would often be used to get home, especially on blue days. On the other hand, the pollution made appalling visibility if we were sat under a high pressure system for a few days, so map crawling was necessary.

Just before you feel that you have missed an opportunity though, pollution in the air reduces the sun's effectiveness at heating the ground (insolation) so look for good visibility days (or excellent ones) as there will be a considerable improvement in the generation of stronger thermals. In recent years, a clear example of the

effect of pollution was during the days that the airline industry was shut down due to the ash cloud from Iceland. The ash was well out of the way but the lack of contrails ensured a series of beautiful clear blue skies and really exceptional thermic days. Equally, winter air from the arctic circle is clean, clear air and during the poor gliding year of 2013, April produced some outstanding cross-country days.

Temperature

If we look at a simple weather forecast in the newspaper or online it will indicate the maximum and minimum temperatures. Assuming an average humidity of 40–60% for the UK, we can work out the approximate cloud base for most places. The bigger the difference between the minimum temperature (occurring just after dawn) and the maximum temperature (occurring some time after mid-day) the higher the cloud base.

Cloud base is the above difference divided by 2.5 (average environmental lapse rate) × 1,000. For example, if the minimum is 10 °C and the maximum 20 °C, (20 – 10) ÷ 2.5 × 1,000 gives a cloud base of 4,000 ft. (Or if you prefer 400 ft per degree difference). Just looking at a basic forecast will give you this information and the nice bit is that the calculation gives you an estimate of the cloud base in that area, above ground level.

> **KEY POINT** Cloud base = max temp – min temp) × 400.

The minimum cloud base for meaningful cross-country flying would normally be 3,500 ft. *Table 3.1 on page 30* shows the average Met figures for RAF Waddington, Lincolnshire. It is clear that the season really is only May to August, which is about 20 weeks or weekends per year.

Thermal strength

To calculate thermal strength the Met-man uses a formula but this is only of limited value to us—a basic guide if you will. In his calculations of thermal updraft the Met-man will simply give the mathematical average from ground to the highest point limited by any inversion, and that for only one place. For example, if 1,000 farmers decided to cut the wheat crop on the same morning then the forecast would be significantly wayward for us, whilst flying over certain areas. However, using our simple calculation of cloud base means that we can calculate the thermal strength for ourselves and recognize stronger thermals on task. Thermal strength is largely a function of cloud base, cloud tops or the inversion, which will be explained later. You will see on a cross-section forecast that as the cloud base goes up, the thermal strength goes up.

2,000ft cloud base gives:
(2,000ft / 1,000 × 1.2) − 1 = 1.4kts
5,000ft cloud base gives:
(5,000ft / 1,000 × 1.2) − 1 = 5kts

This is only for a standard atmosphere with 50% humidity. Also the relative humidity usually changes with height and this may change thermal strength noticeably. Nevertheless, this simple calculation of thermal strength is significant in

The season for flying cross-country in the UK					
Month	Max Temp (°C)	Min Temp (°C)	Cloud Base (ft)	Sunshine (hours)	Rainfall (mm)
January	6.3	1.0	2,100	58.6	52.4
February	6.7	1.0	2,200	73.2	37.8
March	9.4	2.5	2,700	100.9	47.4
April	11.7	4.0	3,000	143.7	44.4
May	15.4	6.7	3,500	201.8	47.7
June	18.3	9.7	3,500	185.7	55.3
July	21.0	11.9	3,600	200.0	44.5
August	20.9	11.8	3,600	191.9	57.6
September	17.7	9.8	3,100	140.7	51.5
October	13.6	6.8	2,700	109.4	53.4
November	9.2	3.6	2,200	70.8	52.1
December	7.0	2.0	2,000	52.4	55.1

Table 3.1

ANALOGY **The Bullet.** If you want a bullet to travel farther then you must make the barrel of the gun longer to give the bullet the maximum time to continue to accelerate.

As with the analogy of the bullet in a long barrel, the deeper the instability layer, then the greater opportunity there is for the rising air to accelerate upwards and equally importantly, the sinking air downwards.

Thermal strength potential is directly related to how high the cloud base is. As a guide, multiply the cloud base (in 1,000's of feet) by 1.2 and then subtract 1 (for the nominal sink rate of the glider).

that it confirms that in any particular area you can recognize that you are in a strong, average or weak thermal for that particular day. Of course the most important contribution to your speed around a task is determined by your average rate of climb. If you find yourself in a weak thermal (that is one which fails to satisfy the previous calculation of cloud base and therefore predicted thermal strength) and if you have the height to move on to stronger looking cells, then you need to do so, and the decision should be easy to make.

KEY POINT Thermal strength potential = (cloud base in 1,000's of feet × 1.2) − 1.

Cloud amounts

When the sun radiates onto the ground the energy is dissipated. Some is reflected and lost, whilst the rest heats up the ground. The ground will heat up the air in contact above it, whilst some of the heat is conducted downwards within the earth's surface itself. This last effect is important as it subsequently provides heating to the air when the area is covered briefly by cloud shadow, or later in the day as the sun's power is reducing. These storage radiators continue to provide thermals for us whilst the surrounding areas cool quickly. Understandably then, the potential for the day to be extended is reduced with more cloud shadow over any area. This calming, stabilising effect on the atmosphere is caused by any cloud at any altitude. Also, another aspect to be aware of is if the clouds develop and extend vertically (towering cumulus) then the day should last longer, but the cut-off can be abrupt.

Cloud cover may be described as octas (eighths) or the sky is split in to tenths. In both cases the amount is coded in words—clear, few, scattered, broken or overcast.

Scattered sounds good but this word is used to describe 2 to 5 tenths (or 2 to 4 octas), in other words up to half cover. Only at mid-day does half the sun shine on the ground, thereafter this reduces with any vertical development of the clouds and cloud shadows grow. So 50% cloud cover will actually give 60% or 70% shadow. Just consider what half the sky covered looks like by looking at *Fig 3.3*. Hard to believe isn't it? Of course the day will not be that good or last that long.

Wind

Less than around 8kts of wind produces good thermals but a long way apart. In light winds of 3 to 7kts, the vertical wind of the thermals is more powerful than the surface wind and dominates (controls) the local areas. The surface wind has almost no effect on the development or control of thermal sources. So with these light winds mechanical mixing of the air at the lowest levels is inadequate. The sky is often blue or, alternatively, fixed column thermals develop which control the air over a large area and sink dominates a large part of the sky in between. Note that as towns get hot they generate a steady

flow of thermals rising up and forming a cloud shadow, which has a big effect on thermal sources. Neither the cloud nor shadow is blown away so a large fixed (stays essentially over the same bit of ground) column (a vertical column of linked bubbles) thermal is generated. The huge amount of descending air flows down and out at the lower levels constraining any other bits of hotspots generating a thermal. It is also worth noting that with these lighter winds sea breezes drive farther inland and kill huge areas which earlier in the day had been good. The sea breeze driving cold sea air over the ground makes a low level inversion and thermals are killed or not generated at all.

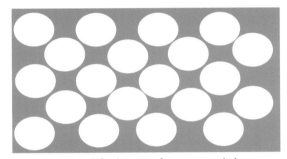

Fig 3.3 A simplified view of a scattered sky.

Greater than 15kts of surface wind gives tighter thermals and makes things generally more difficult, particularly on both into-wind legs and cross-wind legs. Streeting can help the former whilst wave effects can help or hinder the latter. So, 8–15kts is an ideal wind. You may still find useful streets in these winds but then they are not so dominant to make other cross-street legs too difficult.

KEY POINT Winds of between 8–15kts are ideal for cross-country cruising.

When to launch?

To make the most of any day when endurance might be required (five hours or a big task) then it is best to get airborne just after the day has started to develop. It should then only get better or easier, depending on your point of view. But do not launch before the grass is dry as before this point the sun's energy is used to evaporate the moisture, rather than heat up the ground. Also, do not get airborne until after the surface wind has increased and veered, and is showing some degree of variability as before this point there will be insufficient thermals. When the surface air mixes with the higher level air the surface wind will increase, showing that thermals are around and that ground hotspots will have an influence on the thermal structure. Also, when the wind is variable it indicates that the air is mixing. As an aside, if you can, choose a direct line down the middle of the country. This has the advantages of avoiding any sea breezes and is usually the hottest part of the country.

> **KEY POINT** Launch just after the day starts to develop, when the grass is dry and the wind has a degree of variability.

Effects of humidity on air density

If we did not have water vapour in the atmosphere we would not have clouds and every day would be a blue day. In fact we would not have weather as we know it, just variations of temperature and wind. The transfer of energy by evaporation and condensation contributes hugely to the various motions, which we chase or avoid.

Firstly the level of humidity and instability determines the amount of cloud that is likely to be produced. Too much cloud kills the sun and shortens the active day whilst too little makes it a bit of a blue day. There are many quite cheap instruments which indicate relative humidity and a figure of 40–50% is good inland.

There is often the suggestion that thermals expand as they climb. Putting real numbers in to the combined gas law equation means that a 200m diameter thermal at sea level will expand by about 15m to 215m by 5,000ft. So it does expand which at first would appear to be beneficial to us but in reality the expansion is not significant. However practical experience tells us that below 1,500ft we need to turn tightly and accurately to stay in a thermal, carefully controlling speed and angle of bank e.g. 40–45° and we often have to readjust to remain centred. We can climb

efficiently above this height using a slightly reduced angle of bank because the thermal has stabilised.

Photo 3.1 Preparing to launch at Ocana, Spain.

The relationship of IAS and TAS, however, are also subject to the same gas laws and gliders fly only relative to IAS yet the radius of turn is dictated by TAS. An indicated speed of 50kts gives a TAS of about 55kts at 5,000ft and our actual achieved turn diameter holding 45°AoB increases by 28m from 135m to 163m. The benefit of the *bigger* thermal therefore does not exist!

> **KEY POINT** With increasing height a thermal expands slightly but a glider's turn radius also increases.

Air is simply a mixture and no doubt you will have seen smoke lingering in the sky. It can often be seen when it has climbed up to the inversion and loiters before eventually dissipating. Humid air does the same but we just can't see it in its vapour form. Humidity is a huge contributor to very local air density. It makes the weather by moving vast amounts of water about the sky and changing state from water vapour to cloud and occasional precipitation. This matters a lot to us and the clouds help us understand the sky. For a volume of dry air which has a mass of 88 tons, the same volume of humid air could have a mass of about 74 tons whilst that heavily contaminated with carbon dioxide could have a mass of about 100 tons.

ANALOGY **The bathroom ceiling.**
Imagine a ceiling and condensation forming on it. All drops which fall off would be the same size (surface tension vs gravity). As you will be aware, you don't get a fine spray in one place and a bucket of water in another. If the ceiling had a varied surface temperature then the cooler areas would produce more drops and the warmer areas less, or none (cold spots/hotspots). If the surface was uneven then we would see the drops run and form where there were bits hanging down. If a breeze was introduced it would force the developing droplets along towards any barriers. Equally important is to note that the droplets would form and fall from the same place each time. This is just like bubbles in your beer or glass of coke, which form continuously from the same points, even when you swirl the liquid around. The whole process is governed by physics and in the same way thermals are governed by physics and are effectively the same size, forming at the same locations on a blue day (buoyancy versus gravity).

For now just bear in mind that all thermals are also governed by physics and are initially about the same size, about 200m across, regardless of how strong, or to some extent, how high they are. Equally though, in just the same way as snowflakes are essentially the same yet each one is slightly different, so no two thermals are the same but all have well defined similarities. You can also find larger significant areas of rising air, which will be covered in later chapters.

Finding thermals

Never has there been a better time than now to be able to analyse the structure of the thermic sky using the logger traces. We can therefore confirm our suspicions of not mentally mapping out the sky quickly enough. Part of the issue is that many glider pilots only start to look at the sky after they have pulled off the launch mechanism. Prior to this there are many opportunities to seriously

study the sky. Many clubs require ground duties and this gives you the opportunity to study and see results. As a winch driver, watch where the glider you have just launched has gone. Would you have gone that way and did they climb successfully? Before even getting airborne on a club day, just after 'eventualities', you should start thinking and have a plan on where you are going to find your first thermal. Simply turning the wrong way after release will change a successful climb away and a successful task into a frustrating circuit.

If you take an aero-tow, it is worth counting the number of thermals that you randomly pass through. Mentally note their strengths, and to some extent the sink, because it tells you how strong the cores are. Try to relate them to areas on the ground along with the wind and the cloud. To find a thermal you need to use the following:

Photo 3.2 Learning to feel and read the sky on an aero-tow.

- ► Ground.
- ► Clouds.
- ► Gliders.
- ► Birds.
- ► Feel.
- ► String.
- ► ASI.
- ► Smell.
- ► Ears.
- ► Vario.
- ► The map and preflight planning.
- ► Common sense (not luck).

ANALOGY **The lava lamp.** There is another opportunity to have a good

idea as to how the sky works in terms of water transfer—by watching a lava lamp. Despite the controlled environment of a very steady heat source and no wind, the lava lamp does not generate a steady stream of equal blobs with temporal continuity. The lamp and heated glass act as the heat source and once an amount of wax has warmed sufficiently it rises. When the blob reaches the top of the glass chamber it cools and once dense enough falls down again like the evaporated cloud.

The interaction between rising and falling blobs also gives us a visual interpretation of the clashes and sidesteps made by both rising and falling air. Occasionally a hot cell is restrained by the warm wax above until it finally escapes as a smaller blob and accelerates quickly upwards in just the same way that hot air can be held and ejected. There is some variation in the size of blobs but not by much, and none are either huge or tiny. As each blob rises the motion of the fluid around the blob is clearly seen. However to make the lamp work as a decorative item the glass is of a specific shape which encourages convective flow which is not the case in our wide open atmosphere.

You will not be surprised to hear that we do have some difficulties interpreting the weather ahead in the UK. We often assume that the air is the same wherever we are, but this could not be further from the truth. Consider the effluence from a power station. The smoke from the furnace chimney and the steam from the cooling towers drift downwind making a street of cumulus and at the lower levels a stream of polluted air with heavy particles of *stuff*. We can easily see the effect of extensive cloud shadow and hence increased humidity which forms in a street line for sometimes tens of miles downwind. To a lesser extent the pollution downwind of towns and the higher humidity from woods have a direct effect on our fragile climate and hence large lumps of air, modified by features upwind, generate blue holes or dynamic soaring conditions.

Statistically the cloud base for our soaring season is 3,500ft, which just so happens to be close to the height of the mountains in the west of the UK. Our good cross-country weather wind direction is generally northwesterly (north is best but less frequent). In a similar way then, this mountain range causes huge variations in the blocks of air escaping through valleys and around hills and hence to our task routes flown to the east of the hills, the Cheshire gap being a classic example. Just consider those rarer occasions though when the cloud base is closer to 5,000ft. The whole world is open and wonderful and suddenly the overall sky structure is fairly predictable. Sadly, however, this is not the norm even in mid-summer!

One significant point that might not be obvious to you is that there is greater mass in a thermal during May than July and thermals will be stronger. It is the same in autumn. Perhaps this is not what you would instinctively think?

Also, thermals can be more powerful than you think. For interest, a glider produces some 10–20kg of drag in order to fly and a glider weighing 500kg falling at 1kt requires a 4hp motor to stay level. Hence some gliders use a jet motor which gives a static thrust of the order of 20kg.

4

Thermal structure

We had planned to set off early in the morning to catch the ferry out of Bilbao but my crew, Dave and John, decided that it would be better to leave late that afternoon and find a hotel near the port so that we would be nice and fresh in the morning. After 5 hours, as we arrived at the port to dump the trailer, we found fellow contestants who were staying overnight in their motor-home. My crew booked a local hotel via email and then were happy to accept the kind offer to demolish a bottle of scotch between them.

At 22:30 we set off, following the satnav, for a hotel 6km away. Twenty minutes later we were on the motorway to Madrid having somehow missed the required turn-off at a huge junction. Turning back at the next junction, which was some distance away, took us back to where the trailer was, a round trip of around 45 minutes. We then did it again despite following a second satnav. It was now midnight and as my two drunken passengers were not helping I found a couple of police cars parked at the side and I went off leaving Dave and John with strict instructions to be quiet.

The policemen's English was as useless as my Spanish, and they kept looking over my shoulder at my two giggling passengers, but they eventually understood what I needed. They punched the hotel address into their equipment and simply got me to follow them at high speed. Thirty-five minutes later we returned close to where we had initially intercepted them, having done the same route for a *third* time. I gave the hotel phone number to the police and eventually a truck from the hotel came and guided us to where we should have been.

This chapter will concentrate on describing what thermals consist of. To begin with, perhaps quite alarmingly for some, we will disprove several previous theories. This radical approach is necessary before we can move on to describing in detail what a thermal actually is. You will see that instead of the very simplistic and incorrect models that many of us have believed in, the thermal is actually a toroidal vortex.

Incorrect theories

Whilst we usually think nothing of the air around us, wind is a very powerful force. Wind was used to drive galleons, it moves sand dunes and produces huge waves on every ocean and sea. We are familiar with the development of high and low pressures which generate the wind that brings us our weather. The same processes cause sea breezes and are instrumental in the development of thunderstorms. When directed vertically wind is just as powerful. The physics driving the huge effects that we see still apply at the lesser scales and contribute to streeting and any large area of ascending air.

Before we can possibly *feel* the air we have to have a clear understanding of just what is happening. On stable days, over flat ground there is no turbulence generated by any modest wind over obstacles and our gliders cruise in trim effortlessly whilst we calmly unwrap a chocolate bar using both hands. On a thermic day, however, the world is full of bumps and every bump has been caused by the interaction of hot air rising and cold air descending.

The simple sensations and indications, whilst we transit through the middle of a thermal, are the result of sink followed by lift (which increases then reduces) and then sink again. The sink and lift are often of about equal value if we pass through the centre (core) of the thermal. This can lead us to some misconceptions when we apply simple physics to some of the model diagrams we see in books.

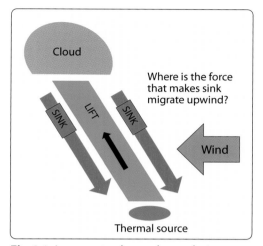

Fig 4.1 Incorrect column thermal picture.

In *Fig 4.1* the suggestion is that the rising air is a leaning column drifting with the wind, yet the sink is moving upwind. This latter action is not possible.

In *Fig 4.2* there is an implication that the thermal is getting bigger as it climbs. So where is this extra air coming from? Also, it implies that the thermal at the top is as wide as the cloud. Furthermore, there is no logic in the sink that is

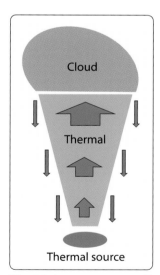

Fig 4.2 Incorrect expanding thermal concept.

indicated in the diagram. If you did put sink into the model this air would have to expand as it moves down to fill the space. Of course a climbing thermal can not make additional rising air so this model also fails.

For now, consider that *Fig 4.3* is a more accurate thermal concept, as will be explained later. We generally believe that most thermals appear to be generated by the ascent of hot air from the ground. If it was this simplistic, then the rate of climb would be simply proportional to the initial temperature. We will look more closely at power stations later, but if cooling towers produced a 2kt thermal from the 30°C air that they emit, then the boiler chimney at 300°C would produce a thermal several times stronger, and this simply does not happen. Equally in winter, when the air is

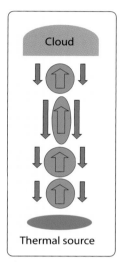

Fig 4.3 A more accurate thermal concept.

bitterly cold, the thermals should be stunning but we know that they are not.

If we consider the flow of hot air upwards, like that from a hair drier, then we quickly realise that this is not how our system works in nature because there is no associated back flow. Even if we allow the hot air to be blown vertically upwards, there is no familiar sink. We can see this kind of flow from the tall thin boiler chimney at a power station but the motion abruptly changes within a hundred feet or so and changes to that of bubble vortices.

We know that a thermal is relatively warm air rising but in simple physics to double the speed of anything we need 4 times (2 squared) the energy to drive it along. An 8kt thermal would need 64 times the temperature disparity with the surrounding air, and that simply isn't the case. We'd feel the heat. The air above a cigarette lighter at some 800°C would also rise at around 30kts—but it doesn't. Reversing the basic mathematics would suggest that a temperature difference of 2°C would produce a pathetic and insignificant thermal.

So what of the natural thermal generated over the countryside? In *Fig 4.4*, if we assume that a thermal rises simply from a wide ground source with the strongest rate of climb in the middle, then after 3 minutes the centre climbing at 6kts will be at 1,800ft whilst the edges climbing at 2kts will still only be at 600ft. Meanwhile, there is no suggestion as to how the warm air is being replaced nor any suggestion as to how sink is generated.

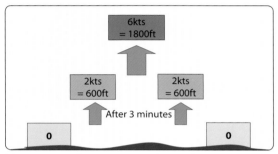

Fig 4.4 Another incorrect thermal structure concept.

Clearly then the simplest model of just warm air rising up is fundamentally wrong!

> **ANALOGY** **A bucket of water.** If you empty a bucket of water down a long drop, as the water accelerates the air resistance causes it to break the surface tension holding it together as a single mass and breaks it up into little pieces, effectively causing rain. The descent of cold air, having no structure, falls in a similar way. Of course the faster it falls the greater the effect.

> **ANALOGY** **The waterfall.** With water flowing over a waterfall, as the water accelerates towards the fall the flow becomes laminar at this point. As it flows over the top it continues to accelerate and the width reduces. In a very similar way then, warm air collects over the hotspot and as the warmest

sections start to ascend, it draws in air from abeam and underneath as it accelerates upwards.

Thermals are toroidal vortexes

Fortunately our ascending bubbles of warm air do have structure and do not go up fast enough to break apart. The cold air above has time to move out of the way and the lack of conduction within air enables the bubble to retain its temperature difference and buoyancy.

If the rising bubble of warm air does start to penetrate particularly cold air the bubble changes shape becoming more pointed (streamlined) and accelerates like water over a waterfall, before reforming a vortex bubble at a greater height (usually towards cloud base).

We know that the ground warms the air at different rates and causes local air temperature disparities. *Fig 4.5*, *Fig 4.6* and *Fig 4.7* show these relative temperature disparities compared to the immediate environment. The centre hotspots expand upwards, become less dense and once the centre spot has reached its trigger temperature, it rises.

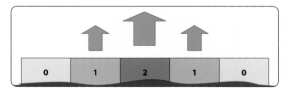

Fig 4.5 Uneven heating of air over a ground hotspot.

Once moving upwards the hottest parts will accelerate like flames from a bonfire. The central updraft draws in adjacent buoyant warm air around and thus from below, which subsequently draws in cooler air from the surrounds. This cold air rush is important to the initial thrust of the bubble.

The air above the rising bubble will be cool so it will sink around the edges, generating a downwards flow on the edge surrounding the thermal. Meanwhile the partly warmed air on the edges within the thermal source will move in behind to slipstream the first trigger.

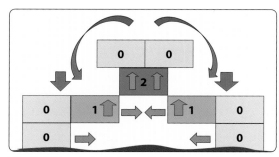

Fig 4.6 Simple build-up of the thermal vortex.

So, as the warm air rises it is replaced by air from around the base and descending around the head of the thermal. A vortex motion will be generated, as a toroidal vortex. This motion is fundamental to every thermal and can be seen in smoke rings, above bonfires, on the top of power stations, in nuclear explosions and even in the expansion of dying stars. Thermals are no different.

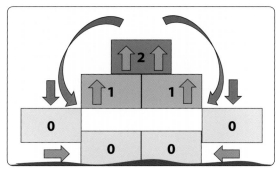

Fig 4.7 Cold air motions thrusting the hot air upwards.

Air is a terrible conductor and radiator of heat, which is a very good thing or it would be likely that our sport would not exist at all. As a result the hot air remains insulated as it climbs and essentially only goes straight up.

Three types of thermals

Just for now, consider that there are three *basic* types of thermal.

- ▶ Weak ones, such as rising air over evening forests with no associated sink. These are used primarily on evening final glides and consist of air which does not achieve the

critical requirements to generate a vortex.
- ▶ Bubbles.
- ▶ Columns (fixed and travelling).

The bubble and the column

Before moving on to discuss all aspects of thermal structure it will help if you have a clear picture of the two types of thermals—the bubble and the column. The key difference is that bubble thermals drift with the wind and climb independently, just as hot air balloons do. They are the only type of thermal that exist on blue days because they are generated by ground triggers. They often exist on days with cumulus and you must search *upwind* of the clouds to connect with them.

Column thermals are quite different and do not develop on blue days. They generate a conveyor belt structure of airflow and sit under the cloud. They are the dominant type of thermal on cloudy days and lift will be found *directly under the clouds*, even on windy days. Their structure is fundamental to the development of towering columns and streets.

The bubble

For simplicity consider first that the thermal is a bubble, simply rising as if it were a hot air balloon. If it rises through a band of neutral stability the bubble climbs in isolation and its buoyancy remains steady. We are familiar with the concept that as air rises it cools at 3°C per 1,000ft. But the descending air warms. Consider the bubble being 1,000ft high. The air above the bubble descends and warms at 3°C per 1,000ft, therefore the bubble continues to rise steadily. The air descending below the bubble remains neutrally stable.

> ANALOGY **The ice-ball.** Consider a ball of ice rising in water, as it rises a little ice will melt on the edges but in essence the ice ball will remain intact.

It is important to remember that air is a terrible conductor of heat. So, as in the analogy of ice rising in water, the rising air will continue to float upwards and the mixing with the air around it is minimal.

The vortex generator

There are toroidal vortex generator *toys* available to explore this effect more closely, as shown in *Fig 4.8 and Photo 4.1.* Rather critically though, the shape of the vortex is only stable when round and they can easily be broken and destroyed. If you frame the vortex generator so that the exit hole is any other shape than round, it does not work. There are no oblong or square shaped vortexes.

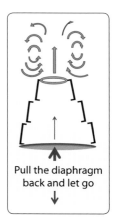

Pull the diaphragm back and let go

Fig 4.8 The vortex flow generated by the vortex toy.

Photo 4.1 A toroidal vortex generator toy.

This is important with our understanding of the air motions around us especially if you think that thermals may be oval shaped. Other shaped thermals will be covered later.

Properties of a vortex

Compare the performance of a balloon to a vortex bubble. A balloon that is thrown across a room will not travel far but a vortex bubble will still be moving after about 10m or more.

There are two other important aspects to the vortex. Firstly, *anything held within the vortex travels with it.* Introducing smoke into the generator shows us this and of course if the vortex is holding hot air it too will remain with the travelling vortex. Secondly, *the speed of travel is directly proportional to the initial push (trigger).* If you reduce the spring pressure within the toy, the rotation within the vortex is slower and the bubble generated simply travels slower.

The rotational motion of air acts with similar properties to that of a gyroscope, which is probably quite a surprise to most people. This motion has a property called rigidity (just try toppling a spinning top) and this can be seen in the rotation of a dust devil. However, the physics of a dust devil is not complementary to a thermal vortex, although the general principles of

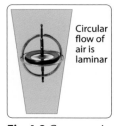

Circular flow of air is laminar

Fig 4.9 Gyroscopic properties/rigidity of a dust devil.

a gyroscope remain. A dust devil uses the *low pressure* to sustain it whilst a thermal requires a *low density* within its core. The dust devil is covered later but what is important is the precessional properties of a gyroscope. If you push down on one edge of the spinning disc the gyroscope will lean as though the force has been applied after 90° of rotation of the gyroscope.

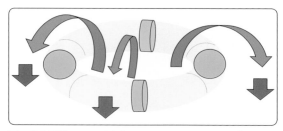

Fig 4.10 The toroidal vortex acts as a continuous loop gyroscope.

Fig 4.10 shows a thermal vortex. This thermal bubble has the rigidity of a toroidal vortex. The buoyancy is the upwards driving force, which is resisted by the aerodynamic zero lift drag.

Thermals are made up of a continuous looped air gyroscope, called a toroidal vortex. This rises as though it is a basic bubble and air displaced by the thermal passes along the outside giving us the telltale sink which surrounds all thermals.

KEY POINT The thermal structure is a toroidal vortex.

The air not directly connected with the vortex generates sink as if the vortex is a bubble. This is shown by the red arrows in *Fig 4.11.*

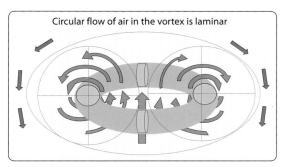

Fig 4.11 Two-dimensional continuous loop gyroscope.

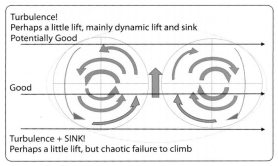

Fig 4.12 Flying through the toroidal thermal at different heights.

Consider the different airflows, feels and gusts that we would encounter transiting across the thermal bubble centre at different heights, as shown in *Fig 4.12*. You can see that the bottom of the bubble would not be a good place to be.

Dynamics of a thermal

Buoyancy is achieved due to both the higher temperature relative to surrounding air and the higher humidity relative to the surroundings. Also, the higher pressure relative to the surrounding air causes expansion. In addition, there are two motions within a thermal: the vortex motion within a bubble and the vertical motion of the bubble or column. It is important to note that these thermals have considerably more mass and momentum than a gaggle of gliders.

KEY POINT The air mass lifting a gaggle of 20 gliders, that weigh a total of about 10 tons, descending through the air at

1kt, will be unhindered by the weight of the gliders. An average bubble thermal of 200m diameter and vertical displacement of 200m has a mass of about 6,500 tons. This massive amount of air is in the region of 650 times the weight of the gliders and if the thermal was rising at 3kts it would have about 2,000 times more momentum than the combined momentum of the gliders. So, don't worry if another glider joins you in a thermal as it won't affect you!

Consider a droplet of water falling into a bowl of water. There will be some reaction but it is small and local, because the density of the water in the bowl is just the same as the droplet. Even on a bigger scale like a huge chunk of an iceberg falling into the sea, there will be just a local effect. Similarly, a thermal will have a local effect on its immediate surroundings, but the mass is still relative to the considerably bigger mass of the air it is trying to disturb. The bigger mass will win and the thermal will therefore be moderated by the surrounding air that it is trying to push aside. It will willingly give in and drift.

As an aside, regardless of the size of the thermal source (e.g. a large bonfire, a thin chimney of a power station or large field or town) 200m is a good guide to the approximate diameter of a standard thermal, regardless of how strong it is. Of course the strength of a standard bonfire simply does not provide us with anything more than a bit of hope. There simply is not enough air mass at the start. This does not mean there are not bigger thermals and this standard thermal size of 200m will vary slightly according to temperature, pressure and humidity. Minority bigger thermals do exist but they require additional analysis for which there is no space here in this chapter, but their structure and development is covered later. So a thermal bubble is about the size of a football stadium, but obviously taller.

KEY POINT 200m is a good guide to the diameter of a thermal.

Bear in mind that it takes just 6 seconds at a speed of 60kts to transit the 200m across the middle, from zero lift through the core and back out through zero lift again, and 2 seconds each side to transit through the sink. Therefore, if you don't react quickly you will jeopardize your ability to centre!

Before considering any movement of the air in and around a thermal you should understand that *rising air primarily only has a vertical force acting on it*, buoyancy; in other words a force straight upwards. If strong enough, it also exhibits an *explosive* high pressure force of expansion around the core where the horizontal temperature gradient is at the highest value. Just to be clear, hot air does not go down or sideways without some external force being applied to it. One thermal cannot be independently pushed sideways to join another without the force equally affecting the adjacent air. Therefore it cannot drift into another and coalesce into one larger thermal. A faster climbing thermal can catch up a slower rising thermal though.

Sinking air has one main force acting on it, weight, so it moves downwards. Again, cold air does not go up or sideways without some external force being applied to it. It does not form vortex-ring motions or rotate.

The warmth of air can only be transmitted by convection (conduction or radiation is minimal in this situation) and therefore it has to physically move to make somewhere else either hotter or colder. For example, the air *under* a lit match does not get hot, nor does a hot air balloon generate a thermal *under* the basket. Any air warmer than its surroundings will not go down. Similarly sink cannot be generated in the air above a cold lake.

Between the strong updraft and the downdraft is an outwards flow, otherwise known as the *gust*. Beyond this the air is turbulent and feels like driving over cobblestones where the air interacts with the outer edges of the bubble. It is all of these forces within the thermal that we must try to sense and feel.

Drag

There is one other thing to grasp and that is that everything which travels through the air is restricted by drag. In terms of an aircraft the drag is divided into two distinct parts:

▶ **Lift-dependent drag**—generated as a result of producing lift.
▶ **Zero lift drag**—generated regardless of any lift being produced.

Zero lift drag is made up of three forces:

▶ **Profile drag**—the frontal surface area viewed in the direction of travel.
▶ **Interference drag**—turbulence between the deflected airflows interacting around the object.
▶ **Surface friction drag**—the area also known as the boundary layer.

Hot air moving through cool air is subject to the zero lift drag aerodynamics detailed above but has three additional properties. Unlike solid objects, *warm air can freely change shape*. Also, *it can mix with the surrounding air* and, perhaps most importantly, *its rotation reduces what would otherwise be surface friction drag*. However, it is easier to simply consider the warm rising air as a single entity, like a hot air balloon. Whilst the additional gas properties are significant, their effect complicates matters but this will be covered later.

First to the bubble (vortex ring). If you imagine a solid ball or balloon going through the air, an eddy will be set up which must generate a vortex motion. However, the faster the thermal rises, the stronger the vortex, therefore the stronger the sink around the bubble. There are two airflows to consider, one of the sinking air passing by and the second within the bubble vortex. The sinking air is not air that has risen, it is air which has moved out of the way and rushed around the rising air, as shown in *Fig 4.13*. Whilst we often talk about climbing in strong or weak thermals, little is discussed about the structure of sink except that we had a bad bit somewhere, the distribution of which for several reasons can vary considerably over the sky at any one time. For our rising thermal, the sink therefore always matches the rate of climb of the part we call a thermal. It is important to note that it is the sinking air which determines the structure of the soaring sky and this is one of the most fundamental points to remember in any subsequent analysis.

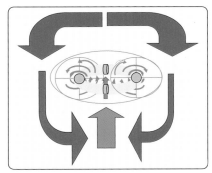

Fig 4.13 Airflow around the rising bubble.

The column

As well as bubble thermals there are two types of column thermals, which are both made up of bubbles. The two types offer slightly different properties to us. *Fig 4.14* shows the first case, of a bubble rising through a layer which is *unstable* and is probably the most important aspect to understand. As the bubble climbs through the unstable layer the temperature difference increases, accelerating the thermal upwards and narrowing the head but also generating an accelerating downward flow. The descending air warms but not sufficiently for the height lost so its relative density increases, which subsequently enables the thermal to grow downwards. This increases the mass of the thermal and for a time changes its shape to be more sausage shaped. The reduction in frontal area is more streamlined and allows the acceleration to continue. Additionally the reduction in drag from underneath allows the thermal to grow downwards.

As the bubble climbs through the unstable layer the temperature difference increases. Initially the bubble is 1 °C warmer than its surroundings and as it climbs 1,000ft it becomes 2 °C warmer. This accelerates the thermal upwards and narrows the head but also generates an accelerating downward flow. The descending air, which was initially stable, warms after descending but becomes cooler than the ambient air so its relative density increases (it becomes 1 °C cooler than ambient). This enables the thermal to grow downwards as air within the descending tube of cold air rises and increases the mass of the thermal from below. For a short time the growing thermal changes its shape to be more sausage-shaped. The reduction in frontal area is more streamlined and allows the acceleration to continue. Additionally the reduction in drag from underneath allows the thermal to grow downwards.

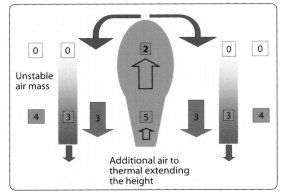

Fig 4.14 Vertical growth of a bubble into a column thermal.

The second type of column thermal development comes from the vortex within a vertical string of bubbles which results in the rapid acceleration of the air. As a bubble catches and passes through a slower bubble it will narrow and accelerate. This can happen several times on passing further bubbles and generate a powerful thermal, which to the pilot feels like a column. Of course, there is also the possibility that the thermals may break apart.

Fig 4.15 shows a vortex generator producing an accelerating thermal. The air within the generator is already rotating and accelerates further passing through the narrow exit.

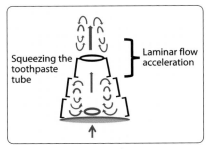

Fig 4.15 Vortex acceleration.

We are familiar with the very smooth laminar flow on the forward part of a wing and the turbulent boundary layers behind. A fundamental difference between the bubble and column thermals is that the flow in a bubble often appears quite turbulent but the rotational air is fairly laminar whereas the column allows for the development of a laminar flow up through the core allowing it to flow faster. When air is accelerated it tends to become laminar and when decelerated it becomes turbulent.

> **ANALOGY** **The bonfire.** Above the central part of a bonfire a laminar flow can be seen as the very hot air accelerates away from the flaming logs. This slows and the outer edges become turbulent at some stage higher up.

As in the analogy of the bonfire, where you can see the airflows in a column thermal, you will feel the gust on the boundary between the laminar flow and turbulent edge, but it will be more abrupt than that. The accelerated laminar flow is a further contributor along with the reduction in cross-sectional area (profile drag) to rapid ascent and due to the reduction in external surface area (surface friction) drag. It will still generate the gust outwards on the edge between the laminar flow going upwards and the interacting turbulent air which is rising more slowly (boundary layer).

Also, if a thermal is rising into a more unstable layer it will narrow and accelerate and we must tighten and hang on within the laminar flow. It is likely that the thermal will reform with a central gust accelerating upwards, as it often does at cloud base and within the lowest level of clouds where the structure will be rather like that of a thermal generated at ground level. Column thermals are intolerant to windshear and will not form or if they have managed to start, the development will cease at the point of shear.

The gust

In every thermal there is a horizontal gust. Between the rising and descending air there will be an interference boundary layer, shown in *Fig 4.16*, which feels like flying over cobblestones. The warmer air within the thermal at the top will now be at a slightly higher pressure than the

surrounding air and therefore the bubble will try to expand outwards into the descending air. This horizontal gust is only close to the central core where there is the largest change of temperature.

It is fundamentally incorrect to suggest that there is a horizontal acceleration when the glider hits a vertical updraft. The gust on the ASI is a horizontal gust hitting the glider at that time. If the glider did in fact accelerate by 6kts in half a second then we would feel this, similarly we would be well aware of the subsequent deceleration.

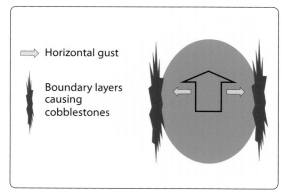

Horizontal gust

Boundary layers causing cobblestones

Fig 4.16 Thermal structure and expansion.

Pure solo vortex thermals

Pure solo vortex thermals are a rare occurrence. You are most likely to have unknowingly seen the clouds generated by pure solo vortex thermals but less likely to have knowingly climbed in one. They are triggered by very specific air motions associated with rapid sink at the lower levels hitting a rising thermal, along with sympathetic topography. In other words you cannot tell by any conventional means that one will be generated at a particular point over the ground. It means that as it hits the layer normally associated with the generation of a column, one is not generated as the sinking air does not descend sufficiently to allow growth. The cumulus cloud generated is classically indicated by a cumulus which clearly decays quickly from underneath at the local cloud base whilst the rest of the thermal rises quickly in a well formed classic but climbing cloud base cumulus shape. Overall the cloud shape is akin to a rising jelly fish.

If you do encounter one there will be no cloud above indicating its presence and you have to respond quickly to get on board. There will be no gliders thermalling above you and anyone joining much underneath you will be disappointed and a bit confused that someone is leaving them behind so quickly.

Thermal shape

When viewed from above it is quite reasonable to assume that most thermals tend to be circular, as depicted in the previous diagrams. The air at the top is at a slightly higher pressure than the surroundings and is always trying to drive itself out as well as ascending due to the lesser density.

There is a view held that bigger clouds must be fed by bigger thermals. If that were so the structure of clouds would remain the same regardless of size. In fact when we look at any cumulus cloud it rapidly becomes clear that they are all made of multiple bubbles, as shown in *Fig 4.17*. Bigger clouds simply display more bubbles, not bigger bubbles.

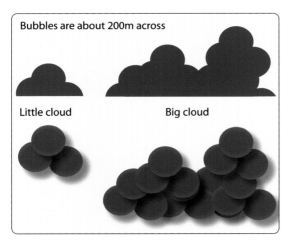

Fig 4.17 Clouds made up of individual bubbles.

If thermals always rose as standard bubbles our sport would be a little simpler. If you shoot a large number of bubbles from a bubble gun, they do not all follow the same trajectory. In fact they disperse quite considerably even in a closed room. When a thermal source produces a constant stream of thermals then it would be quite wrong to suggest that they all go on the same flight path.

The break-up of the vortex

Both the column and the bubble can be broken and this often happens, much to our dismay, despite the fact that we can still see a cloud above us. So long as the thermal remains circular then the bubble will retain its rigidity. As it climbs into a small windshear the forces endeavour to push the top of the thermal over, as shown in *Fig 4.18*. This force has no significant effect on the upwind or downwind sides of the thermal, but precessional forces affect the rotating air on either side causing the thermal to try to become oval and the structure breaks immediately. We see this clearly when a smoke ring collapses. Looking at clouds we can see that an inversion also destroys the vortex.

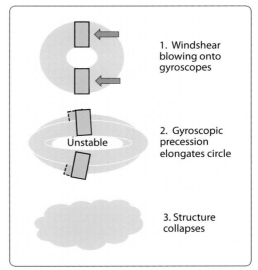

Fig 4.18 Plan view of windshear destroying the vortex.

Despite the break in the vortex, the air is still warmer than the surroundings and it will continue to climb, although initially the structure will be a muddle to us because there is none. The warm air continues to rise but as a shimmer without structure and the breaking vortex scatters the air outwards. Of course this slight windshear nearly always coincides with the thermal rising into a more stable level, where it will slow and broaden anyway. We can often get the impression that the thermal has become elongated. Effectively, the rising air will drift towards an elongation, shaped by the descending air from the cloud above, but the overall strength will have significantly diminished. All bubbles reaching the more stable air will do the same so we can have an extended area where there appears to be several thermals. We often experience this approaching cloud base under a large elongated cloud mass with little vertical development and find it impossible to climb the last few hundred feet to cloud base. There is another consideration whilst climbing in a broken or breaking bubble thermal—the fact that we are descending down through the air and it will eventually leave us behind. If we are falling at 2kts through a 200ft high shimmer then we fall out of the bottom after one minute. Fortunately there are clues that this has happened as we lose the normal indications of the thermal. The thermal shear is not present so we lose wing flex, the gust on the ASI and if we get any string deflections they are usually only spurious flickers.

The vertical shape of thermals

One aspect which is hardly touched on in all the gliding literature is the vertical shape of thermals. If we consider any fluid object moving through the air then we find that a teardrop type of shape develops naturally and this will offer significantly less drag than a flat plate shape. Viewed in the direction of travel the shape is round but may become teardrop shaped when viewed from one side. Other shaped volumes of air do form but they are far less common. It is necessary to start with a basic idea before identifying how the shape can be modified.

Any increase in pressure (such as an explosion) demonstrates that the outflow is displaced evenly from the central point. This is seen when thermals are produced by bonfires or cooling tower chimneys, whilst clouds of individual thermal cells are also essentially generally circular in shape. The generation of these thermals are, however, formed from a fixed point and are not disrupted by any conflicting activity in the environment. Of course this assumes that the thermal is climbing into neutrally stable air. In an unstable band of air sinking air interacts with

the rising air. This may reinforce the strength of the rising air and can also modify the shape of a thermal whenever it interacts with it, as shown in *Fig 4.19*. Here, rapidly descending cold air is modifying a normal thermal.

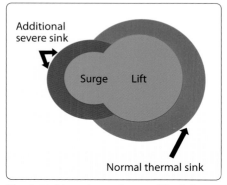

Fig 4.19 Plan view of a modified thermal.

Fig 4.20, viewed from the side is more complicated. Firstly, the normal shape of a bubble thermal will be essentially toroidal but it can distort a small amount to be egg shaped or teardrop shaped. Thermals can be influenced to a small extent by adjacent sinking flows generated from other bubbles, without destroying either cell. If you are lucky, then the sink from one thermal will modify an adjacent thermal. If they are too close, the interaction destroys both.

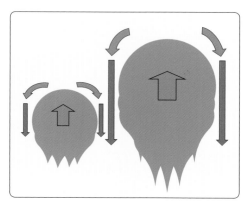

Fig 4.20 Interaction of adjacent thermals.

Stronger thermals

Imagine trying to make a balloon travel quickly through the air by hitting it hard. It will rapidly slow due to drag and then descend slowly, regardless of the size of the balloon. The density of a big balloon is effectively the same as a small balloon; likewise, the size of a thermal does not depict its strength. An incorrect commonly held view is that bigger thermals are stronger thermals. If you try to ascend a helium balloon quickly, drag will determine its speed in the same way as other balloons. A thermal is no different, its speed will also be determined by buoyancy and drag..

Once a thermal leaves the ground its energy is fixed and it is the initial thermal source, size and trigger that determine this energy. The trigger determines the strength of the thermal and the source size determines its volume.

If we time how long it takes between the initial development of a cumulus cloud and the time at which it stops continuing to develop, by knowing the average rate of climb we could then work out how tall a bubble thermal is. For example, if the development lasts for 2 minutes with a 3kt thermal we could then consider the depth of the thermal bubble to be around 600ft.

Of course once the trigger has sprung and all the local warm air has been dragged in the general direction of the thermal there will be a lull in proceedings until the next pulse. So, a good source will produce a series of bubbles which will each climb as a separate entity, entirely independent of each other, but they may overlap horizontally.

Sink

Contrary to some suggestions, cloud does not fall. If it did, fog would clear by going down. What we can see around the edges of clouds are the winds generated by the vortex and windshear.

Consider the cloud at the top of a thermal. As it pushes up into the drier air the cloud droplets will start to evaporate into the dry air next to it, which is already descending. It takes 540 times as much heat energy to change a water droplet into a gas than to heat the same water droplet up by one degree Celsius. This large amount of energy is taken from the dry air, which rapidly reduces in temperature, so the air next to a cloud increases in humidity and becomes rapidly cold. It is therefore denser and heavier than the air around it so it descends, hence clouds make sink. As shown in *Fig 4.21*, the higher the cloud top (and

the drier the upper air) the stronger the sink will be because the rate of evaporation will be higher.

Of course whilst cruising in your glider at lower altitudes the cloud may well have fully evaporated and hence the occasional scenario of not knowing where the sink has come from! Just like thermals, sink can vary and even accelerate downwards slightly.

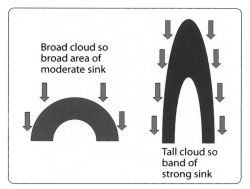

Fig 4.21 The higher the cloud the stronger the sink.

Evaporation of the water droplets takes place around the edges of the cloud first and from the centre last. There is no formation of a descending vortex and the sinking air lacks any kind of rigidity, unlike a rising thermal. This is an important difference. The exception to this rule is when there is precipitation. Rain, hail or snow generate a central downflow of air, similar to a column thermal in reverse.

Because of the upflow in the centre the majority of the sink is experienced below the edges of the cloud. The sink is predictable but quite variable as it depends on so many things. It depends on relative temperature and humidity, the size and shape of the cloud and how broad the base is. It also depends on how the cloud was generated. It is also important to note that when there is any light precipitation at cloud base which evaporates before reaching the ground the sink will become more severe.

ANALOGY **Pouring milk.** Consider pouring milk from a jug into a cup of tea. The milk accelerates downwards from the jug. We could just drip the milk out or pour a stream along with raising or lowering the height from which we drop it. (Cold air descending through an unstable layer will act in a similar way and accelerate). When our milk hits the tea, as the relative densities are very similar, the milk disperses horizontally mixing with the hot tea. It also cannot descend below the limits of the cup.

Similar to the cup of tea analogy, the volume and strength of the sink will depend on the size of the cloud and the height from which it is descending. It will effectively pour down and if the air is unstable, accelerate downwards. It will not expand and the turbulent boundary layer is narrower than that of a thermal as there are no horizontal motions. We get far less warning of approaching sink despite the fact that the effective lag on the vario is considerably less in indicating sink than lift, it just appears, but both the strength and displacement can now understandably be quite variable. When the previously relatively cold air approaches the lower levels or reaches a stable layer it disperses outwards, flooding the area. Of course when this descends down towards the lowest levels it then effectively kills off weaker thermal-generating areas, and pools over lower ground.

Where there is a considerable development of cumulus cloud coupled with a decrease of wind strength with height above cloud base, but below cloud tops, large areas of mammatus cloud may be seen adjacent and upwind to the large cumulus. Mammatus is best described as upside-down

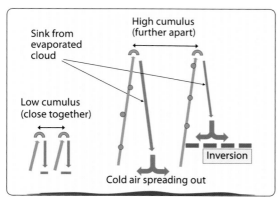

Fig 4.22 Sink.

cumulus. Venture under this cloud entirely at your peril as it is the best indicator of a large area of sky offering sustained sink.

In *Fig 4.22* the higher cloud base generates a taller column of descending air within any unstable bands and this spreads further afield when it reaches the lowest levels, killing embryonic thermals. It is not just hot air going up which generates ground level gusts.

We can now briefly introduce the organization of sink above and around clouds. *Fig 4.23* shows that the higher the cloud the wider the gaps between thermals. The structure of the thermic sky is controlled by the sink. Ignoring wave, there are three types of sink:

► Mass subsidence. This may be ignored in the UK but in areas of the world where cloud bases are very high it becomes significant.
► Sink associated with the thermal. This may be from a bubble or column thermal.
► Sink associated with evaporating clouds.

It is worth noting that sink does not develop vortices. Any rising bubble of air can generate a bow wave above it and the same thing can happen just above the forming clouds. Clouds may be relatively narrow but often broaden out and present themselves as flat mushroom shapes. When this occurs, the air above is displaced sideways, and eventually falls or cascades around the sides of the cloud like a waterfall. This explains why the sink you experience as you approach or leave such a cloud is quite strong, yet there is no corresponding strong lift anywhere under the cloud. In fact sometimes there may be no useful lift at all as the displacement is being triggered solely by the extension (local mini spread-out) of the cloud above cloud base and its evaporation. You should always check the top of the cloud before you get under it in order to see if it is still being fed from below by a narrow head of thermal activity.

Summarizing then, the cloud will be much bigger than the thermal underneath and if you analyse the tops to note where any peak is you will stand a better chance of contacting the thermal core. Make sure that you route via the clear air rather than under decaying cumulus.

KEY POINT Look for the highest part of the cloud tops to find the thermal underneath.

Sinking air does not rotate or generate vortices. For thermals this means that there must be an equal volume of descending air to replace the volume of rising air. The huge volume of column thermals will only be generated and get taller by effectively growing downwards as they climb into an increasingly unstable layer, as explained previously. But then once fully developed they also generate an equal and additional volume of cold descending air which cascades down and floods the lower layers over a considerable area. It is quite reasonable then to assume the greater the volume of active cloud, the greater the volume of sink will be, no matter how it is generated. This descending air is therefore a major contributor to the thermals developing farther apart as the cloud base steadily moves up. In light winds, fixed column thermals develop and the thermal width will broaden (volume of rising air increases) and the huge volume of sinking air will kill off the weaker areas for miles around. Perhaps strangely then it is the huge volume of sinking air which controls the thermic sky.

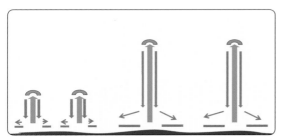

Fig 4.23 Column thermals, the higher the cloud base the wider the gaps between thermals.

On the left side of *Fig 4.23* there is a small flow and volume of descending cold air which does not extend too far away from the column core. On the right the taller columns cascade a huge volume of cold air which spreads much farther away from the core forcing the thermals to spread out. In column thermals, the higher the cloud base the greater the volume of rising air, therefore the greater volume of descending air. The controlling force when the air is unstable is this huge volume

of descending air and this causes thermals to be farther apart when the cloud base is higher.

Volume and development of the bubble thermal

Just before we move on to thermal triggers there are some very important basics to understand.

We have a pretty good idea that thermals are 200m across but to know the volume we have to know the height of the column. Accepting for the moment that all thermals are essentially formed by bubbles of air leaving the ground and rising, we will now look at the volume of bubble thermals. Stood on the ground we occasionally feel the gust which feeds the initial launch of a thermal, but even if the gust was as much as 10kts (1,000ft/min) for 6 seconds, the draw of air is usually only about 100ft horizontally over the ground. Actually if you investigate the area from which a vacuum cleaner draws air it is surprisingly small, despite the blast of air which comes out from the other end. In other words blow generates a more powerful influence than suck.

Watching the clouds and sky at any time allows you to develop a sixth sense of what is probably going on in the air below.

If we watch a cloud for a few minutes we will see that after the initial wisp a cumulus cloud will develop and then dissipate. The whole process may take around six minutes with the cumulus cloud being in a state of development for only three minutes, dissipating for a further three minutes. So a 2kt thermal (200ft/min) means that the bubble was only 600ft tall. Even if the development was five minutes then it was only 1,000ft tall. As the cloud starts to develop, the tail of the thermal will also be climbing behind even though it was disconnected from the ground six minutes ago, leaving perhaps only a little turbulence behind, but no thermal underneath. If the thermal was a little stronger though, assuming the same cross-sectional area, then the column will be taller—3kts for three minutes still only makes the column 900ft tall. This tells us two things. Firstly, why on some days despite seemingly flying under every cloud we can reach, we don't find a climb and secondly that there may be a shift in the wind somewhere in the climb and that the air is not unstable enough to produce column thermals. On some days it definitely pays to stay up near the clouds and uncharacteristically use, or bounce, every thermal.

So from this simple picture we can calculate the volume of air in a standard thermal and relate this volume to the thermal source, let's say a field. If we consider a thermal to be a sphere then a standard thermal of 100m radius has a volume of 4,190,476 cubic metres. Now consider the size of field that would generate this thermal. A typical field in the UK is 500m square. So the volume of air in the thermal divided by the farmer's field surface area of 250,000m^2, gives a depth of the initial warm air of just 16.8m.

When we compare this deduction with what we feel on the ground and experience flying at low level this all makes sense. How often do you find that from low key to final there is often a broad *thermal* just too late (too low) to use but you subsequently end up relatively high turning final? Another question though is more telling. How often are you in a flat glide below 500ft? Probably this is likely to be (up to now) only during the late part of a circuit. As you do more cross-countries or more importantly, final glides back to base for a straight-in approach, you will often get significant benefit from flying over what would appear to be good thermal production areas with no significant sink and even some gentle climbs. Having height in hand, speed is increased and you safely cruise during the last few kilometres because of the surplus speed. As a result, during the late stages of the glide you continue to gain energy and you go even faster. This is usually taken to be an error of setting off too high 30km back for the final glide. This assumption is incorrect. Do not assume that it will always work. When you really need it—it won't!

The effect of anything which shields an area from the wind to encourage the build-up of hot air and therefore allows the generation of the appropriate volume of hot air to produce our thermals is worthy of notice. Such shields might be trees, buildings, small ridges and wind farms.

Of course not all fields are 500m square but the slope, area and shape orientated to the wind contribute to the volume and strength of the thermal produced. A large round or square-shaped field surrounded by physical boundaries like trees or buildings in light winds will produce a strong thermal, whilst a long field in line with the wind will generate a weaker yet almost continuous stream of bubbles.

5
Trigger actions

- ► Looking for triggers
- ► Thermal triggers
- ► Identifying thermal sources
- ► Hills make their own weather

During a nationals race Dave's initial helpful task in the air was simply to provide cartons of juice. This first opportunity for him to impress was to be met with failure as, having handed over the desired items and having been given back control, I found that the straw, being too short for the carton, disappeared inside.

At this point the vario suddenly hit the stops down. The winter vario agreed so it was not an electrical issue and the flight resembled something akin to an upside down winch launch, with the averager hitting 22 down. I looked to see if we still had the wings attached! But, just as suddenly, this all reversed and my attention was drawn to 18 up on the averager, whilst Dave was distracted by the half-finished carton of orange which went hurtling back in his direction, spilling juice all over his trousers. And so we climbed out of this extraordinary situation.

The flight was analysed in the evening and we discovered an unusual sky structure. This was confirmed later in the week whilst flying over the same area. It was strong, yet surprisingly very local, wave!

Now that we have a real understanding of the ups and downs of the air we can consider trigger actions, an often-used couple of words with a vague and confused meaning. The thermal structure is entirely embryonic in the lowest levels and can only be understood by looking at the things we can see, which are simply ground features, topography, wind and cloud structure.

Looking for triggers

At a low altitude the normal glider instrument indications and feel are different to those when entering a thermal at height. This knowledge can be more than a little useful if you ever find yourself a bit low. We avoid flying our gliders at very low altitude with the intention of thermalling simply because it is far too dangerous. As a result, we have very little experience to judge just what is happening to the air motions lower down. Nevertheless this is where most thermals are born, so some understanding will help if we are disconnected from the usual cloud indicators and now have to start looking at the ground and trying to determine where we might get that saving climb.

Of course investigating the air motions at heights less than 500ft is exactly the area where our concentration is focussed on landing.

However, we do routinely enter this height band on every flight including final glides so it is worth exercising any spare mental capacity to note just what is happening.

In this regard the common seagull is indeed a blessing. After all, they routinely glide at extremely low altitudes yet have a polar curve similar to a *T21*. The soaring flying techniques that they use are similar to our own and apart from classic thermalling they do 'S' turns, ridge running, dynamic soaring and MacCready dolphin, although it would seem that they have yet to discover wave. They display visually to us the lowest structure of developing thermals which is similar to the thermals we use at higher heights.

To try to understand what is going on we might first consider cold spots, so we will start with something simple that we can see—fog. We know that thermals generated from the ground require a temperature contrast. When we get fog we can see it sitting in valleys but also in the little dips as we drive along a road or along the side of a river bank. It is often patchy but it shows us the pooling of cool air at ground level. It takes either a wind of over 8kts to shift it or a lot of heat. We also know that over flat land when an area near fog warms in the sun, a light breeze will develop and draws the fog over the clear area, cooling that area. It then slowly subsides back to where it came from and the cycle might repeat. During a summer day with a light wind we should be able to anticipate where there might be bad air with almost the same accuracy as predicting good areas. For example, a large area of cloud shadow covering a valley can't be good.

In *Photo 5.1* whilst there is no fog it should be clear that any cold or relatively cooler air will pour into the valleys and there is unlikely to be much in the way of thermals. Routing along the valleys *cannot* be a good idea.

Photo 5.1 Avoiding valleys.

In many aspects of physics there is a critical point at which something will or will not occur. Boats will start to skim the surface at a set speed, tyres will aquaplane at certain speeds related to tyre pressure and the airflow over a wing ceases to be laminar at a critical angle of attack. In a similar way then, thermals develop only after a certain critical point has been reached and we rather loosely call these *trigger actions* which are often linked to trigger temperatures. One such action is a significant temperature difference (about 2 °C) over a small area. Trigger actions are the supporting *boot* which then starts a chain of events and these trigger actions can be split into two types.

The first is a thermic trigger caused by sufficient disparity in the temperature of adjacent lumps of air, over a relatively small distance, causing the hot air to rise. The second is a forced trigger where air has been driven upwards, for example wind going up a hill or hot moist air being pushed out by a power station. The air above may have the potential to be unstable yet in a dormant state,

whilst the air below is stable. Once triggered a ripple of instability can continue like the turbulent wake generated from a moving boat. Of course we always talk about the warm air but we must remember that this is just in relative terms. Descending cold air will also act as a trigger.

> **ANALOGY** **Smoke rings.** Smokers can always blow smoke out of their mouths, but if they do it in a particular way they generate a smoke ring. Otherwise the smoke just drifts.

Just as in the smoking analogy not all rising air becomes a vortex. An effective thermal source must generate sufficient warm air and the trigger must support the formation of a vortex.

Thermal triggers

Subsequent references to hot, warm or cold air are simply air temperatures relative to the adjacent air. There can be good large areas for thermal generation but then more specific points where the thermals are triggered.

> **ANALOGY** **Boiling water.** If you look at a pan of boiling water you will see that the bubbles occur in the same spot every time, even if you stir the water.

From the pan of boiling water analogy it should come as no surprise that our thermal sources are largely from the same place, time after time. However, this is only on a blue day because cloud shadow will alter the thermal contrast on the ground. Thermals depend on buoyancy and float upwards in a similar way to the bubbles in the pan. Physics limits this buoyancy and even with huge heat sources the rate of ascent soon slows due to drag. You can't keep hot air down and you can't keep cold air up.

Consider a blue day with little or no wind. You should be able to recognize which areas will get hotter than adjacent ground and identify potential thermal sources. You need to have a significant thermal contrast between two adjoining areas of ground (or water) to generate a thermal trigger. In reality the trigger requires about a 2 °C contrast.

There are opportunities for a larger differential to be generated and obviously these thermals will kick off with more gusto and may generate a stronger thermal.

Source size, colour, material differences such as crops or tarmac, dryness or dampness, shape of the heated source, angle to the sun and orientation to the wind are all important along with the overall instability of the air. If the furrows of a ploughed field are aligned to both the wind and the sun the thermal, kicking off from the downwind boundary, will be stronger than if the wind, or particularly the sun, is across it. Although we are not considering the wind effects yet, wind blowing up a hill can be a strong trigger action. Equally a long field aligned to the wind will funnel air to the trigger point compared to a broad field across the wind. Triggers to help the generation are important and they can also occur at altitude causing middle airspace instability.

Identifying thermal sources

Of course it is easy to identify a thermal source from a small village some 500m across but whilst a bigger town will be a good producer of many thermals it will be difficult to find a specific trigger source on any particular occasion. Patrolling the downwind edge will be your best bet whilst looking for any telltale surface wind deflections. This is rather like anticipating where drops will start to run on a window covered in condensation.

In the past I have flown many radio-controlled scale gliders up to a 5m span and this has allowed me to explore thermals and thermal sources at very low altitudes, at and around 50ft. The best time to launch my model has always been just as there was a lull in the surface wind, indicating an approaching thermal as the air is drawn into the area upwind of my position, where the thermal is lifting from. Bearing in mind that the launch elastic of 50m allows one to get the model about 300ft up and 200ft forwards of my position on the ground, then this gives an objective indication of the surface size of the air feeding into the thermal. To emphasise, the average thermal at ground level is not miles wide, but merely a few hundred metres, narrowing as it rises towards overhead the trigger point. Another point regarding thermal

generation in lighter winds is that a large bush or high tree on a hedge row or the subtle high spot of a field can be the trigger point.

Obviously not everyone has the desire to go out and buy expensive radio-controlled models to explore thermal development but then the birds do a better job of showing us the thermals. Gulls can be seen almost anywhere in our country and demonstrate the structure of thermal and ridge lift. They do not always turn in the same direction either, even in the same thermal at the same height. Recently reintroduced to the UK are red kites, which routinely thermal from some 20 or 30ft over relatively open fields, often in the lee of buildings or trees. They can be seen to eventually climb up and connect with thermals at our kind of operating heights.

Fortunately we have a few other things to help. We know that when standing on the airfield, in light winds, we can feel when a thermal is passing through because we feel the gust. You might even notice the lull when it was upwind. To avoid inaccurate wind indications due to turbulence generated by the mean surface wind flowing around ground obstacles, the Met-man's wind sock should be attached to the top of a 30ft mast. Yet if you watch it, the wind sock will still often be seen swinging around a bit. If you look at a trace of wind speed and direction, as a glider pilot knowing that the air was unstable at the time, the indication might make more sense and can be useful. During the time of deflection, air is being drawn into the area where the thermal is lifting up from. The deflection angle will be determined by how far away and where the thermal hotspot is. The period of the deflection is also important if we are to estimate how large the thermal bubble might be. We can feel these changes in surface winds below 200ft on the approach, but of course don't let this detract you from making a safe landing. Various smoke sources that we see also give a good indication that there is a local surface disturbance going on. Smoke sources from high chimneys are less effective indicators because the chimney top is often well above the air that is being drawn in. Over flat ground there needs to be the development of an adequate thermal contrast before the bubble rises. Small limited areas only produce weak thermals as in *Fig 5.1*. Assume that a difference of 2 °C is required to generate a thermal vortex.

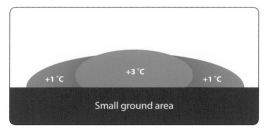

Fig 5.1 The temperature contrast to trigger a weak thermal.

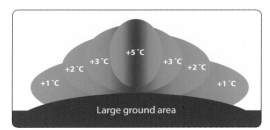

Fig 5.2 Strong thermal from a big ground area.

Despite the loss of several power stations in the UK, such as the well known thermal source at Didcot, spare a celebratory drink for the replacement thermal sources that are appearing throughout the world. Solar farms are 20% efficient, which means that in simple terms the rest is reflected light and heat. As we are not blinded by the reflected light this is an 80% efficient hot air thermal generator then! There are a lot of solar farms around and more appearing every year. Housing estates with roof solar heating panels will become better areas for us to explore for more reliable thermal source generators. Those who have already experienced these thermal generators will have noticed that they work really well on blue days. Task planning and setting will become easier in the future and such areas will be good as fall-back thermals, just as stubble field fires were years ago.

Wind farms on hills increase the effectiveness of the area as a thermal generator. In *Fig 5.2* a

large area and volume of air is allowed to be warmed before the critical 2 °C trigger adjacent air temperature is reached. Once triggered, all the warm air around is sucked into the central area producing a solid and strong thermal.

Photo 5.2 Thermal sources.

In *Photo 5.2* the thermal source was being generated by the large grey hangar type buildings, just behind the tail of the lower glider.

Look out for whatever may be generating the thermal. For example, golf courses are always well drained and trees act as useful barriers. Pig farms generate quite a lot of heat and you can usually smell them! Looking at *Photo 5.3* you can see some potential thermal generators.

Photo 5.3 A variety of thermal generators.

ANALOGY **The jet engine.** With a thermal the initial rise from a central hotspot draws adjacent warm air in from the sides rather like a jet engine draws air from a wide area and directs it into a narrow column. Whilst we would obviously avoid the rear of a running jet engine, air is not being invented by the

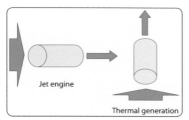

Fig 5.3 Jet engine.

engine. There is just as much air going into the front as is being pushed out of the back. Thermal generation is similar to this and the draw may encompass a far greater ground area than the diameter of the rising thermal.

In calm conditions or when the vertical speed of a thermal at low altitude exceeds the surface wind, fairly well rounded bubbles of hot air tend to develop. However, when the surface wind exceeds the thermal speed the vortex fails to establish itself at lower levels. At times, continual centring is required chasing gusts, and an uneven rate of climb is achieved. Once the thermal has climbed sufficiently to be released from the lower level wind effects the vortex will develop.

In *Fig 5.4* the thermal contrast to generate the trigger is where the hottest air climbs over the barrier. Make sure that you look out for these downwind barriers that are effective triggers.

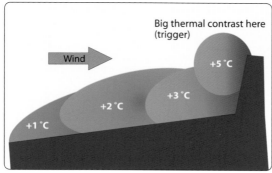

Fig 5.4 Hot air dammed up against a high barrier.

In Photo 5.4 the stubble field on the wing tip is the thermal source. The wind is from the top of the picture and the line of trees and water form a barrier and air fence for the thermal to be triggered.

Photo 5.4 A stubble field that is generating thermals.

Photo 5.5 is taken from a low altitude where it is often simple to identify where a thermal is generated. However, the skill on a blue day is to recognise these areas from a more comfortable height. Look for smoke to indicate the wind direction; in this case the wind is from the left. The tree line acts as a barrier and trigger for the hot air generated by the brown fields.

Photo 5.5 Low altitude thermal searching.

The initial development and structure of a thermal can be quite fluid and makes thermalling below 500ft difficult, especially if there is any degree of wind. Consider a cut rape field (a very dark dry surface full of black sticks) surrounded by trees. The air above the field will become very warm but will struggle to release upwards. Once it does, however, the cold air above the trees pouring into the hole will generate a very powerful vortex. The same applies to some quarries but not those which are full of water.

Another aspect which is worth being aware of is that once a bubble has been triggered it can set off a series of bubbles from the same point in a series of regular pulses.

Photo 5.6 shows a complex hotspot with quarries, a town, irrigated fields and hills. All of these could potentially trigger a strong thermal.

For a natural weak thermal it is common for a vortex to form shortly after leaving the ground, but perhaps not go up much because the upper air is only just unstable. It will just drift downwind largely rotating within itself, before collapsing.

The surface wind (where we stand) will be lighter than the wind at 500ft up so as the warm air rises the thermal is blown over, as shown in *Fig 5.5*. The barrier may be cold air from a lake or a damp area.

Photo 5.6 A complex hot and cold area.

the initial column of air and cold air undercuts, shearing off the bubble from the source.

A barrier offers a wind break and the downwind side of the barrier may generate a hotspot which at various times breaks away in a strong bubble. The direction of the wind in this situation becomes important in determining the length of the thermic day. If the wind is mainly from the west, the day will die quickly as these hotspots fall into shadow as the sun moves around to the west. If the wind is from the north or even has some east in it, then the day and stronger thermals will last longer, particularly during early and late summer.

Hills make their own weather

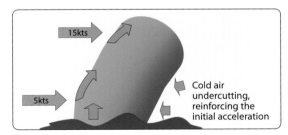

Fig 5.5 Surface vortex, first 500ft, some wind.

ANALOGY **A wet towel.** Consider a wet towel drying on a line, the top can be totally dry whilst the bottom is still soaked.

Windier days present a more complex build of thermals. On any flat surface where warm air would develop there will be a wind chill effect. This will allow a lot of air to be warmed slightly rather than generate a specific hotspot. The wind will push a build-up of warm air against any vertical barrier which then becomes the trigger point. It is important to note that if there is no barrier along these flat lands then there will be no trigger. The lower wind gradient will tend to push over

As with the wet towel analogy, upper slopes will be drier than lower ones. The geology often means that the top surfaces are well drained and rock offers a deep heat sink for the production of thermals later in the day. Unlike flat ground, hills have a significant effect on the production and structure of thermals. The south-easterly facing slopes offer a near perfect angle with the sun in the morning whilst the south-westerly facing slopes produce strongly in the afternoon.

Sink from the unstable layer flows not straight down but is deflected as it hits the slopes to run as water would, generating various complex winds and eddies in the valleys, destroying the production of column thermals at the lowest levels.

Cold air trigger

In *Photo 5.7* the trigger is clear. The hills on the left were producing a stream of ridge thermals in addition to the one I climbed in over the dam. In light winds the water ripples give a clear indication of any active local surface winds caused by thermals. The ripples can also be caused by rotor on the lee of the hill and can indicate cold air blowing down the slopes. It is worth taking note, however, that if there is any significant breeze, the cold air over the lake will run downwind through the valleys very much as if it were water, or even up gentle valleys. This again will generate triggers at various locations but immediately over the valleys will be poor and likely to be sinking air. So from the choice of hill-generated thermals I climbed from the dam in the forced air over the reservoir.

Photo 5.7 Looking for a thermal trigger.

Hill-top trigger

As we climb the atmosphere becomes thinner and often contains fewer pollutants. Meanwhile the temperature of the air is significantly cooler whilst the wind is often a little stronger. Since solar radiation also increases with altitude, those

surfaces exposed to the sun heat up rapidly whilst those with less exposure stay cool. Just consider the significance of the angle of the sun shining on a south facing slope to that of the adjacent north facing slope. For the entire day the heating effect on the north face will be significantly less, increasing the difference in relative temperatures. This is further exaggerated due to the reduced drying effect on any damp areas.

With a slight northerly breeze on an east-west orientated ridge the thermal contrast at the top of all hills will be very significant and generate an almost constant stream of ridge thermals. So if you insist on working the hills low down, or inadvertently arrive there and require a *thermal*, stay on the south side of any hill.

When it is a bit windy the hills come alive in a different way. Column thermals are often killed as they drift into the hills, but there are benefits nevertheless. Depending on the particular weather conditions the hills can generate a reliable source of strong thermals, streeting, hill lift and local wave. The volume of warm air rising on the sunny side is continuously added to and warmed by the hillside. The cool air at the bottom may be involved in the cycle, but not necessarily, and a continuous string of thermals leaves the top of the hills, rather like the thermals produced by a power station. The cold air descends on the other side of the hill, possibly encouraging the next thermal source on the upward slope downwind of the valley. Being cold it acts as a strong forcing trigger, before it flows down the valley.

As can be seen in *Fig 5.6* the sink generated by the evaporating clouds falls to the downwind side of the ridge and does not interfere with the thermal trigger. On blue days the sink tends to be in the middle of the valleys and thermals may be produced by both side of the hill during the best period of the day.

Snow

Occasionally there might be snow on the ground and the great thing about snow is that in freezing conditions it does not melt and soak the ground with water and cool vast areas with evaporation. However, on adjacent land without snow the

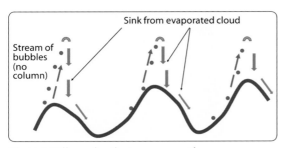

Fig 5.6 Hills make their own weather.

ground will heat up quite readily and hence trigger the easy generation of thermals, even in winter.

If you fly over a hilly or mountainous area which has significant snow but there are clear dry areas, you may find some good thermal bubbles from really obvious places. The contrast between the snowy cold and the warm brown or black clear surfaces is perfect for the generation of thermal contrast. A clear long ground area or tall gully that has little shadow is usually effective.

Hill-top instability

The sky shown in *Fig 5.7* is classically seen in the mornings before the day has warmed sufficiently for the air to establish an unstable layer emanating from the valley floor. At height though, the potential instability may already be active. As air is forced up over the hill or mountain good looking thermals and cumulus develop, usually presenting a short but decaying street. Despite the sky looking good you cannot connect with the thermals well below the clouds because *they*

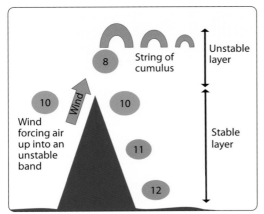

Fig 5.7 Instability may only occur above the tops of the hills.

do not exist. You need to stay above ridge height because if you get low you will be in the fields or making it back home in dead air.

Thermals approaching hills

If you are sat on a hill surviving on weak ridge lift, waiting for a thermal to come through, beware. As a thermal drifts towards a hill the sink associated with the vortex is often powerful enough to destroy the hill lift being generated by a moderate wind.

Bubbles hitting hills

Bubble thermals developing on low land and drifting onto the sides of steep hills splodge themselves to the hillside and the volume of hot air may well be added to. However the essential structure of the vortex is destroyed. The associated sink surrounding the rising bubble is confined to three sides and does not have access between the rising bubble and the hillside. As a result the sink on the three sides increases and the centre becomes somewhat gusty and chaotic because the normal vortex structure is broken. From *Fig 5.8* you should be able to see that a figure of 8 pattern is not just safer but a more effective way of climbing from below ridge height, and staying in the bubble.

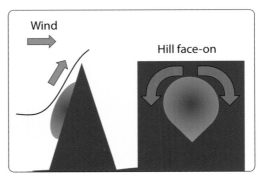

Fig 5.8 Fly a figure of 8 to climb above ridge height.

On the other hand narrow gullies completely prevent the vortex formation and the hot air drives up the side like an uphill river, without any associated sink. A powerful stream of thermals may develop from the top of the gully or hill. When the wind blows along the ridge, thermals only develop from the hilltops.

Columns hitting hills

As a column thermal drifts towards a hill the column is briefly reinforced as the bottom of the core transits the hilltop, as shown in *Fig 5.9*. It depends on how high the hill is above the valley floor along with the instability between the hilltop and cloud base to determine what happens next. In the UK it is normal for the column to be broken but, on rare occasions, if the cloud base is sufficiently clear of the hilltops then the column might survive.

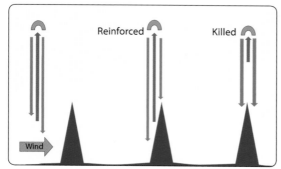

Fig 5.9 Columns hitting hills.

On a blue day there is no sink generated from decaying clouds and thermals can be produced from both windward and the lee side of the tops of the hills; essentially anywhere in good sunlight, as shown in *Fig 5.10*. Between the hilltops and over the valleys there will be sink.

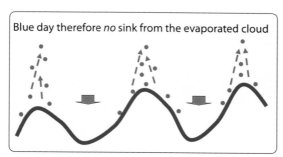

Fig 5.10 Blue thermals over the hills.

When there is a significant wind above the inversion the thermals pushing up mirror the contours of the hills. This action can generate shear wave as shown in *Fig 5.11*.

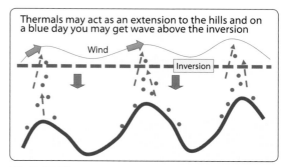

Fig 5.11 Blue wave.

In *Photo 5.8* we are running a line of ridge thermals with a light northerly wind from our left, wooded lower slopes on the southern sunny side on our right and following the hot rocky areas on the top. Cruising at around 100kts we eventually took a climb back up to 11,000ft about 15km later.

Photo 5.8 Running along a ridge.

So, as you can see, getting high and staying high is not the only way of doing business. The same principle of running along a ridge at low level also works when it is seriously cold.

6
Centring

During one run to the turning point, I tried to let my commentary demonstrate the continual multi-tasking functions being carried out, mentioning the three suitable areas to land as well as an airport some 15km south, the lift sources and trigger points along with the wind and the various ridges. At this point my P2 spotted a wasp that was the wrong side of the canopy, so I delegated bluntly, "That's a job for you Dave, deal with it!" This offered Dave a separate multi-tasking challenge as he looked down at the fashionable (no socks) sandals, bare knobbly knees, baggy shorts and his loose, short-sleeved shirt.

Whilst so far we have looked at the common basic thermals of bubbles and columns, this chapter further explains motions within a thermal. In order to identify just where the core is when you hit a thermal you need to use all of the information available—sound, feel and instrumentation. But all of these useful indications can be misleading if you are not fully aware of the likely structure of the turbulent air that you have just entered. Fluids and gasses in motion can display rigidity in just the same way that a gyroscope can. Consider a simple tidal wave or the huge surfing waves at the seaside. If this flow is directed into a second plane a swirling motion will be generated. Just like a gyroscope then, after the initial trigger the motion may continue for some time, giving it other properties which are not present in a single plane.

The vortex

To start with we have to find out if we can make an air vortex. A smoker (without hot air) or a cloud produced by an atomic bomb, certainly display the motions of the doughnut ring, but how can nature produce this flow? To help us, *Fig 6.1* shows a vortex generator that you can buy or make yourself. Air is forced through a narrowing tube and expelled with the fastest air motions being in the centre. Does the shape look familiar at all? Round off the straight lines and you get cumulus!

In the thermal that we climb in it is important to bear in mind that the rotation of the cloud is not necessarily an indication of what the air is doing underneath. It is simply showing us the air motions of the outside edges of the cloud.

As the vortex rises the edges of it can be accelerated by the sinking tube of air from the evaporating clouds above, a bit like whipping a spinning top. This will add energy to the vortex and it will accelerate upwards.

Vortex thermals are formed on blue days but they tend to be quite weak because with no cloud evaporation the accelerating downdraft is not present.

If a significantly strong vortex is generated into the air it will travel a considerable distance at great speed before being destroyed. The ascent of hot air into cooler air, however, continues to provide energy to the vortex bubble and maintains a strong vortex up to cloud base and beyond. The rising vortex can be further enhanced by strong sinking air but can be destroyed quickly by another vortex.

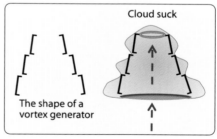

Fig 6.1 The vortex generator shape of a simple cumulus cloud.

Accurate flying?

There is often a suggestion that we should try to fly the glider as accurately as possible whilst thermalling. There is also a suggestion that when the glider hits a thermal the upwards draft will cause an acceleration because we see the ASI surge upwards. Our body is very sensitive to accelerations so if we did accelerate by 6kts in half a second, rather like the initial part of a winch launch, we would all know about it. In this case it is an illusion. Indeed, go farther and ask a student to close their eyes whilst you hit a thermal. The response is not a sensation of horizontal acceleration, simply because there is no acceleration. It is no different to the way the ASI fluctuates on the ground responding to gusts. So, if you are not centred perfectly then it is not possible, practical or beneficial to try to fly an accurate speed as the horizontal gusts generated by the thermal will inflict airspeed fluctuations. It is considerably more important that you maintain a steady attitude and use these gust fluctuations to give you an accurate indication, with very little lag, as to where the thermal centre is.

Seen from above there is always an outward flow from the core of a thermal and this is shown in *Fig 6.2*.

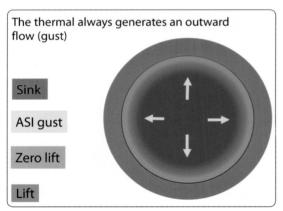

Fig 6.2 Thermal structure showing outward flow from the core.

Now consider *Fig 6.3*. Before arriving at the climbing part of a thermal you must go through the sink, which effectively tells you how strong the thermal will be. You will then pass through a horizontal gust which is indicated accurately on the ASI, with no lag. The string deflection will indicate if this is from one side or the other.

This gust is also indicated on the vario through the total energy compensation. In a bubble thermal the outward gust occurs at the thermal shear. In a column thermal the outward gust occurs at the boundary between laminar and turbulent air flow.

Horizontal gusts, however, can mislead the pilot as they indicate a climb or descent on the vario due to an increase or decrease of total energy. This is why the vario fluctuates whilst stationary on the ground on a blustery day. But then again, the horizontal gust is an important indicator that you are close to the thermal core and that you should be turning very soon, or if detected in the turn, then you must re-centre by increasing the bank immediately.

When encountering sinking air remember that there is almost no lag associated with the indication and your sink. However, when we encounter lift there is an apparent lag. For these reasons we are told to respond to the feel of lift rather than wait for confirmation from your instruments. To fully understand we must remember that the forces of lift and sink are accelerations and these forces are not instantaneously converted into new vertical velocities. The vario is a vertical speed measurement device, not a vertical accelerometer. On transiting the sink around the thermal, the force applied is the sum of the sink pushing down and the downward weight of the glider after lift forces are taken into account. There will also be a brief reduction in AoA so the lift generated by the wing will suddenly reduce. Hence there is effectively no lag on the vario entering sink. Having established a high rate of descent, when we enter lift an upwards force is applied. We must take into account our glider's residual downward weight. Note that this now means taking the difference of the two, not the sum of the two. The new upwards acceleration has to convert the

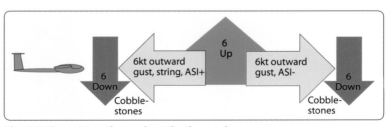

Fig 6.3 Transiting through a 6kt thermal.

downwards speed of the glider firstly to reach zero vertical speed, and then to reach a new upward climb rate in the thermal. No wonder the poor vario appears to be behind the game. Blaming the vario for lagging is no fairer than blaming the ASI for not showing an instant change from 50kts to 100kts when we quickly lower the nose to the 100kt attitude!

> **KEY POINT** The variometer is a good indicator of sink with almost no lag but it can be used to confirm your suspicion that you might have flown through lift some time ago.

Modern Instrumentation

There are various instruments that can assist you to fly your glider efficiently and give a vast amount of key information. One of the most useful instruments is the multifunction electronic display. For thermalling, these have a thermal assist to indicate both visually and aurally where the core of the thermal is, once you have completed a turn or so. They will indicate which parts of the turn produced the highest rates of climb and where the strongest point was. In map screen they show a snail trail showing where the strong areas were in relation to the world. This thermal assist in thermalling is exactly that though. The system will not find the initial thermal for you and responding to your feel will achieve greater and faster results. At the top of the climb they will indicate what the average rate of climb was and this helps confirm your mental mapping of the core. Setting the MacCready with the achieved rate of climb will also indicate the suggested block speed, if you think the next thermal will be of equal strength.

The TE system indicates a change of energy by combining changes of climb or descent with changes of speed. Ideally, if you do a loop in smooth flat air the variometer should not indicate a climb but a slight change in RoD as performance is gained or lost. If the calibration of the total energy probe and instrument are correct, then this reduces stick lift which can be demonstrated

with the TE switched off. As a rule though, always fly with the TE on.

In cruise or speed command mode the vario simply indicates the theoretical best speed to fly, adjusted for the weight/MacCready/bug and the momentary air you happen to be passing through at the time. So that you are not encouraged to continuously pitch the glider there is a silent audio dead band. Beyond these values a variety of tones are used to indicate that you are flying either too slow or too fast. These sounds and the value of the dead band can be altered by the user so it's important to know what the setup is if you are flying in an unfamiliar glider.

Vario lag

We spend a lot of money on vario systems. We accept that the vario accurately displays a rate of climb of 0.1kts, which is 10ft per minute or 2 inches per second. That is more accurate than civilian GPS systems and yet we still are led to believe that it lags by 3 seconds. Can this be correct? Obviously not, but the instrument does have problems being so accurate as to mislead us if we don't know what is really going on.

Once again, remember that the vario will accurately measure a rate of climb or descent of 2 inches per second. Now consider how far the tail moves and at what rate, rotated about the glider's centre of gravity when we pitch up from cruise speed into a thermal. If the vario feed is mounted on the tail the instrument will receive a temporary false pessimistic indication during the pull up and an optimistic indication as we push over or even when we allow the glider nose to fall in a high banked attitude at the top.

> **KEY POINT** Varios may give misleading indications with high pitch rates.

> **ANALOGY** **The bouncing ball.** Consider a vario mounted in the centre of a very large (about 50m diameter) steel ball. If we dropped the ball we could detect exactly when it hit the ground because the ball would not absorb any of the bounce and the vario would

immediately reverse from falling to bouncing back up. Now consider if the vario was mounted in an equally large sponge type ball. As the impact would be absorbed by the soft shell the vario would slow, eventually stop when the ball had reached full compression, and

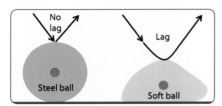

Fig 6.4 Perceived lag.

then accelerate upwards. The instrument would appear to have lagged but in fact it would accurately indicate what the middle of the ball was doing.

The vario tells you what the glider is doing, not the vertical velocity of the air. It is when the rate of change of the vario is at a peak that you are passing through the most active part of the thermal. Despite spending hundreds of pounds on a good electric variometer many consider that they still lag by some three seconds. This is not true! They simply measure and indicate essentially what the glider is doing, with inertia, momentum and dynamic lift contributing to the indication.

In *Fig 6.5* the arrows in the blue circles show probable vario indications. The car has a springy suspension that absorbs the force acting on it in the same way that a glider mushes through the air as it hits rising air. As the car goes down the steep hill the vario will indicate the sink with no lag but, as it starts climbing over the hump, it will take a while to indicate the climb. Once again, as the car begins descending there is no lag. Similarly, in a glider there is no lag when entering sink but it takes time for the upward force of a thermal to act and actually convert the descent

into a climb. Most people mistakenly call this 'instrument lag' but the instrument is not lagging.

KEY POINT Variometers do not lag when entering sink.

Hitting a gust

Consider what happens to our glider as we transit through a strong thermal. As we hit the strong sink the glider picks up considerable inertia downwards without delay. As we hit the rising air there is a considerable amount of work that has to be done to reduce the rate of descent and achieve a climb. For this reason the vario alone is a very poor indicator to be used for identifying strong thermals. So, in a strong thermal we usually ignore the bleats but respond aggressively to the feel we get from gusts. It is also important to note that there is *no airspeed gust* as we transit out of the heavy sink and into the edges on the outside of the thermal.

Importantly, if the change in inertia is small then the *perceived lag* of the vario can be ignored. Consider how we use the vario in wave, ridge lift and weak thermals. Once established in a smooth thermal small corrections towards centring

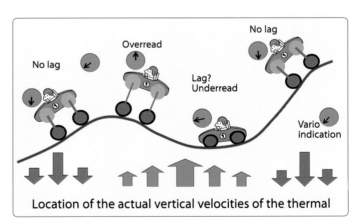

Fig 6.5 Vario lag.

around the core can be reasonably achieved using the vario. So, techniques that use the vario to centre in weak thermals, with a strength of perhaps 1kt, will work quite well.

Search for strong thermals by feel and use the vario for weak ones.

Feel, and more about vario indications

If you fly your glider at maximum weight for the first time and don't make the necessary corrections to the instrument systems, coupled with the new feel of the glider, it is likely that you will think that you are no longer capable of thermalling.

If we hit a gust flying at 45kts the thermal has to overcome the downwards momentum of the glider. At 90kts the glider has double the momentum and will respond far less to the same upward gust. Equally there will be dynamic lift generated. The AoA will briefly increase for no change in speed and more lift will be generated, indicated as a climb. At the higher speed the increase in AoA will be less, so the vario will again under-read for the same thermal. It is therefore more difficult to assess the strength of a thermal without experience of *feel* for the particular glider that you are flying and a thorough understanding of your instrumentation.

The combination of the pitot gust and static pressure changes gives an indication of changes in total energy. However these indications will suffer a time delay if the detector sources are fitted towards the rear of the glider and further indicated errors will occur if the static and pitot tubes are placed at significantly different fore and aft positions, as shown in *Fig 6.6*.

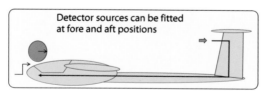

Fig 6.6 The vario is only as good as the information that it receives.

Static pressure detected at the nose will differ from the static pressure detected at the tail during manoeuvre, as indicated in *Fig 6.7*. Ideally they will cancel each other out to improve accuracy. More importantly, sat on the fin the static system

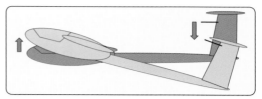

Fig 6.7 Instrument error and lag.

has dynamic errors as the glider pitches. With this situation, pulling up into a thermal, the vario under-reads and whilst pushing the nose down it over-reads, giving the appearance to the pilot that he has just hit a sharp edge to the thermal and is now in sink. If the pressure sensors are at the back of the glider the vario will indicate what the back of the glider is doing.

The underread on a pitch up is exaggerated further by the loss in performance of the glider during manoeuvre. At the top, whilst pushing over, we get an overread.

This may all appear complicated but it can largely be overcome. Set your glider up at a normal inter-thermal cruise speed and manoeuvre (pull and roll) as if you were entering a thermal. Most electronic varios have a facility to easily correct any over or under-reading. If this is not available then you will have to carry out your own assessment of the level of over or under-read and apply a mental correction to all thermal entries. Remember that you are only making adjustments to the total energy compensation here. There is no instrument compensation for thermal gusts. Bear in mind that there will be significant differences between flying dry and fully ballasted with a heavy glider. Making consistently similar control inputs by feel and noting the corresponding indications, rather than chasing the instruments, will likely give better familiarity with the human-machine-thermal interface.

Thermal searching

Firstly consider the often suggested method for searching for a thermal. Giving a thermal a glancing blow the suggestion is that we do a gentle turn to try and feel the central core. Does this make sense? The lag associated with the delay before the vario indicates that we are climbing means that most of the thermal is already behind us, as shown in *Fig 6.8*. Now considering that we need to hold around 45° AoB to just maintain the thermal once centred then to use lesser bank, to search, is not logical. On the other hand, turning hard offers the opportunity to remain connected or reconnect with the central core earlier.

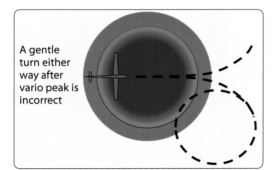

A gentle turn either way after vario peak is incorrect

Fig 6.8 Incorrect concept of thermal centring.

Feel

It is one thing to say feel the air, but how do we do this? The well-established opinion in the world of biologists is that birds have 5 senses like us, but they must have a 6th sense, one which detects climbing and descending or they would not be able to soar as well as they do. They still do not fly in cloud, and few fly at night. It would also appear that they have not discovered wave. Birds fundamentally use each other to help centre on a thermal and commonly fly in pairs to do this, as can be seen with eagles and buzzards, although this might equally well be to search and attack prey as a pair.

Our body is a very sensitive tool provided we give it a chance. In any steady flight we are able to detect very slight changes in acceleration (g) and specifically changes in rates of rotation about all three axes. Our feel is limited though.

> **ANALOGY** **The elevator.** Travelling in the lift of a high rise building we feel the acceleration at the beginning of the ascent and equally the slowing at the top, but whilst we travel up at a steady speed we feel nothing.

In our glider we can feel a change from a high rate of sink to a slower one, but we cannot detect that we might still be going down or indeed climbing. Equally, we can detect a marked change in rotation but be unaware of small steady rates of rotation, hence the need for instruments to fly in cloud. If we are flying with no control inputs then all bumps and shakes must be induced by the air movements around the glider. In this way we can feel what the air is doing and sideways shoves along with fluctuations on the ASI are just as important as vertical gusts. Equally, whilst banked over hard, gusts that hit the glider can be related to the vertical and horizontal real world. We must look out to correctly orientate our sensations, so a strong sideways gust on our glider can be interpreted to the vertical and will contribute to mapping out just where the thermal core is. Make sure that you hold the stick lightly so that you can feel these accelerations.

In significantly turbulent weather however, our sensitivity is reduced. It is also reduced if we endeavour to keep the speed on datum and the string continuously in the middle. Do not *over-fly* by trying to correct perceived errors or continuously shake the stick, as you will deny your senses of feel.

Different gliders have a different feel. Light old wooden gliders like the *T21* and the *Olympia 2* are so light that they respond to each and every gust. The more modern heavy glass gliders like the *K21* and *Astir* make it harder to feel the air and the glider response is further reduced with heavy pilots and filling the wings with water. Of course soaring birds must use this *feel* but must also have an additional sense, that of steady state climbing or descending. This is a motion that we have converted to our visual and hearing senses by using the audio vario. Turbulence means that the air is unstable, but it does not mean that you are in a thermal.

Centring techniques

Ignoring mechanical turbulence, all conflicts between rising and descending air generate a horizontal gust and this is always from the lift to the sink. This is equally significant during any straight glide.

Approaching a thermal you will experience the following, in order:

► Downdraft.
► Cobblestone turbulence.
► Speed gust increase (and possible string deflection).
► Lift.

The speed increase will also be detected on the variometer in the total energy system as a climb, but do not be fooled as you are not climbing yet. It is important to realize that if you are in rising air without a gust you are not near enough to the centre of the thermal or the thermal is collapsing. Transiting deeper into the centre you will normally find yourself rewarded with a stronger climb. Cloud shape should be a useful indicator here and as always, when in doubt, go for the darkest or upwind areas. It is very important to note that the string deflection is only temporary and lasts for about one second so you have to look for it and anticipate committing to an immediate response. If you don't hit the thermal head-on then you may feel the wing lift and see the string indicating a brief sideslip (Atkinson's string theory) because this means you are close to the core.

> **KEY POINT** **Atkinson's string theory**. When approaching a thermal core, *make an immediate turn in the opposite direction to any significant string deflection.*

The bigger the gust the stronger and tighter will be the thermal core. Remember that the force required to move the string is tiny, at any speed, compared to the force required to lift the wing. Indeed, the outward gust may be detected by the string in an area that is not strong enough to lift the wing.

In *Fig 6.9* we are tracking straight through the middle of the thermal. The yellow track from a right turn, using just 30°AoB, would give us an extended period through the sink and even beyond the edge of the thermal. We actually need

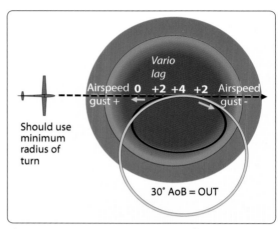

Fig 6.9 Using 30°AoB is a poor technique!

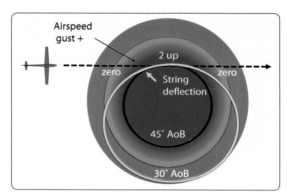

Fig 6.10 Entering beside a thermal core.

to turn as hard as possible as soon as we have passed through the core.

In *Fig 6.10* we are cutting the side of the thermal. Using just 30°AoB is potentially even worse in this situation as we track through a considerable amount of sink on the edge of the thermal. If you are sure that you have entered a thermal and the glider is going up you must turn hard to anchor your position and ensure that you remain within the good air. It is far better to be a bit out of balance and climbing than in balance and sinking!

> **KEY POINT** Don't consider searching for a thermal using 30°AoB.

Once established in our thermal we usually use about 45°AoB. If we are not centred then we briefly reduce the bank and then return to 45°AoB to ensure that we stay in the thermal. From this knowledge we know that we need to hold a radius of turn at less than 60m or we will be wide and climbing slowly or worse still, out of the thermal and in sink.

Consider another case when you miss the optimum line. If you pass through only sink it will take about 4 seconds (at 60kts) for you to reach abeam the centre of the core, so at this time the thermal could be immediately on either side of you.

An advanced technique is to interpret the sky and deliberately offset your track slightly to one side or the other. Then, if you can identify that you are on the edge of a thermal you will automatically know which way to turn!

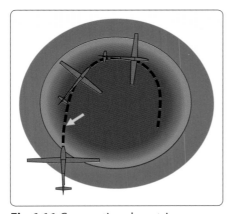

Fig 6.11 Conventional centring.

Fig 6.11 shows conventional thermalling. If the lift is increasing as you turn, keep increasing the bank. The right wing lifts and the string is pushed left, so turn right and tighten the turn until an optimum turn is achieved. If the lift increases in the turn, keep increasing the bank.

The vario measures sink accurately with little lag. *Fig 6.12* shows conventional centring using the worst indication as a reference. A feature of any vario is that it will tell you, without delay, that you are in sink. Therefore, 90° after the highest sink value, roll out and after an appropriate pause, roll back in.

If you recognise that you have passed through the centre because you feel a strong surge underneath, you must turn through at least 180° as tightly as you can, before reducing the AoB to 45°, as shown in *Fig 6.13*.

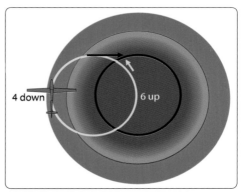

Fig 6.12 Conventional centring using the highest sink values as a reference.

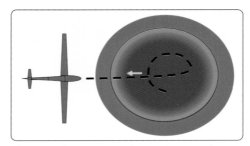

Fig 6.13 Conventional centring passing through the centre.

The vario has almost no lag in indicating when the glider sink rate increases or whenever the rate of climb reduces. With that in mind, as we turn there will be a point where we are climbing the slowest, as shown in *Fig 6.14*. We need to make a small adjustment to establish the turn, away from the poorer area, so that the central core of the thermal is also the centre of our turn. Bear

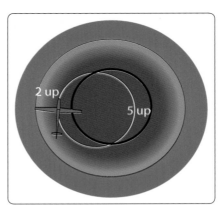

Fig 6.14 Re-centring by using the lowest vario lift values.

in mind that we only want to move about 20 or 30 metres away from the least beneficial area, it makes sense to simply reduce the AoB briefly an appropriate amount. So, to re-centre, 4–5 seconds after the vario indicates the worst climb rate, reduce the bank for about 1–2 seconds before returning to the original bank angle.

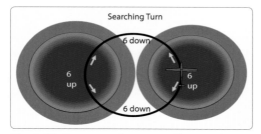

Fig 6.15 Encountering two adjacent thermals.

Depending on how hard you turn you can suffer the initial confusion of encountering two thermals at the same time, as shown in *Fig 6.15*. This situation can sometimes be indicated on thermal assist devices and a turn reversal at the strongest point might be your best option. Bear in mind that the technique of re-centring 90° after the worst point does not help if there are two adjacent thermals. In *Fig 6.16* the pilot wrongly perceives what is happening and ends up outside the core. At point **A** the glider encounters a gust. This is indicated on the ASI but it is important to realize that *from this point onwards* the glider will be affected by outflow from the core. At point **A**

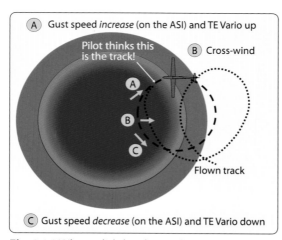

Fig 6.16 Where did the thermal go?

this slows the glider's progress towards the core. But, at point **B** the glider is under the influence of the same outward flow, which is now a cross-wind. Finally, at point **C** the glider encounters a negative gust indicating that it has entered a tailwind, which subsequently blows it out of the thermal.

In summary, the indications of gusts on the ASI and the string deflection will always give a clear direction as to where the thermal core is. Bear in mind that, with crosswind gusts, the string will always point away from the core. On entering a thermal if the ASI shows a gust increase and the string remains straight then the thermal core will be directly ahead. When passing to the *side* of the thermal core as the string deflects the core will be on the opposite side of the deflection. When leaving the thermal the ASI gust reduction will indicate that the thermal core is directly behind the glider.

Misleading indications of the total energy system

If we use only the vario to centre and assume that there is a delay between reality and the indication after about 40° of turn the TE vario will indicate a climb when we actually have simply hit an airspeed gust. We assume the thermal is some way behind us, when in fact it is of course immediately in front of us. We might also misunderstand the decrease in gust as an increase in sink. Our mental mapping of where the core is will be quite wrong. The TE compensation will be different for different weights of gliders, which further confuses our mapping.

Some people are inclined to dolphin in a thermal—don't. Apart from the fact that it makes it hazardous for others using the same thermal, it does not help the average rate of climb because it takes you away from the core, particularly if you do it on ASI gusts. Slowing down briefly does decrease your radius of turn but slowing down on vertical acceleration is much more beneficial to use as a centring technique and then other pilots will be happy because you will indicate the central core position!

Feeling a thermal

A very common statement is to "feel the wing lift up". But how do we know that it is not the other wing being dragged down? The key is in the associated sideways feel. If the glider is simply brushing past an area of sink the wing in the strongest sink will simply fall away and there will be no gust or string deflection.

> **KEY POINT** Lift is usually felt as a surge and slight sideways shove and includes the all-important string deflection.

So this is what we are feeling (feel, hear, see) if we fly *directly through a thermal*.

- ▶ Feel and hear (on the audio) the sink.
- ▶ Feel cobblestones.
- ▶ Hear and see the speed increase.
- ▶ Hear the audio vario up.
- ▶ See the string deflection and wing lift.
- ▶ Hear and see the speed decrease, audio tone reducing.
- ▶ Feel the sink.

And this is what we are feeling whilst *turning within the thermal*.

- ▶ Feel, and hear (on the audio) the lift.
- ▶ Hear and see the speed increase.
- ▶ See the string deflection and feel wing lift.
- ▶ Hear the change in audio vario up.
- ▶ Feel the tail go up (or nose yawing down).
- ▶ Hear and see the speed decrease.
- ▶ Hear the audio as the lift values reduce.
- ▶ Feel the reduced climb rates.

Stronger thermals are narrower so the stronger the thermal the tighter you must turn. The turn radius is the important factor and this is achieved either at fast speeds with high angles of bank or slow speeds with less angle of bank.

In stronger thermals we often get other indications of the gust. If we are a little slow as we hit the gust whilst heavily banked the string will give an indication of a large sideslip. This also can cause the ASI to underread (even below any normal flying speeds) and hence the very

slow indication. This loss of pitot pressure is also detected by the TE and results in the vario suggesting you are in strong sink (you are not). Shortly after the airflow has restored itself the ASI will recover to give an accurate indication whilst the vario suggests you are climbing like a winch launch (you are not). You need to ignore the indications and maintain a sensible attitude whilst taking note that you have just transited close to the core centre. Likewise, at about this moment the tail is hit by the vertical gust forcing the nose down relative to the world and if you already have a lot of aft stick in the turn you may well run out of elevator to stop this.

Thermalling with other gliders

We often find ourselves thermalling with other gliders and this gives us the opportunity to really be efficient in the climb. If we observe another glider and note how they rise or fall relative to us we get a clear visual picture of where the best rate of climb is. If the other glider is moving up on the horizon we must slacken off our turn (usually done by reducing our bank a little—which the other pilot will notice) to get to where the other glider is. If the other glider is going down relative to us then we must tighten our turn (usually done simply by pulling a little harder whilst maintaining 45° AoB) to prevent flying out of our good air and into the other glider's poor air. Working together in this way the small changes in our turn relative to the thermal core allow us to optimise the climb.

At this point it is probably worth emphasizing the difficulties of thermalling with other gliders. Throughout your training you will no doubt have been taught that you should look out and avoid other gliders. Even whilst being taught thermalling you might have had a glider within a few hundred feet of you, but it is more likely that you will have been thermalling effectively on your own whilst the instructor has taught you the vagaries of the motions you can feel. An aspect often missed is teaching students how to thermal effectively with others. Pilots of both gliders wish to climb as quickly as possible, but they need to keep the spacing in this very dynamic situation in order to remain aware of where the

Photo 6.1 Looking out for other gliders.

other glider is, yet adjust turns together to remain in the better air.

To avoid overtaking another glider it is a normal reaction to slow down and increase the bank. Does this work when both gliders are thermalling? If you are overtaking someone on the inside, just like increasing bank, slowing down will simply make the situation worse. Doing both might be disastrous! With an overtake you must manoeuvre to the outside of the turn to ensure a safer separation.

> **KEY POINT** Do not increase bank or slow down if you are overtaking on the inside of a turn! Instead, manoeuvre to the outside of the turn.

Photo 6.2 Blind spots occur before turning.

Following close to someone is fine as long as you acknowledge that you are following and that you have to give the leading glider full freedom to manoeuvre. It is difficult to continuously monitor someone who is behind you so avoid lingering in the blind spots.

Turn radius (m) and rates of turn (degrees/sec)					
	40kts	**45kts**	**50kts**	**55kts**	**60kts**
35°	61.7m	78.1m	96.4m	116.6m	38.8m
40°	51.5m	65.2m RoT 20.3	80.4 RoT 18.3	97.3m RoT 16.6	115.8m
45°	43.2m	54.7m RoT 24.2	67.5m RoT 21.8	81.7m RoT 19.8	97.2m
50°	36.3m	45.9m RoT 28.9	56.6m RoT 26.0	68.5m RoT 23.6	81.6m

Table 6.1

Table 6.1 shows the turn radius in metres and rate of turn (RoT) in degrees per second achieved with various angles of bank and speed. The nine shaded cells are commonly used thermalling speeds and angles of bank. The table shows how a small change in either can have a relatively big effect.

For example, consider the two green shaded cells. If we slow down from 50kts to 45kts and increase our bank from 40° to 50° we almost halve our turn radius and increase our RoT by 50%.

It should be clear that small changes in either angle of bank or speed, as you fly around the thermal, will soon change your relative position to other gliders with you if they are not making similar changes.

Photo 6.3 indicates action being taken to manoeuvre to the outside of the turning *K18* ahead. In addition, it is worth noting that the old and slow machines will out-turn the high performance modern gliders.

Photo 6.3 Avoiding the glider ahead.

Remember, whilst in a sustained turn, if we try to avoid the glider ahead by either slowing down and/or increasing the bank angle, we simply increase the rate of overtake and rate of closure. Referring back to *Table 6.1* you can see that a glider flying at 45kts and 50° AoB (*K18*) out-turns a glider flying at 55kts and 40° AoB (*Duo*).

The best and only key visual clue to avoid closure is to ensure that your nose is never tracking at, or ahead of, the glider in front as indicated in *Fig 6.17*. In the same way you can anticipate gliders tracking you and their closure rates by noting where their nose is pointing and their relative angle of bank.

In *Photo 6.4* we can see that because pilot **A**'s nose is pointing ahead of pilot **B** there is a *lead* being generated. If pilot **A** increases the AoB then he will no longer be able to see glider **B** who, at that moment, might not be aware of this. This is a potentially hazardous situation.

Just like stalling or spinning, thermalling with other gliders is not

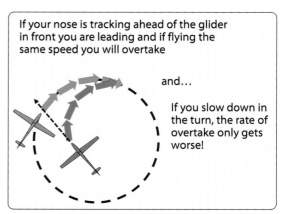

Fig 6.17 Avoiding collision.

dangerous but it should be clear that it is simple to generate a dangerous situation. Firstly, avoid the blind spots where one of you cannot see the other. The *blind* pilot does not know what you are doing or where you are. In this situation they must be given absolute freedom of manoeuvre and it is your responsibility to ensure mutual safety. Even when you can both see each other it is easy to get into a challenging situation if you concentrate and adjust on the thermal centre but you are unaware that you are generating a lead on the adjacent glider(s). In these situations it is often the case that one glider is allowed to be the leader who concentrates on centring, dictating where the gaggle goes, with the others just following.

As a point of interest, we can see in *Table 6.2 on page 74* the turn radii and rates of turn of slower flying devices, and this table could be applicable to hang gliders and paragliders. Once in position,

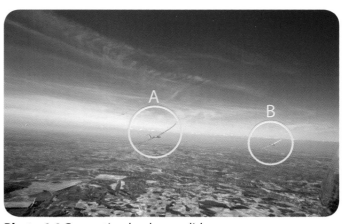

Photo 6.4 Generating lead on a glider.

if everyone maintains the same rate of turn the relative positions will not change. The speeds and angles of bank commonly used in thermals by gliders are shaded green.

Slow speed turn radius (m) and rates of turn (degrees/sec)						
	30kts	35kts	40kts	45kts	50kts	55kts
35°	34.3m RoT 25.5	47.3m RoT 21.8	61.7m RoT 19.1	78.1m RoT 17.0	96.4m RoT 15.2	116.6m RoT 13.9
40°	29m RoT 30.5	39.5m RoT 26.2	51.5m RoT 22.9	65.2m RoT 20.3	80.4m RoT 18.3	97.3m RoT 16.6
45°	24.3m RoT 36.4	29.1m RoT 31.2	43.2m RoT 27.3	54.7m RoT 24.2	67.5m RoT 21.8	81.7m RoT 19.8
50°	20.4m RoT 43.3	27.8m RoT 37.1	36.3m RoT 32.5	45.9m RoT 28.9	56.6 RoT 26.0	68.5m RoT 23.6

Table 6.2

7
More on thermal structure

► Reaching cloud base
► Lapse rates
► Effects of thermals at cloud base
► Disappearing thermals

It's not always a good idea to trust your P2. Whilst we were in a slow climb of around 1 kt my P2 was adamant that he could see another *Duo* about 5 km away, in the haze, outclimbing us. Without really looking at the sky he insisted that we should rush off and join the better thermal. We set off from just 1,500 ft, somewhat optimistically at 80 kts, in the direction of our thermal. As we got closer I asked my P2 what he thought the black mark was on the back of the glider's fuselage. As he had no immediate answer I explained that it was a *turbo*! My P2 was awarded the appropriate wooden spoon prize the following morning. In the pursuit of learning there are no secrets and this is not the first time I have seen this mistake!

This chapter continues to look at other contributing aspects of thermal structure. It is normal to simply consider that a thermal is air that is rising because it is warmer than the surrounding air. The higher level of humidity within the air carried up by the vortex will also contribute to the overall buoyancy and will assist a thermal's strength at height. This means that even when the actual temperature of the air within and outside of the vortex is the same, the vortex will continue upwards. Physical processes at and above cloud base will also have significant effects on the column.

Reaching cloud base

When the bubble gets to cloud base the dry air immediately above is cooled as the water droplets of the cloud evaporate, so the dry, colder air moves outwards and downwards, as shown in *Fig 7.1*. Although the cold dry air was stable before, it is now next to humid air and being denser and cooler, rapidly cooled from the evaporating cloud droplets, it descends into the moist air where it continues to sink as it remains relatively heavy.

The air of the rising thermal is less dense and warmer so the descent of the cold air will continue. The severity of the sink will also depend not just on the height of the cloud cells and the thermal temperature difference but also the relative humidity. The drier the air around the cloud the faster the evaporation of the water. Thermals can get stronger (but not bigger) with

height as they climb into drier air, and sink can become quite severe lower down.

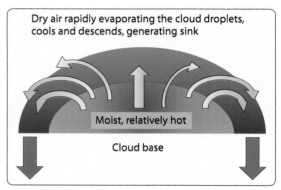

Fig 7.1 Cloud evaporation generating sink.

The downwards flow, shown in *Fig 7.2*, is controlled by the thermal core ascending and the surrounding environmental temperature. Strong lift from a strong thermal will give strong sink. If

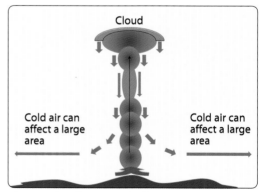

Fig 7.2 The downwards flow in a thermal (no wind).

the thermal is weak with a broad area of lift then the vortex may be broken.

Lapse rates

The term *adiabatic lapse rate* is often misunderstood:

▶ The wet air lapse rate means that if a bubble of moist air is raised 1,000 ft then it will cool by 3°C. In simplistic terms, this is considered to be any air rising from the ground up to cloud base.

▶ The dry air lapse rate means that if a bubble of dry air is raised 1,000 ft then it will cool by 2°C. In simplistic terms, this is the air above cloud base.

▶ The actual rate of temperature change with height is called the environmental lapse rate which, amongst other things, can vary within or beyond these two rates, whilst relative humidity can also vary with height.

On a good day we find that the air at ground level is moist with an average level of humidity (about 60%), pushing up into often drier air towards cloud base. This means that the moist rising thermal becomes relatively lighter than the air around it and the thermal becomes stronger, solid and more developed. The other aspect of importance in this situation is that the cloud readily evaporates, reducing the risk of over-development and spread-out, but possibly causing severe sink.

In the same way that water can exist at temperatures below zero without freezing, the environment can set itself up such that relatively cold air is sitting above warm air in a tentative steady state. Once there is a trigger or upset the air then starts churning and cumulus clouds develop without the need for sunny hotspots. In this way we can get a complete overcast sky made up of cumulus which is *all* active. It is middle airspace instability. Practically, when underneath the cloud, look for the darkest bits which indicate the strongest climbs. Also, don't get low as there will be little or nothing down there!

Fig 7.3 shows a real cross-section for Warton from 3 March 2011 indicating the variability of temperature with height. It also shows three freezing levels. So, whilst there is a commonly held view that as height is gained the temperature reduces, this can be far from the truth. You will notice that early in the day there is a freezing level at 200 ft and another at 1,000 ft. Meanwhile the temperature is +3°C at 2,000 and +2°C at 5,000 ft giving a strong inversion somewhere in that band. Later in the day there is instability within the band generating cumulus at lower levels (2,000 ft). There is another unstable layer indicated around 8,000–11,000 ft.

It would now be traditional to introduce the tephigram. You may be delighted to learn that I will not! They used to be real soundings but now they are simply predicted and they are of no use

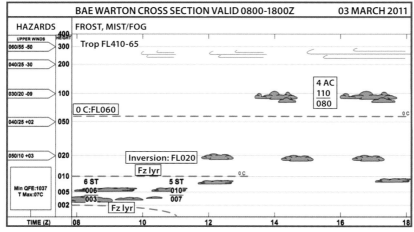

Fig 7.3 A cross-section.

to us in the cockpit. Keen task-setters may wish to continue to use them but there are more than enough people with clever computer software programs costing millions of pounds (the Met Office) who will give us the information that we want with two clicks of a mouse button. All we need to do is to look out of the window and have an understanding of what we actually see and to recognise the good, the bad and the limitations and opportunities of what is available ahead.

Fig 7.4 shows the lapse rates of rising (in green) and sinking (in blue) air. The green thermal gets weaker as it climbs. Note that sinking air can accelerate downwards and is sometimes called sink slugs. This can reinforce the next thermal hotspot or kill potential thermals. Whilst we can understand that warm air might slow as it climbs cold air can accelerate as it passes downwards, giving a larger strength of sinking air than anticipated.

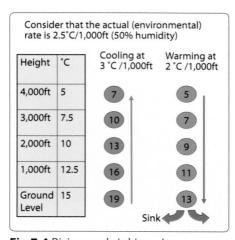

Fig 7.4 Rising and sinking air.

Finally, thermals may accelerate upwards from cloud-base because the rate of cooling of the air then becomes only 1.5°C per thousand feet and the thermal may become more unstable and yet again reinforced by the surrounding cold descending air.

Effects of thermals at cloud base

Humid air above cloud base within the cloud produces heat as the water vapour condenses. This causes the air above to accelerate upwards and *suck* air drawn in from below upwards to the accelerating thermal above, as shown in *Fig 7.5*. The higher the cloud the greater the suck. Because the acceleration is so marked it will also suck up air from around the base of the cloud and you will likely experience a wider thermal that is considerably larger than a 200m central core. As subsequent air is drawn into the cloud from the higher levels the rate of climb will reduce because the surrounding air will be cooler and drier than that coming up the middle. Cloud suck will only occur if the thermal accelerates above cloud base and you will see tall cumulus. If there is little development above cloud base then the thermal will weaken as you approach it.

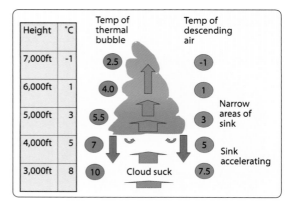

Fig 7.5 Cloud suck.

Fig 7.6 considers the cross section of two separate thermals. The top cross-section is for a standard thermal, at cloud base, which is rising without affecting the adjacent air. The lower cross-section depicts as stronger thermal. Note that both thermals have about the same widths of lift and sink. However, the sink of the stronger thermal is so cold that it induces an upward flow of the environmental air outside of the thermal. This weakly rising air, caused by the descending air, can form false thermals, indicated by weak, pitiful cumulus. Consider for simplicity that a 1°C temperature difference equates to 1kt of lift or sink. You can see that the bottom thermal will have a 1kt area of lift generated outside the thermal itself.

Tall clouds can cause small areas of excessive sink. Broad clouds, trapped by an inversion

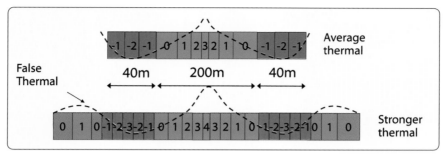

Fig 7.6 Thermal cross-sectional structure.

and spreading out, can generate large areas of moderate sink as shown in *Fig 7.7*.

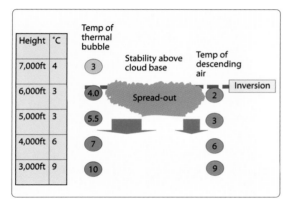

Fig 7.7 Spread-out.

Spread-out occurs when the air is sufficiently unstable and moist and there is an inversion not far above cloud base preventing the clouds developing upwards. The cloud is forced outwards and a considerable blanket of cloud develops, perhaps over a large area, cutting off the sun. The thermal activity may reduce or almost die.

Disappearing thermals

Let's now consider two types of thermal collapse. The cause of the first example is a bit of a *mystery* and the second is purely caused by *windshear*.

> **ANALOGY** **Toothpaste.** With a tube of toothpaste the contents only flow out so long as you are squeezing the tube. Once you stop squeezing, the flow stops.

The mystery of the disappearing thermal!

On some occasions whilst climbing up in a column thermal with a few other gliders the thermal appears to collapse and gliders even a few hundred feet below also detect this, seemingly at the same time, and leave. At first glance it is difficult to understand why this should happen. The hotter rising air can't suddenly disappear and looking up at the cloud above it still appears to be okay, whilst gliders underneath you are, at the moment of confusion, still turning.

Consider a 4kt thermal; the surrounding sink is falling at 4kts so the relative speed between the lift and sink is 8kts. If the sink stops falling around the rising air the squeezing and controlling influence generated by the temperature difference is removed and the warm rising air is no longer contained or accelerated. It will expand outwards and therefore slow down, generating turbulence and climb more slowly as the temperature difference between it and the now adjacent environmental air has reduced. The controlling force is always the huge volume of descending air. The repositioning of this descending air will break the column, as will windshear. A glider some 200ft beneath us will experience the condition very shortly after us, far less than the time it takes to do one really hard turn and about the time it takes you to realize that there is a problem. If you then spend a further turn wondering if you have just fallen out of or temporarily lost the thermal, then the actual effects are now being experienced by other gliders well beneath you. A small amount of momentum in the rising air and the push from underneath from the still rigid yet rapidly decaying column generates a short but chaotic turbulent band.

The action of windshear on a column

Fig 7.8 shows a normal column in a stable state drifting with the wind. As it passes over a hotspot it becomes a stronger column that punches above the inversion into a stronger wind. The higher column is broken because the cloud and its subsequent sink are removed from the top of the column. The cold descending air no longer descends around the rising column.

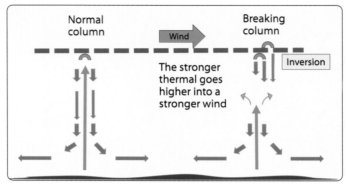

Fig 7.8 A column thermal breaking up and disappearing.

8
Daily changes

My student had been making good flying progress but the LX instrumentation was new to him and remained a little bit of a mystery. An inter-club league allowed us the opportunity to consolidate things on Saturday's task so that on Sunday he could take full responsibility for this aspect as though he was flying the task solo. Our kit in those days was unusual in that the front and back units were effectively independent and, to instil confidence in my student, I did not set any task information in the front instrument.

Off we went on what might have been considered a slightly under-set task. He did all the decision-making and navigation, whilst I simply did the stick work. After a fantastic final glide it readily became evident that we were going to win the day.

An hour or so later the second finisher arrived. "Gosh, how did you get around Bottesford so fast?" "Bottesford? We didn't go around Bottesford. Hey P2, erase that smug smile and come here!"

Throughout the day the thermic sky is changing continually. Thermals produce clouds which generate both shadow and sink slugs from the evaporating clouds. These change the relative hotspots which move as the clouds drift. It is up to us to interpret the various patterns that are generated.

Patterns in the sky

As soon as the first low cumulus develops a common pattern in the sky is quickly established. The air leaving the surface must be replaced and this air comes from above and around the rising bubble. As a consequence it is impossible for the development of one enormously wide thermal. The descending cold air spreads out after entering the lower layers or may even reach down to the ground, cooling the near areas but promoting adjacent areas causing a chain reaction in the vicinity. The cloud shadows can further influence the pattern. Bear in mind that a temperature difference of just a couple of degrees may produce a thermal but the difference between *in the sun* and *in the cloud* shadow can be more than this. The areas which develop thermals will be continuously changing and regions considered strong thermal producing areas can be switched off.

It is not possible for the ground to generate a huge area of rising air. A regular patchwork of thermals are generated, indicated by the classic pattern in *Fig 8.1*. This pattern of thermals can also be present later in the day, whilst the lower level of the sky loses the unstable property and

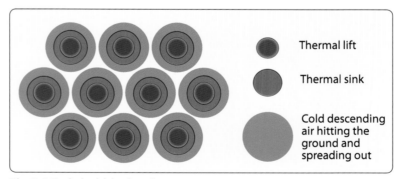

Fig 8.1 Early bubble development.

82

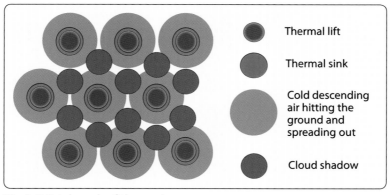

Fig 8.2 Patchwork of thermals.

the only real thermal development takes place at height. This leads to days when the cloud makes the day look good but it is a struggle lower down,

Fig 8.2 shows that the cloud shadow may fall on the cool areas of the ground and reinforce the hot areas and patterns in the sky. Alternatively, the shadows may fall over the hotspots and disrupt the day.

It is quite normal for an unstable air mass to generate the patterns similar to this, over the sea. Stronger thermals generated by hotspots over the ground increase the number of regular thermals and can generate streets. As the day warms up the lower inversion is driven up and the depth of instability increases, the development of thermal columns or streeting rearrange the sky and some clouds become increasingly large and more developed, thus controlling the sky in the vicinity.

Look at the sky at mid-day, just before you go off on your task. Assuming that there is no significant frontal activity coming your way, then what you see is what you get and it will stay that way until about 15:00 in August, 16:00 in May and July, and 17:00 in June (light winds). This is largely to do with the sun angle and cloud shadows. However, summer is not usually that good. The tropopause is at its highest which allows for a greater depth of pollution. The light winds, which extend to high levels, mean that the concentration of pollution can build up over a number of days and we get quite hazy days with reduced visibility and less surface heating. Thermals have less mass in the warmer daytime temperatures. The night time temperature struggles to drop due to the short nights so there is a narrowing between minimum and maximum day temperatures. Perhaps if you

were lucky enough to fly cross-country when the Icelandic ash cloud grounded all of western European air travel, you might remember the pacific blue skies and the magic strong thermals with high cloud bases.

As the angle of the sun changes, casting shadows over significantly different ground areas, then the structure will start to change and can easily become *out of phase*. Initially the light winds mean that the sink and lift are sympathetic. As the surface wind increases and the sinking air mixes, then the structure may change into wandering columns. However, as the cloud finally dissipates the driving cold air disappears and the thermal structure breaks down.

Having acknowledged that as the cloud base moves up the thermals are farther apart, a simple rule of thumb can be made depending on the performance of your glider. If the sky was uniform then the height lost when moving on from your current thermal would be in proportion to the cloud base. The 15% rule of thumb is a guide to how much height you will lose between thermals.

KEY POINT Expected height to lose before the next thermal = Cloud base × 15%

So, if the cloud base was 2,000ft then you might anticipate a thermal after losing 300ft. Similarly with a cloud base of 5,000ft then you might anticipate to lose 750ft before your next thermal. Whilst the sky is not equal it should at least stop you worrying that on *better* days you just don't seem to hit thermals quite so often. Of course the sky is not equal and large areas can be either very productive or a bit of a dead area. This may be because the ground is not heating sufficiently, perhaps damp, and there are almost no thermals or it is overcast so that the sun can't heat those good areas.

Cloud amounts throughout the day are a significant factor. Remember *scattered* in the forecast would appear to be good but means that cloud could cover up to half the sky. This is far too vague for our purposes.

An incorrect suggestion is that if a thermal fails we should seek another by moving to the sunny side of the cloud. The reference to the sun is misleading as the sun does not control the drift of the next thermal, it is the wind both below and above any inversion that does this. The northern hemisphere's prevailing wind is westerly and we normally only find ourselves on a cross-country in the afternoon when the sun is also in the west. So moving towards the sun will often work and is, of course, effective only in a westerly wind. To find the next thermal you should seek something on the upwind side. This could be in any direction and is definitely not related to the sun.

Photo 8.1 shows that thermal bubbles can be quite adjacent, as indicated by this close but scattered pattern next to a better thermal. Cloud patterns are important because they tell you the current structure of the air underneath. These

weak bubbles are probably false thermals and clearly have very little vertical depth and no column development.

Bubbles mirroring the heat sources

Quite often thermals are generated from the ground upwards by the heat from the sun, producing *bubbles*. The clouds in this case mirror the ground distribution of thermals but are delayed by around 10 minutes plus drift. In this case the clouds give us an immediate history lesson. Transposing cloud down to the ground, allowing a displacement for the sun and 10 minutes of drift, gives us a picture of which areas of the ground generated the thermals. This assumes no other weather-influencing aspects such as streeting, sea breeze, wave, precipitation, and not too much cloud over-development. Equally, because you are only looking at clouds which have proven thermal-making potential, areas of the sky lacking in clouds display ground areas that are weak.

Random column thermal sky

In the case of *column thermals*, which are a result of an unstable layer of air, they do not necessarily extend vertically to the surface, nor are they necessarily connected with any convection generated from the ground. As a result, the cloud pattern is not related to the ground. However, column thermals can subsequently generate instability down to ground level. The clouds are often not directly linked to known thermal hotspots although the middle airspace instability may be reinforced whilst they pass over hotspots.

Photo 8.1 Weak wisps and false thermals.

Large areas of lift

Just like water can remain liquid at temperatures below freezing, the atmosphere can be in a state of limbo despite being theoretically unstable. Once the ball starts rolling cold air cascades down wherever it can find an adequate shove. Huge areas of cold air sink and the warmer air does its best to climb up in traditional thermals around the sinking area or larger general areas of lift. In this situation you often get a very large broad band of gently rising air, perhaps 500m or more across, but within this is a number of specific strong centres (bubbles) in which you can turn and climb faster. You may move from one centred thermal to another without entering sink but the thermal strengths can be widely variable.

Sink structure

Just before we look further into the association of lift and cloud it is worth considering sink and cloud. One of the best visual displays of sink profiles is displayed by virga clouds. These clouds are essentially dying cumulus and show precipitation in the form of ice crystals, rain, snow and hail, but the precipitation evaporates before reaching the ground. From a glider pilot's point of view they display an area of considerable sink which extends beyond the visual bits and can be related to some extent as the structure of sink under all dying cumulus. It would be reasonable to expect the cold air generated by the evaporating ice/rain to continue down and interact with the lower unstable layer. There is a lack of form in the virga cloud and also a lack of structure to the sink.

Of course, continuing the trend, whenever a street collapses a reverse streeting will develop. It may well be better to cruise home between the dying cloud lines.

How cloud height affects our flying

Now we will analyse how our pattern of climbing and cruising varies with different cloud base heights, and therefore different thermal strengths. In the following examples we are considering just bubble thermals. We are assuming the following:

▶ Climbs are made from 1,000ft agl.
▶ The thermal is rising at 1.2 × cloud base (in 1,000's ft).
▶ Our glider has a 1kt sink rate.
▶ In these diagrams there is no 'minus one' (for the descent rate of the glider) as we are just considering the rate of climb of the air.

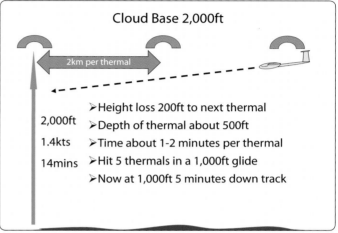

Fig 8.3 Lower cloud base therefore thermals close together.

2,000ft cloud base gives 2 × 1.2 = 2.4kt thermal. Cruising at say 65kts (120kph) at 150ft/min descent = 6.6 minutes to descend to 1,000ft (13.2km down track).
The time spent climbing 1,000ft at 140ft/min = 7.7 minutes = about 19 turns.

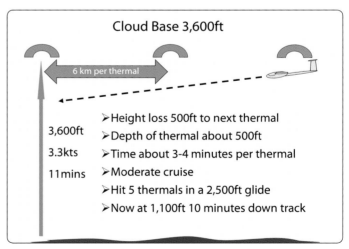

Fig 8.4 Average UK cloud base May – Sep, clouds 4km apart.

3,600ft cloud base gives 3.6 × 1.2 = 4.3 kt thermal.
Takes 8.3 minutes and the next thermal is not too far away.
Cruising at say 71 kts (131 kph) at 175 ft/min descent = 14.8 minutes to descend to 1,000ft (32.3km down track).
The time spent climbing 2,600ft at 330 ft/min = 7.8 minutes = about 20 turns.

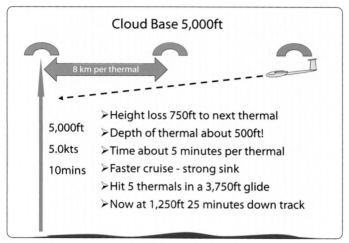

Fig 8.5 Strong day in the UK, clouds develop big gaps.

5,000ft cloud base gives 5 × 1.2 = 6 kt thermal.
Cruising at say 77 kts (143 kph) at 200 ft/min descent = 20 minutes to descend to 1,000ft (57km down track).
The time spent climbing 4,000ft at 500 ft/min = 8 minutes = about 20 turns.

Because you are flying significantly faster in this last example you will gain height on the pull up so you will need less turns. As the thermal will be tighter a higher rate of turn and a greater degree of accuracy is required to maintain the centre correctly.

KEY POINT We spend about the same amount of time climbing regardless of thermal strength!

The proportional *time* cruising increases as the thermal strength increases. This latter effect is mainly because whilst we are considering a linear increase in thermal strength, the performance of our glider with increasing cruise speed is not linear, double the speed and we only go less than half of the distance forward. This is important when we start to consider the benefits of dolphin techniques and our decision making.

Bear in mind that the calculations offer a guide to average thermal strength, from the ground to cloud base. There can be some significant variations resulting in both weaker or stronger thermals and a variation of the same thermal with height giving the well talked about ideal operating band. The optimal operating band will differ depending on several variables such as the type of thermal being used—bubble, column, street, the wind at different heights etc.

But of course the sky is rarely uniform because of changes in ground features, cloud shadow and topography. Consider a day when all thermals are exactly the same strength as they climb. Now introduce into this simple ideal world a poor green area which is largely covered with cloud, but a sunny hole appears making a local hotspot. A trigger point will be achieved and a weak thermal will leave the ground. As it climbs though, it will not be hot enough to continue the same rapid climb and will quickly weaken to produce a relatively weak thermal for the rest of its climb to cloud base.

Now consider the reverse scenario. A hotspot which is temporarily held down because the whole area is hot and it quite simply has not got the energy to trigger, for example a sunken dip in the ground which gently gets hotter. Eventually when it does break away it climbs into a relatively cold band of air where it accelerates quickly upwards drawing hot air up from beneath making an unusually strong thermal. Again this particularly strong thermal also produces a tall cumulus cloud which in turn starts a chain of events revolving around cloud base which can then trigger further instability and create a great situation!

A further consideration is the concept of not using too many thermals and trying to operate between the top and bottom of the ideal height band. This simply comes from the fact that many up-and-coming pilots are likely to take two turns to centre (which is a huge penalty to the overall average climb rate), so you are better centring once (one loss of time) and taking the climb all the way to the top. Unfortunately, if you don't connect at the bottom of the band with the next climb you are then forced to continue down into a known poorer band and have to take a slower climb for a while.

SeeYou and other computer programs have that rather depressing statistic of the total height lost on a flight whilst thermalling but take heart, you might not be as bad as the data suggests. On the other hand, if halfway along in the cruise you encounter a strong climb then it would be sensible to take it, because even if there is some loss of efficiency it will still be better than dragging yourself out of the weeds. By looking at the losses, we can work out what weaker value would be an acceptable climb in the ideal band. It is equally important not to cling on too long on days when the cloud tops do not extend very high, the thermal strength tends to reduce as you approach cloud base.

To avoid going into a protracted series of calculations it should be obvious that to push too hard for too long, getting low and running out of options, is just not a comfortable way of making progress on a cross-country. We know that having to accept a slow climb will mean a

huge loss in average speed and we immediately become aware of this by looking at the same piece of ground for what seems like ages. Although we might have experienced an unusually strong thermal we cannot push on blindly assuming or hoping that this is the new norm. We might have had a 5kt thermal and pushed on but 3kts at 3,000ft is better than 2kts at 2,000ft and 1kt at 1,000ft.

In conclusion, to stay in the comfortable zone where the ground and fields are not remotely in the picture, anything which gives you close to 80% of the average rate of climb or better, calculated with reference to the height of the cloud base, will do.

KEY POINT Consider using any thermal that will give you at least 80% of your expected average rate of climb.

The bubbles on the left of *Fig 8.6* are the temperature of a thermal starting at 15°C at ground level. Each of the vertical columns on the right are different actual temperatures with height. Green indicates instability and that the thermal will climb, whilst blue indicates the air to be stable at that height.

However, working a well-defined height band probably only applies to days when the thermal strength and cloud base are especially strong and high. Even then, in the UK this ideal is rarely achieved over the complete route of a

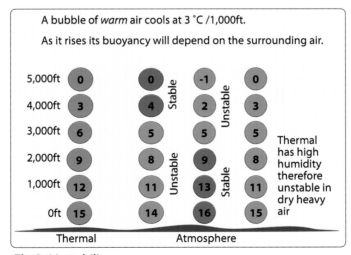

Fig 8.6 Instability.

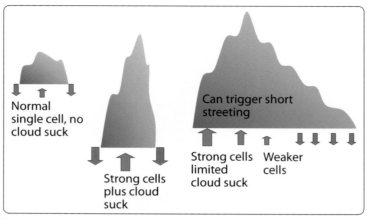

Fig 8.7 Very simple cloud shapes with an indication of where the lift or sink might be.

large task. There tends to be a lot of variability in the conditions, both throughout the day and at different locations. As a result, generally avoid getting low. There can be occasions when staying low to push into a brisk wind, which increases significantly with height, can be beneficial but this depends on just how low you are prepared to go and still feel comfortable. It is much better to get back slowly than not at all.

It can be quite a challenge to determine where the lift or sink might be. *Fig 8.7* shows that this can be in different locations underneath the clouds. Until you gain experience at reading the sky and distinguishing between the various thermic sky structures, when cruising cross-country it makes sense to hold between cloud base and halfway to the ground. During this time use the clouds and cloud shadows to develop your skills at reading the sky. If you find yourself at lower levels you may need to start using ground features to assist in finding your next thermal.

The inversion

There is always an inversion even if it is at the tropopause but there are usually others much lower down. An inversion puts a flexible lid on the vertical development of the climbing thermals. Strong thermals may penetrate well up into weak inversions where the wind speed and direction is different. This displaces the sink generated by the evaporating cloud and can have hugely significant

effects on the subsequent structure of the vertical motions of the sky.

More on cloud structure

The structure and development of any cloud depends on the continued feed of hot air and the motion of descending cold air within the unstable band. When the sink of the evaporated cloud is considerably displaced from the rising air a mechanism may be triggered which leads to *very large thermals*. Individual cells become just a part of a massive structure.

Consider the perpetual motion in *Fig 8.8* and *Fig 8.9* which is dependent on a thermal breaking the inversion and a change of wind speed with height a little above cloud base.

Any change in wind speed and direction above cloud base and before cloud tops is really important as it determines where the descending cold air from the evaporating cloud will fall.

The two developing mechanisms generate thermal triggers laterally making a very broad band of lift which can be utilized as a street, essentially cross-wind. A broad cloud does not mean that there are a lot of thermals feeding it underneath and it definitely does not indicate that the thermal is very wide.

Great care needs to be taken to interpret the very big clouds and the associated bubbles or columns feeding them. A large cloud fed by column thermals will remain looking good as it drifts

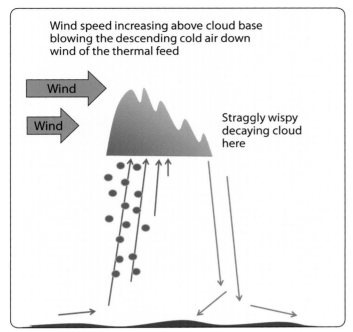

Fig 8.8 Tall large area cumulus—wind increasing with height.

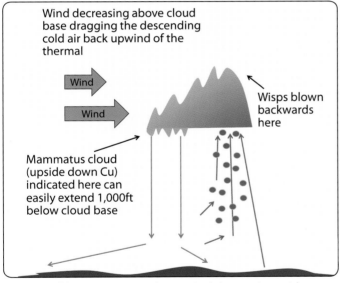

Fig 8.9 Tall large area cumulus—wind decreasing with height.

downwind. A large cloud fed by bubble thermals will essentially maintain the same position over the ground, rather like lenticular clouds.

Bubble thermals often cycle through quite quickly depending on what is making the cycle.

Their death is often caused by cloud shadow, the loss of the trigger action by a large downwash of cold air (hotspot in a ground depression), or by the dragging of all available warm air by a stronger thermal source nearby. Thermals generated by islands in lakes cycle (pulse) as all the warm air available is replaced with cold air.

Another important aspect is how quickly a cloud is developing. The faster it is forming then the greater amount of thermal activity is feeding it. Be cautious as the faster it grows then the faster it is likely to switch off, ignoring developing rain and thunderstorm clouds.

A broad cloud may have a towering column above it which sucks or draws all the air at cloud base towards it. Of course although the hottest part has taken off upwards, it might not be in the middle of the cloud. Other clouds of course do not show such a strong surge in one area. This variation of thermals is par for the course and often determines just how close to cloud base we care to go.

The *theoretical* stronger thermal is not necessarily because the air nearer the ground is significantly hotter. It can be because the sinking air surrounding the rising thermal is significantly colder. On any day, therefore, take a look at the thermic sky and interpret it briefly. Consider where, if you had to decide now, which cloud(s) you would press on to. Look again 3 minutes later and keep repeating. Note the changes. With practice you will teach yourself to genuinely read the sky rather than guess and hope. This can be done anytime looking at any good sky, anywhere in the world. It is an excellent way to pass the time on a high speed train, which has comparable cruise speeds to a glider.

Temperature changes

The surface temperature during the day and seasons can change considerably from well below freezing to a sultry 30°C. This does not affect the thermal production as it is simply relative temperature which triggers it. A simple calculation results in a narrower thermal diameter in winter but then the same physics determines the aerodynamics of our glider. At any given indicated speed, as the air temperature reduces we are able to turn the glider at a reduced radius of turn for the same angle of bank and the rate of turn also increases. Therefore, in winter we do actually turn tighter which is just as well as this closely matches the shrinking of the thermal. In conclusion, our ability to remain within the core of a thermal remains largely the same whether the air is hot or cold, at altitude or at low heights. There is a slight benefit, however, in colder air. At lower temperatures the density of air is greater. This gives the air of a thermal generated in cold air a greater mass and therefore greater momentum. The relative ups and downs that we experience will therefore feel more robust.

9
Streeting

The run from the start line at Bicester had been fantastic, holding 90kts in a heavy *DG300 Elan* and not a single turn, whilst maintaining cloud base to the first TP at Nympsfield. I'd been trying to force myself to look out at the clouds but flying at cloud base in relatively poor visibility had absorbed most of my attention. I occasionally checked the air-data computer for an estimate of the distance to run. The cameras were ready and it was just a case of looking down for the club house and the TP sector. There it was but "what a big club house and that ground looks alarmingly close in the mirk." Of course the cloud base had been steadily reducing so I was now below 1,500ft. Despite the next leg being northerly I headed back east for 20 miles, to the other side of the hills, at a much slower pace!

And along came the wind and changed everything. Although a wind of 8 to 15kts is a good thing.

Windy triggers

The wind is best imagined as a river flowing over rocks. Turbulent eddy currents, which will differ depending on topography, will be present but these only affect the lowest levels where thermals are generated. At lower heights then, at less than 800ft, misleading mechanical gusts are present within the thermal-generated gusts and can lead to disorientation as to where the thermal core is. These misleading gusts will reduce as height is gained.

The wind may also force thermals to break off the ground earlier and although it will generate some upward vigour, the thermal will have less volume. It will initially become strong, narrow and not too tall as it does not have enough volume. Sometimes sheltered areas do generate hotspots. A ploughed field may be protected from the wind but this is only part of the equation. The sheltered bit will produce a strong but small thermal, not reinforced by the exposed area of the field. As the climbing cores develop they will be narrower initially with significant sink. These thermals are quite challenging to climb in.

Efficient glides

There is a commonly held view that the person who climbs only in the strongest thermals is the fastest around a task, but that is only part of the story. If you can make efficient glides, making good speed but losing less height than the polar curve suggests, you will spend more time cruising on course and less time climbing. In this case you will definitely be quick. So efficient routing is also important, hence the need to understand streeting and linking the energy together. It is often called straight line flying but actually involves far more weaving and not that much on-track straight line flying.

In *Fig 9.1* there is a choice; to fly **A** to **B** and climb in the big strong thermal or to simply fly the connected weaker thermals without stopping and turning.

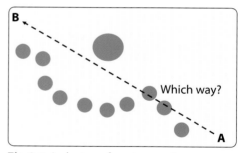

Fig 9.1 A choice of routes, perhaps not through the strongest thermal?

Consider the following simple questions regarding streeting:

► Is there more than one kind of streeting?
► If this is the case, how do we identify each

type of streeting?

► Are streets always in straight lines?
► Do streets exist on blue days?
► Do streets drift?
► Do streets turn?
► What is a street surge?
► How do we best use streeting?
► How can a thermal suddenly become stronger at height?

The sea breeze

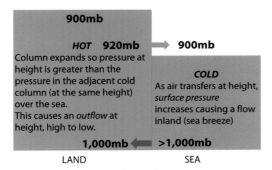

Fig 9.2 The mechanism of a sea breeze.

The mechanism of a sea breeze has a very powerful effect on the local and surface wind, often for tens of miles. In the same way the different properties of hot and cold columns of adjacent air can generate a circular cycle. Once that cycle has started the effect can generate repetitive ripples or waves in the air. This circulation is the equivalent to mini sea breezes, but with no sea. It just needs an adequate volume of cold versus hot air to set up this domino effect. The mechanism shown in *Fig 9.2*, generating a cycling motion driven largely by the cascade of descending cold air, is largely fundamental to the generation of most streeting.

The Met-man only considers one kind of streeting, classic streeting. There are other situations when the sky conveniently organizes itself into something which we can use and this is not always in line with the wind. Any line of useful energy to follow which results in not stopping to climb, but instead offers the opportunity to climb or maintain height as you progress down track, can be considered streeting.

It is particularly important to understand that this cycling motion produces a weak upward vertical wind, which is strongest down the central line, generated by the surrounding descending air. This allows regular thermals to be reinforced in their upwards travel within the central region, whilst those beyond the edge are either destroyed by the windshear or cannot compete against the downwards flow. The destruction towards the edge is not an issue as it supports the overall width of the upward band.

You need *some wind* and normally an *inversion* for the following streeting:
► Power station streeting.
► Inversion induced streeting.
► Blue day streeting.
► Wave induced streeting.

And with the following you *don't need the inversion*:
► Cloud shadow streeting.
► Hill streeting.
► Sea breeze streeting.

Power station streeting

Natural streeting and the streeting caused by power stations are often different. The great news is that power station streeting is clearly visible from the thermal source at chimney top level and its progress up to cloud base and the cloud street development downwind. This allows a useful starting point to get to grips with the structure of both thermal bubbles, columns and a street. It also demonstrates to us the ascent or the development of thermals in different air masses. What can also be seen is the way thermals change during the day's environmental change in temperature, from stable to unstable conditions as the day develops and back to stable as the soaring day dies.

There are key advantages to be able to see the thermal activity produced from a power station. The main heat sources of a power station are not associated with the sun, shadow or sink slugs. The humidity of the air is artificially increased and the thermals may be stronger on low humidity days. On the other hand on high humidity days the cloud base will be lower.

Consider Drax power station in the UK. The top of the boiler chimney contains four exhausts less than 2m across. Despite the effluent design temperature being significantly hot, this only gives relatively poor thermals. The six main cooling towers are each 20m across at a design venting temperature of 45°C. The brown field required to generate an equivalent thermal would only be about 300m square! So despite their appearance, power stations are not quite as good as they suggest, but are better on dry days due to increased humidity, if they are working at full capacity. Coal stacks may possibly generate a better thermal source on blue days as the power stations will not be working hard. This streeting can be useful if it happens to be aligned going your way, so perhaps plan the task with this in mind.

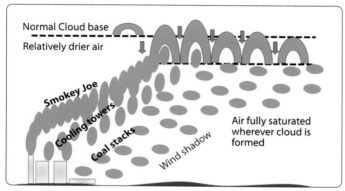

Fig 9.3 Power station streeting.

Fig 9.3 shows streeting downwind of power stations. In reality, the thermals out of the hot thin chimneys will expand (hot but heavy air full of contamination) with no vortex. The cooling tower thermals will form strong vortices.

There is no reason why a large powerful ground hotspot should not be able to produce a thermic structure to the sky similar to that produced by a power station.

Fig 9.4 shows a simple suggested concept of the thermal structure in streeting. Whilst the stronger thermals push through the inversion they also bounce off it, whilst the evaporating cloud and sink cascade

down the sides. Weaker thermals fail to penetrate the inversion and can break the street at that point.

Often there are other influences that conflict with this simple picture. We know from experience that we can use lift 30 or 40 miles downwind from a power station if the streeting has become established, and charge along it either way.

In *Fig 9.5* the power station is puffing into an *unstable* layer and column thermals are developing downwind and generating a street. If you are flying along a street like this make sure that you don't stray away from the good air because the bad air is really bad!

In *Photo 9.1* a twin spiral is being generated leading to the development of a street and castellations. The arrows indicate the spiral flow on the near side to the camera.

The reality is that power stations and other fixed hotspots do produce a steady stream of thermal bubbles, even with no sunshine, and these can quickly grow and modify into column thermals. Obviously the power station introduces a large amount of water vapour into the air and this contributes to the fullness of the clouds immediately downwind. Farther away the thermal air is drier so the clouds are not as big, yet the thermals may still be strong.

Photo 9.2 shows that the spiral cloud soon starts to separate out and produce columns. In the background, despite all the steam coming out of the top of the towers,

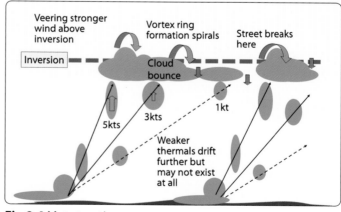

Fig 9.4 Met streeting.

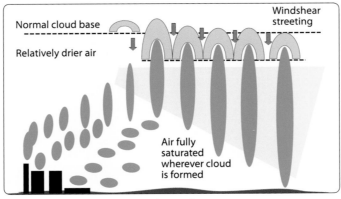

Fig 9.5 Power station streeting column.

steam can also be seen subsequently descending indicating the sink as castellation develops.

Photo 9.1 Twin spiral generating an embryonic street.

Photo 9.2 Castellation development.

Streeting conditions

The most favourable conditions for the formation of cloud streets occur when the lower moist layer of air is unstable but is capped by an inversion of stable air. The upper wind will be stronger and usually veers from the lower level winds. This condition often occurs when all the air is descending such as under high pressure (anticyclonic) conditions. Convection occurs below the inversion, with the rising air in thermals below the clouds and sink in the air between the streets. Whilst they are usually straight lines and favour a 10 to 20kts wind, they can make a paisley pattern when the wind driving the street encounters interference. These cloud patterns are known as *von Karman vortex streets*.

Fig 9.6 shows thermal activity when the inversion is not far above cloud base. In this case the active line of the street is not as wide as the cloud and a good proportion of the cloud on the edges will give you sink. Although it often streets on blue days the upper structure is very similar to this and it is important to make every effort to stay down the centre.

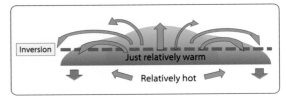

Fig 9.6 Broad and blue day streeting.

The effect of wind slants the thermal line relative to the ground which normally causes a string of bubbles or, with an inversion, streeting. This is never a slanted column. A string of bubbles can accommodate each other at regular intervals but don't overlap, as shown in *Fig 9.7*.

Fig 9.7 Bubble stability.

If a strong thermal hits a weak one centrally as shown in *Fig 9.8* they can be briefly complementary. It can accelerate and narrow. To hit at any other point can destroy both vortex structures.

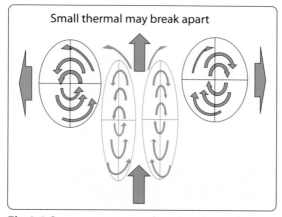

Fig 9.8 Strong vortex accelerating through a slower vortex.

Vortices can be sensitive things. A strong one will pass effortlessly through the middle of a weak one but any misalignment will break both.

Strong cells passing weaker ones can be reinforced by the combined adjacent descending air as shown in *Fig 9.9*. In this event the weaker vortex can be destroyed. If the air mass is not

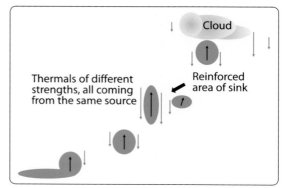

Fig 9.9 Thermal structure with wind.

especially unstable, once a thermal structure has been broken it can't reform into a vortex.

ANALOGY **Bouncing balloons.** A ball can bounce along the floor in the same way that a helium filled balloon can bounce along the ceiling.

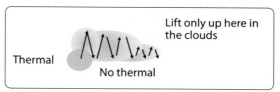

Fig 9.10 Cloud bounce.

Fig 9.10 shows the initial or last bubble thermal from the ground, after which the cloud will continue to look good due to an induced bounce, depending mainly on the humidity above and below the cloud base. Similar to a helium balloon bouncing along the ceiling the thermal will bounce. Beware, despite the appearance that there is a line of energy to fly along, there will only be a line at cloud base.

ANALOGY **Helium balloons.** With a mass launch of helium balloons they don't all obediently drift up the same diagonal line, but drift apart quite significantly as the various horizontal eddies in the air affect each balloon slightly differently.

Just as with the analogy of helium balloons drifting apart, thermal bubbles are moved around by the horizontal eddies in the air. Once the street is established the thermal bubbles will be drawn into line.

Streeting models

Fig 9.11 shows the initial development of a street. The mechanism of cloud bounce still applies, however, the stronger cells in the street climb well above the inversion. The descending air from the tops of these clouds is deflected to the sides by the subsequent strong thermal coming up. This action reinforces subsequent cells.

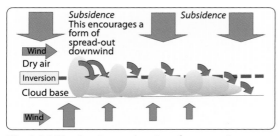

Fig 9.11 The basic mechanism for streeting.

In *Fig 9.12* which is a plan view of vortex streeting, the leading strong thermal (on the left of the diagram) punches highest and restricts the upwind downdraft coupled with any significant change in direction of the wind above the inversion. In this case a two rather than three-dimensional column is generated, in part along the lines of a sea breeze.

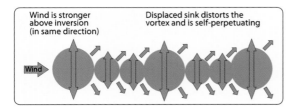

Fig 9.12 Plan view of vortex streeting.

Fig 9.13 shows a three-dimensional model of vortex streeting. You can see how we can fly in straight lines in lift for many miles in these streets made by bubbles.

In *Photo 9.3* (over Lincolnshire) looking upwind there is a clear equal flow out to both sides from the cumulus cloud. And the cloud looks broader just above cloud base so a distinct slowing of the thermal must occur just above cloud base due to

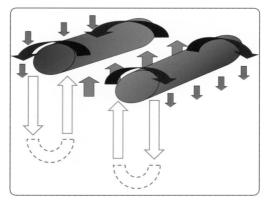

Fig 9.13 Side view of vortex streeting.

an inversion. Notice that the strong thermal (high Cu top) in the street to the left above the flock of birds has effectively broken the street briefly at that point as sink cascades not only to the side but also in the downwind direction.

In *Photo 9.4 on page 98* we are looking downwind at the same street. In both pictures we can clearly see that the parallel streets strongly resemble one another in every respect.

Also, in *Photo 9.4 on page 98* the gaps are starting to fill as the street becomes more established. Whilst we cannot see the clouds of the street we are in because we may be cruising close to cloud base, this photograph shows how we can get a good idea of the structure of our street from the parallel streets by looking both at the clouds and the cloud shadows. On days such as this every shadow is that of a cumulus.

Stronger thermals can trigger a break or make a displacement in the line. Sink from the higher

Photo 9.3 Looking upwind at some classic streeting.

Photo 9.4 Looking downwind at a street 10 minutes later.

cloud is stronger and whilst sink will cascade to the sides any sink tracking farther downwind prevents the generation of the next cell. However it rarely kills the line but more often regenerates the thermal line slightly to one side or farther downwind. In these cases contours, hills and large thermal hotspots like towns adjacent to the sinking air now have a big influence on the subsequent street.

The leading strong thermal punches highest and prevents the natural downdraft upwind coupled with any significant increase and change in direction of the wind above the inversion.

Not all cloud streets are interlinked. They may be straight, meander gently a little like a river or they can be distinctly separate. Meandering streets will break once the sun angle to cloud shadow reaches some critical point, the upper inversion breaks or a different air mass enters the area. This is a time to *use it or lose it* and be aware of any changes.

In *Fig 9.14* and *Fig 9.15* it is important to note that the wind has veered somewhere above cloud base but below cloud tops. This causes the sinking air to favour one side.

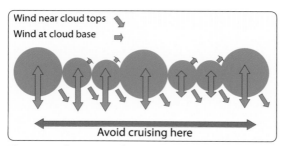

Fig 9.14 Plan view of vortex streeting with a veering wind.

In this case more air rotates and descends on the downwind side of the upper wind. This kind of streeting drifts downwind of the upper wind and across the surface wind.

Where the upper wind veers you get a stronger line of lift to one side. As described in Chapter 11, *Reading the sky*, the formation of cumulus and subsequent evaporation is considerably more complex than the simple models would have us believe.

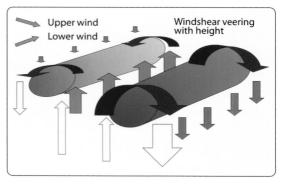

Fig 9.15 Side view of vortex streeting with a veering wind.

How to fly in streeting

On a street the strongest path can be down the middle or either side regardless of the sun and wind vector that we are flying in and has everything to do with the wind above the inversion and the distribution of the sink.

Wind speed normally, but not always, increases and veers with height. Even at a gentle inversion with dry air above moist air this can be pronounced, hence the effects which we have just covered. The instability created, however, with dry air over moist air and with a strong trigger like wind blowing over a high hill or an island in the sea, causes a downwind ripple for many miles as shown in *Fig 9.16*.

This unstable street aligns with the upper wind (not what the GPS equipment will indicate) and so the street will form across the lower surface area wind. It can be triggered by a particularly strong thermal which develops a tall cloud, in which case the street will drift slightly cross-wind. They can also turn slowly, normally clockwise depending on the circumstances.

Photo 9.5 Streeting has been generated from the Lincolnshire Wolds, 25 miles away, and continues well inland and beyond Cranwell.

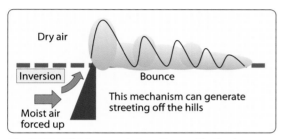

Fig 9.16 Hill triggered streeting with the inversion close to the top of the high hills.

On two separate days I set my powered aircraft up with insufficient power to stay level in order to be representative of my glider. I chased a street from the Barrow area heading into a westerly wind and on the second day I chased a street from north Wales into a northerly. Both routes were to the Isle of Man with a cloud base just below 2,000ft. Both flights would have been completely successful if I had been in my glider but without an amphibious ability it would have been an utterly irresponsible

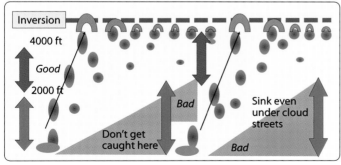

Fig 9.17 Side view of streeting.

thing to try for real! But this does show that there are some wonderful opportunities.

Fig 9.17 shows a cross-section of a weak street generated by bubble thermals. You can see that the clouds and thermal strength diminish after each lead thermal.

Practically, try to cruise at a speed which maintains a comfortable height and never get lower than halfway between the ground and cloud base. If you need to climb at any point endeavour to make it in one of the stronger thermals within the street.

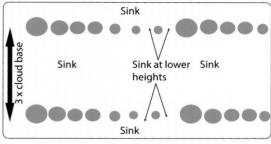

Fig 9.18 Plan view of streeting.

Fig 9.18 shows that it is best not to hang around between the streets. You will find that when jumping from one street to another that it is wise to do this at the narrowest gap and to aim for the strongest cells. As a guide, the distance between streets is approximately three times the cloud base.

Often whilst on a street *cruise* we encounter a larger surge and no matter which way we turn we hit considerable sink, which is frustrating as we wonder where that strong thermal is located. Just remember though, that if the thermal doubles in strength then the radius is approximately halved and the air at the top is now accelerating upwards rather like the initial birth mechanics of a thermal at ground level. Taller decaying cloud on the street causes a strong sink hole on the street line but the thermal is not destroyed. The vortex motion distorts and rising air is reinforced by the sudden temperature difference giving a strong but rarely usable (to turn) local surge. An unprecedented surge on a street is usually far too narrow to turn in. Pull, hold, accelerate and press on before the inevitable strong sink.

The surge is caused by the acceleration of the vortex as it hits colder descending air passing by the upwind edge. The sink tends to be horseshoe shaped during this process.

Always try to remember that despite the desire to turn—don't. Instead, pull up hard and ride the lift whilst you can and accelerate before the inevitable strong sink. Perhaps surprisingly, you can anticipate the surge.

The question is where does this unusually strong *thermal* come from? Well, it comes from the modification of a sink hole clashing with a strong thermal hitting it. The sink is pushed out to become horseshoe shaped and remember that sink does not form a vortex. As a result sink has no physical rigidity either so it can be displaced sideways more easily than rising air. But in this case it does reinforce the thermal core at that point. As you run into wind along the line you will not experience any strong sink before the surge. The sinking air energises the thermal contrast. It does not increase the overall strength of the bubble, the surge may go above the vortex bubble as shown in the side view on *Fig 9.19*. It is important to note that you can't thermal in it because you are unable to turn tight enough. The cloud structure above can give you the clue to its presence but you have to look for it.

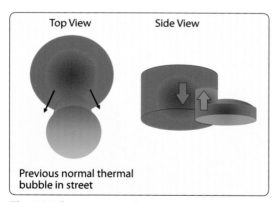

Fig 9.19 Street surge views.

KEY POINT You can't turn tight enough to stay in a street surge.

In all streeting lines associate the lift with your height in relation to the cloud and cloud shadow. Streets are normally about three times the cloud base apart. If jumping streets then leap directly across the narrowest gap or from cloud base directly to the highest cloud on the adjacent street.

The ability to run efficiently down a street is largely dependent on your rate of descent and the polar curve. If any particular glider descends at 1kt and the street is providing an average rate of climb of 1.5kts then all gliders can fly a little quicker and will achieve the same effective glide, but the higher performance machines will simply do it at a faster speed and this is also linked to their wing loading.

Running along any line the balance depends on what you are trying to do. There will be times when it is best to fly slowly trying to gain height for a downwind TP. You will always have a number of options open to you and it depends just how long you wish to run the line and where you are going to next. For example, your next leg might require you to go cross-wind and several miles away from the street or you may wish to leave the street, make a TP and return to the street. Once within a few hundred feet of cloud base you can afford to accelerate and run faster and this is especially significant running into the wind. Just be aware that not all streets are the same and nothing stands still, so adjacent streets may have blocks or reinforcement at different positions along them. The streets either side may be less well defined, start to break up or not exist at all. Caution will be required as the good times may be about to finish. You might be running home and sacrifice height for a good high speed final leg. Be cautious though, as reality rarely lives up to our dreams. At all times it is more important to maintain the centre of the energy line within the street than be concerned about the actual speed that you are flying. Flying efficiently in sink 50m from a line of lift simply does you no good. On every wing gust and string deflection adjust your line a few degrees to remain on the optimum line. Note the *centre line* of energy by interpreting the clouds and cloud shadows and stick with it, chasing the associated line. This might require slight changes of heading transiting from one cloud to another and the line might not be straight down the middle. Cloud shadow is important but almost impossible to use in a conventional way. The priority here changes and it is the gaps in the street which you have to monitor on a regular basis. Put bluntly, a large gap anywhere in a street will be guaranteed sink. Big gaps mean climb as high as possible before you get to the gap and then accelerate. My experience would suggest when running into wind that climbing for a gap is best achieved at the second to last cloud (shadow) in your current line, the lead cloud shadow is often one which is in part disconnected from the main street structure and is breaking. To climb early with a little caution costs almost nothing, whilst pushing for the last cloud and finding a mess can make life difficult!

> **KEY POINT** When into-wind and jumping a gap consider climbing at the penultimate cloud.

More complex streeting

It will usually street on a windy blue day, although you can't see it. So having grasped the basic concept of streeting then you should now have an understanding of the thermal structure on a blue day.

The good news is that thermals will be triggered from the same obvious sources. Recognizing ground features for thermal sources now becomes extremely important. You will find many of them on a map. However it is not quite that simple. There are no clouds so the ripple action or chain reaction of the cloud suck and evaporation generating downdrafts do not exist. Equally important is that there is no cloud shadow to enhance the cold or hotspots. The thermals weaken and broaden before being destroyed with height as the thermal enters relatively warm air at the inversion and stops ascending. This gives weak thermals which may have been quite strong lower down. The thermal strength for the day is much more average so there is little point in pressing on for the significantly better thermal as it is unlikely to be there, unless it has been generated by a known strong trigger point. The bigger decision is how long to stay in high, weak

thermals dumping the water or how low you are prepared to push on carrying the water and rejecting the thermals as they become weaker in the climb.

Lattice streeting

On some occasions the sky can become harmonic, generating both downwind and cross-wind streeting. This is rather like two sets of ripples generated from different spots in water. If you happen to have tasked that way you are a lucky person. It is why sometimes on windy streeting days, going cross-wind strangely presents no problems.

Photo 9.6 Lattice streeting occurs more often than you think.

Streeting associated with wave

If caught low in the lee of hills which are producing wave you may encounter a line of cumulus across the wind which *does not drift*. The upwind leading edge forms very quickly and decays at the back continuously. This is being generated by the rotor. Having wound itself up it acts like a rotating rolling pin as shown in *Fig 9.20 on page 102* and it can occasionally break away and roll downwind, still producing cumulus. You can ride these but never get onto the back of them as you will get a combination of very strong sink and turbulence and will find yourself in a field!

Rising thermals can not climb in the downwash of wave. However, they are released on the upward cycle and this sometimes forms a street and indicates the point where you might connect with

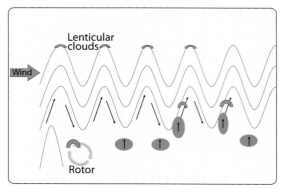

Fig 9.20 Rotor on the lee side of hills can be indicated by cumulus.

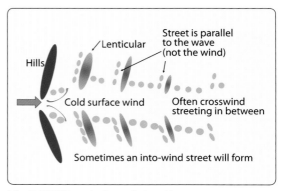

Fig 9.22 Wave induced streeting.

the upper system and go wave flying. So, under the influence of wave which penetrates the unstable layer, a street of cumulus will form across wind as shown in *Fig 9.21*.

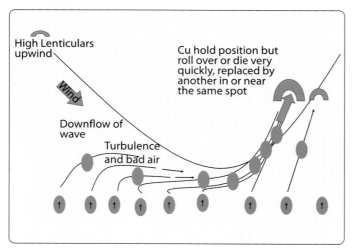

Fig 9.21 Wave induced streeting causing a street of cumulus to form across wind.

Eddies generated by the wind rushing out through a gap in the hills can generate a useful street to run upwind under the wave system, as shown in *Fig 9.22*. This only works if the lowest levels are sufficiently unstable.

Cloud shadow streeting

For cloud shadow streeting to become established it usually requires a change in wind direction below cloud base and there will be no good columns of lift anywhere. Often there will only

be individual bubbles and all will be quite broken and difficult to hold for a full climb.

The sun heats the primary source and the thermal generated forms a cloud. The cloud makes a shadow near the original thermal source which generates differential heating and triggers another thermal and cloud. This process is repeated many times.

Fig 9.23 shows the pattern of cloud shadow generating hotspots. Note that the cloud street appears angled well off the surface wind direction. The advantage is that you can see where the thermals are, or were. More importantly it provides structure to the sky and provided you don't get too low, allows long glides to be made linking the energy. As the sun moves the streeting will rotate or disappear.

Of course cloud shadow simply prevents those nice areas which would otherwise get hot on a blue day from doing so, therefore avoid flying under

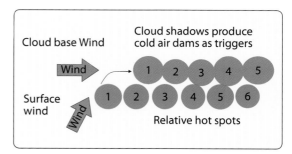

Fig 9.23 Plan view of cloud shadow streeting.

large cloud shadow areas unless they have obvious instability. If it is completely overcast i.e. a day of spread-out, then it is back to using the obvious hotspots as on a blue day, although streeting is unlikely.

The leading edge of cloud that is drifting downwind can produce some very good thermals because it is the leading edge of cold air flowing over the hot ground and undercutting the warm air that will trigger a stream of thermals.

Also note that when a large area of cloud starts to cover an area there will be a sharp wall of cold air approaching the sunny areas. This will trigger numerous thermals which can be run along as a street.

The particular ground being heated is significant and it is far more than just the colour. Sandstone is an airy rock which does not get anywhere near as hot as grey slate or tarmac. The latter two materials retain heat for much longer and will produce late *get you home* thermals, seemingly from nowhere.

Hill streeting

Hill streeting is a term used to describe the lift pattern associated with hills. In the right conditions on a long line of closely connected hills or a ridge then a line of thermals may develop. It is important to understand the following:

► The heating of the same type of ground surface at height is the same as at lower levels but, because the air at height is cooler and possibly clearer, the effect of warming the air is greater. So thermals are likely to come off the hilltops, not valleys.
► The angle between the sun and the ground surface is important and the more perpendicular the better, as this generates more heat at the surface.
► The wind blowing up the slope along with the hot air generated provides a constant flow into the vertical component of the thermal.
► This mechanism is particularly important on blue days.

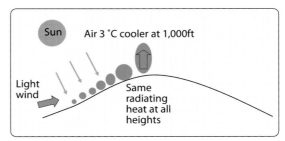

Fig 9.24 The mechanics of hill streeting.

Sea breeze streeting

The sea breeze mechanism causes two types of streeting:

► Streeting parallel to the coast with lower cloud bases.
► Downwind streets caused by the pooling of the cold air in the valleys and so the thermals are generated from the tops of the higher ground which can develop into streeting. The streeting continues inland for as far as the hills and sea breeze can influence it.

The direction and inward penetration of the streeting depends on the strength of the resultant wind (sea breeze versus the gradient wind) and whether the hills offer a high enough trigger above the cold air entering the valleys.

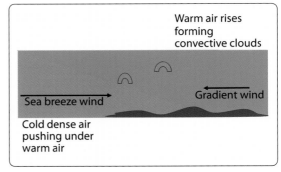

Fig 9.25 Cold air penetrating inland.

Of course a perfect 360° sea breeze is often generated over islands such as the Isle of Wight, producing a huge and wide central core of lift.

It is normal to consider the area influenced by a sea breeze as a place to be avoided, however, where hilly areas are concerned it is simple to determine where lift may be coming from, as shown in *Fig 9.26*.

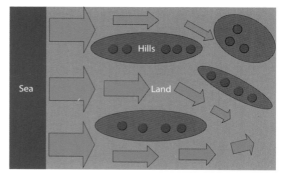

Fig 9.26 Sea breeze thermal identification.

10
Complex thermals

- ▶ Dust devils and rotating thermals?
- ▶ The reverse thermal
- ▶ Cruising and thermals
- ▶ Hill shadow thermals
- ▶ Convergence
- ▶ Accelerating thermals
- ▶ Bubbles or columns?
- ▶ The visual development of columns
- ▶ Death of column thermals
- ▶ Reinforced thermals
- ▶ Elongated thermals
- ▶ Gravity waves and shear wave
- ▶ Blue days

The promised crew were unable to attend on the first day, so help had to be sought to rig and grid. A late start meant that the fleet was launched into a dying sky resulting in an out-landing at RAF Wittering. Having no crew, the short aero-tow retrieve avoided the need to de-rig and rig.

The next day, as the pilot returned to the grid with his crew, they noticed a flat tyre so they dragged the glider off the grid using the trailer fuselage dolly and fitted a new inner tube. The repair was only temporary as an undetected tyre failure had caused the puncture and a further flat tyre damaged the new inner tube. The crew fitted a new tyre and another new inner tube begged from a fellow competitor. Unfortunately haste and zeal split this latest inner tube by trapping it between the two wheel halves as they hurriedly tried to clamp the combination together. Running out of spares meant that an earlier inner tube had to be retrieved from the bin and repaired.

Finally, the now distracted pilot launched amidst the later open class task group. Unaware that both classes were on fall-back tasks he then went off on his original task, making good progress to the first *wrong* turning point, before losing height and landing out again. A high speed tow achieved a landing back at 21:00 just as the street lights were coming on!

By now you will have realized that the model of the sun heating the ground which subsequently heats the air to generate a thermal is too simplistic. After all, chaos theory cannot be that simple or we would not call it chaos. Whilst the wind can generate favourable conditions for the development of thermals it can destroy them too. This chapter looks at some of the more complex thermal structures that we may encounter and the mechanics that drives them.

Dust devils and rotating thermals?

Photo 10.1 A dust devil in Spain.

Dust devils are a common occurrence in Saudi Arabia during summer and I have also seen them in Spain as shown in *Photo 10.1*.

But is rotation a part of our normal thermic sky? If the wide thermal source has some rotation, then the motion of it would, if it were visible, resemble a dust devil. We have to consider how a rotating thermal could form, what would keep it rotating and how we would recognise a rotating thermal should we encounter one.

Rotation of the dust devil

The rotation in a dust devil generates a centrifugal force and the lack of a descending boundary of cold air on the outside means that any buoyancy is not reinforced. The lack of cold air descending means that there is no containment either and the air on the outside is free to fall outwards and mix with the surrounding air, diluting the temperature. At the higher levels there is a downdraft down the middle so the hot air would be cooled from both outside and inside and would further lose any modest buoyancy that it would otherwise have. Dust devils are triggered from a very local hotspot on the ground but understandably don't extend upwards very far at all. As clouds do not rotate we can narrow this activity down to hot, breezy days well below cloud base.

Hypothetical flight through rotating air

Fig 10.1 depicts entering the middle of a column of air, rotating at 10kts. Even with only a modest 10kts of rotational wind the experience would still be unpleasant. There would be no warning sink and you would experience quite different indications and feel depending on whether you hit the middle or one side. Hitting to the right would give a significant loss of speed and the TE would indicate sink. If you hit the thermal to the left the speed would gust up coupled with the vario. Of course if they all turned left this would be useful to identify which way to turn, but the dust devil could be rotating the other way.

If you flew through the middle of this air then you would experience no sink and a huge sideslip. The relative airspeeds of the two wings would be considerably different passing through the middle with one wing likely stalled and a resultant significant undemanded roll, followed by another large sideslip in the other direction as you left the rotating air.

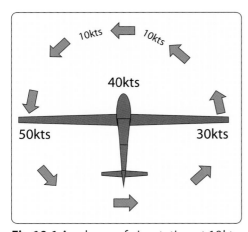

Fig 10.1 A column of air rotating at 10kts.

Dust devils can rotate either way, they are very narrow and in Saudi Arabia they do not extend to more than 4,000ft agl. Rather importantly, they appear to have some vertical motion but little associated sink. They not only carry dust but empty coke cans and dead bushes can also demonstrate free flight. Two other points of

note is that they often display a gentle snaking motion upwards (gyroscopic precessional effects) and they wander slightly cross-wind, probably due to the spin similar to a spinning golf ball or football that drifts to one side. The travelling dust devils in the Middle East would survive for about 10 minutes. I once saw one that was fixed to a motorway sign for an hour, the sign being both the generator and anchor point. Standing in one was very unpleasant and flying at 120kts through the tops in an aircraft weighing 5,700kg was quite rough.

The mechanics of this rotation is easy to understand. We know that nature can generate rotation because of dust devils and in the days of stubble fires you could often see some rotation at the lowest levels. Dust devils that I have observed in Saudi Arabia seemed to develop a rotation by the wind swirling around a small sharp hill, often a dried up river bank with a hot side. This is probably similar to the way leaves pile up on one side of a building coupled with the hot side where the wind swirls. The dust devils would usually then drift for a while downwind and wander a bit left and right as the mood took them. The column might reach 3,000–4,000ft, at which point the rotation had run its course, well before the inversion, which was usually around 18,000ft.

Theoretically, rotating thermals can't exist!

The only time that I can definitely say that I identified rotation in the UK was flying low over the Welsh mountains with the opportunity to explore in an appropriate power plane. This was not a rotating thermal, it was the air swirling around the mountain at a rock-face hotspot. In terms of flying my glider I have never become aware of the situation of pulling up into a strong or weak core and feeling anything other than the mechanical motions of a standard vortex thermal. Furthermore, I have never experienced the sideslip, yaw or roll that I would expect encountering a rotating thermal.

Clouds also show no signs of rotation. If rotation does occur it can only be in the lower levels and not generated by any acceleration, steady or diminishing instability of rising or sinking air otherwise it would be routinely experienced. (Apart from tornados which have a different mechanism). But it might still raise the question—do thermals sometimes rotate?

Mechanism for a dust devil

The mechanism for a dust devil is completely different from that of a thermal. The energy of a dust devil is rotational with no means of self-sustainability beyond the generating mechanism of a central low pressure. The mechanism of a thermal is vertical instability generated through low density and therefore natural buoyancy and of course when the potential for instability stops, the thermal stops. We routinely generate rotational energy into the air by wing-wash so consider something of an appropriate scale like that of a Boeing 747. The standard separation to avoid wake turbulence for a light aircraft behind a heavy aircraft is 3 minutes so the vortex must be breaking at around 2 minutes. This type of aircraft can weigh about 400 tons and at 150kts (2.5nm per minute) on the approach are generating two large powerful vortices (200 tons) which therefore trail out about 5 miles. Not all the energy goes into the two vortex paths generated. In fact, by design, as little as possible does, hence the use of winglets, but there is still a massive amount of air moving at quite a rotational speed. This is far more than in dust devils, yet the wake of a heavy aircraft always breaks up. Therefore, if the much smaller thermals did rotate they wouldn't have the energy to extend very far vertically, before breaking up. Yet, when our 747 hits a thermal it does feel it, hence the manipulation of the throttles that you hear as a passenger whilst on the approach on a thermic day, even when the autopilot is engaged.

Hot air provides a low density for a thermal and a low pressure for a dust devil. As we need the two quite different mechanisms of a dust devil and a toroidal vortex to occur at the same time I cannot see any specific circumstances when the criteria for both exists. Of course an anchored dust devil has a serious conflict with the downwards moving air of the sink generated by the thermal vortex. They simply can not work together and they are not in any way sympathetic.

KEY POINT There is no evidence to support the theory that thermals rotate.

The reverse thermal

It is normal for pilots to feel the need to run away when they see a heavy shower of rain, hail or snow coming their way. However, as shown in *Fig 10.2* there is usually considerable benefit if you fly towards these thermals. Descending air is cooled by the evaporation of water and the downwards flow is dragged along with falling rain. This considerable downdraft makes the surrounding air uncomfortably warm, so it rises. The updraft that is generated is found as a considerable band around the downwind sides ahead of the storm. Within this band will be individual thermal cells. Look for higher cloud bases above and around the main shower cloud due to high, drier air carried with the main updraft.

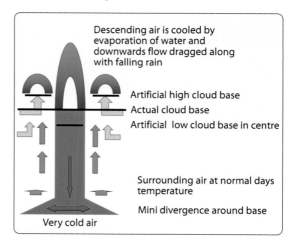

Descending air is cooled by evaporation of water and downwards flow dragged along with falling rain

Artificial high cloud base
Actual cloud base
Artificial low cloud base in centre

Surrounding air at normal days temperature

Mini divergence around base

Very cold air

Fig 10.2 The reverse thermal.

In *Photo 10.2* you can clearly see the strong thermic activity which is developing around the edge of the precipitation.

Cruising and thermals

When cruising and encountering a possible thermal an early decision can be made whether to fly through and bounce or to climb. The first indication on the instruments of a thermal is the increase in the rate of descent i.e. sink. This will tell you whether the thermal is likely to be weak or strong as the stronger the thermal the stronger the sink, and you do have to go through the sink to get to the lift.

Photo 10.2 Cumulus clearly visible generated by the reverse thermals triggered by the downwash of the storm.

It is important to recognize that column thermals can form in very light winds and if the cloud base is high and the clouds are tall then they dominate the sky, grow very large (upwards and outwards) and the huge downdrafts kill off the development of weaker thermals out to many miles, rather like a shower affects the general area. *Photo 10.3* shows how you are likely to get big gaps between usable strong thermals. Also the sinking air does not descend on to its own thermal source so it keeps stoking up.

Photo 10.3 Large thermal sources dominating the sky.

Hill shadow thermals

Another trigger action for thermals can be downwind of a hill, caused by the wind going around the hill and then meeting up on the downwind side with a slight collision vector—convergence. This kind of action is routinely seen downwind of islands and can form long streets. It is an action which occurs around any hill with varying degrees of success in producing a thermal depending on many factors, but mainly the surrounding topography and of course the potential instability of the air. Any time one wind is in significant collision with another convergence will result. This convergence, meeting of two winds, can cause a forced updraft, become a trigger in its own right, and a street may develop.

Convergence

Convergence on a bigger scale can produce some outstanding areas of lift. The minimum closing angle of the two winds is about 20°. Consider that for a wing an AoA of 15° is good at maintaining an optimum laminar flow, above which interference between the airflows occur, then this minimum angle for two winds to interfere would make both physical and logical sense.

Accelerating thermals

If the thermal you are in is giving 2 kts but then accelerates and develops into 4 kts there are several considerations. The drag of the bubble is proportional to the square of the speed so if the speed is doubled this implies that the thermal must have 4 times as much buoyancy to maintain the new speed, if it is to remain the same size. Clearly if the original thermal ascends simply because it is relatively 2 °C hotter, it would now have to be 8 °C hotter and so the increase in thermal strength can not just come from the relative temperature difference between the thermal and the air around it. We would not need a vario because we would feel the temperature difference.

For any shape, drag is also proportional to cross-sectional area (form drag) so a reduction in the thermal radius viewed from above would cause a reduction in drag (streamlining). If the thermal reduced in cross-sectional area (by 3/4) then the drag at the doubled speed will be the same as the drag of the original ascending broader bubble.

As we cannot destroy the mass of the air in the thermal, or give it a huge increase in buoyancy, then as the thermal accelerates it must change shape and become more streamlined and vertically more bullet or sausage shaped.

Stronger thermals are therefore tighter. This acceleration briefly results in a break in the vortex structure which is re-established at a greater height. In a similar way, this is the mechanism causing a street gust. The surge is exactly that and the normal vortex of rising air becomes stretched vertically as the air rushes up into a bullet shape, creating a column of laminar flow at that point.

Bubbles or columns?

The relationship between surface wind and thermal strength is important. In light winds and when there is little variation of the wind direction and strength with height, large column thermals develop if there is a sufficient depth of unstable air. On the other hand, as the wind increases and the thermal strength weakens then the wind becomes the dominant controlling factor and single bubble thermals tend to prevail.

So far we have concentrated on the concept of bubbles (vortex rings). A far more useful thermal for us is the drifting column thermal.

Cloud is history. Sometimes if you observe a large solid-looking thermal cloud, you would consider that the cloud thermal source must be drifting downwind yet surely it is triggered by a hotspot fixed somewhere on the ground. This mystery needs to be explained and understood because it is the most common large, strongly energetic thermal, the best in town, forming a self-sustaining rising column until other external forces break it up.

So why is the vertical shape of a normal or strong thermal important to us? If the thermal reduces in diameter by half then it must be about four times taller, as shown in *Fig 10.3*. So, you could join a strong thermal well below another glider in the same bubble.

ANALOGY **Slipstreaming.** In a peloton the lead cyclist has to do all the work,

pushing against the profile drag, whilst the rest of the cyclists coast in the slip-stream. This increases the pack speed.

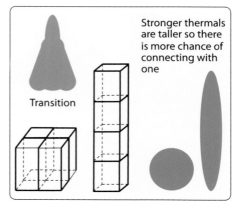

Fig 10.3 Thermal strength, size and shape.

This vertical growth of the column both downwards and upwards is very important. You may recall that the drag of a thermal is dependent on profile, interference and surface friction. In considering the interaction between two airflows moving in opposite directions, it is easiest to simply consider the last two drags as one, and the greater the interaction between the two airflows the greater the drag.

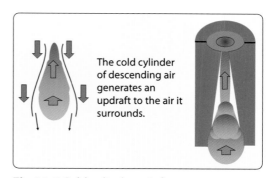

Fig 10.4 Cold cylinder reinforcement.

As the column accelerates and narrows, profile drag reduces significantly. As the column develops, initially it acts rather like the cyclists in a peloton. Once the column has been established the following hot air slipstreams the air above and the thermal will then accelerate to a new state of equilibrium. It may subsequently also widen slightly, so that the increased speed is not quite as good as we might mathematically assume. If the whole motion can stay in a fairly steady vertical state, then all is well.

Our accelerating thermal induces an accelerated downdraft. It is important to bear in mind that this downdraft has no rigidity and is centred by the warm air of the thermal but is also surrounded by slightly warmer air as well. As the cold air descends it becomes denser and encircles air minding its own business which suddenly becomes buoyant and which now rises after the initial thermal. The thermal therefore grows downwards.

The descending accelerating cold air forms a tube shape, containing the warm air and reinforcing the temperature difference, as shown in *Fig 10.4*.

As the column thermal transits over a hotspot the column will be further energised. To us in our glider it appears that there is a new bubble coming up and you often experience this when gliders below start to catch you up as they climb and yet you are in the same thermal column.

Depending on the various levels of instability with height, this development can continue downwards and can extend all the way to the ground. Below about 500ft the downdraft forces air near the surface to be swept up and feed the developed thermal, as shown in *Fig 10.5*. This explains why thermals can *travel* and why they can appear unconnected to a ground hotspot even

at low altitudes. Passing over large cold areas, however, can kill this action.

The real decision is whether you fly off in disgust to avoid the seemingly embarrassing feeling of being outclimbed or do you stay and wait a minute or so and then ride the stronger climb with the others. Of course the opposite rather satisfying situation can occur, with the column collapsing from the bottom as it transits over a poor area much to the disappointment of the glider pilots lower down.

It is, however, perfectly normal for several column thermals to be generated in close proximity over quite a large area, as indicated in *Fig 10.6*. It is simply a function of the specific conditions of air mass instability. As a result, several individually dispersed gliders may climb effectively in an area (up to about 9 thermals within 1 square km) with no single clear mother thermal.

> **KEY POINT** Unlike bubble thermals which are triggered from ground sources, column thermals depend on air mass instability.

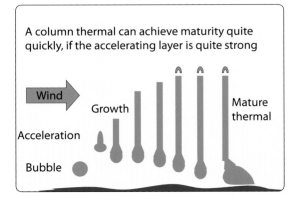

Fig 10.6 Diagrammatic cross-section of the building of column thermals.

The visual development of columns

There are actually many occasions when we can see this development in action and there is no reason to doubt that it occurs in the warm air that rises that we can't see. In *Photo 10.4 on page 112* you can see the smoke demonstrating the castellation developing.

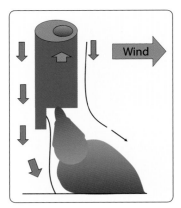

Fig 10.5 A column formed at height acting as a vacuum cleaner at the lower heights.

In *Photo 10.5* you can see the edges of the column descending to the ground, whilst the top continues to move upwards.

Photo 10.4 Castellation developing.

Photo 10.5 Further development of the castellation.

Observing the rise of smoke and steam from a power station or studying photographs usually shows several key aspects of the formation of bubbles, columns and the heaviness of air from the boiler chimneys. Sadly column thermals are intolerant of a change in wind speed or direction with height (shear).

Death of column thermals

ANALOGY **The tap.** Consider the slow flow of water from a tap. As we turn the flow up from a drip (bubbles) it turns into a stream (column). If however, we generate a wind from the side halfway

down, the flow breaks down into drops again (bubbles).

Assuming that the thermal is fairly strong all the way up, then a windshear might separate the two columns, as shown in the right side of *Fig 10.7*, with a broken and difficult area where the transition occurs. This is similar to the analogy of water flowing from a tap. The thermal will weaken at this point but may re-establish at higher heights. This all depends on the rate of change of the wind speed with height and to a lesser extent the strength of the thermal.

If a column thermal is fairly steady all the way up and there is a very small and smooth increase of wind with height (1kt/1,000ft) then the column can accommodate this and bends, as in the left side of *Fig 10.7*.

The real issue is what happens after a column thermal transits over a hotspot. In *Fig 10.8* there is a smooth and slight increase of wind with height (less than 1kt/1,000ft) which the column thermal accommodates. When it transits over a thermal hotspot, however, the faster rising air breaks the top of the thermal column in a whip action, taking the top farther upwind. The initial cloud decays whilst a new one forms slightly upwind.

Sadly, however, the thermal is no longer self triggering and the decaying cloud from

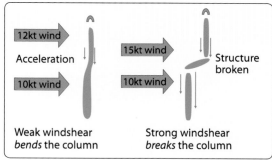

Fig 10.7 Column thermals and their intolerance of windshear.

the strong cell coupled with the lack of hot air rising causes a ripple in the column, the bend of which is too severe and the structure collapses. The column breaks apart. On longer flights this sometimes becomes the deal of the day for a few hours. It is often debriefed as "I don't really understand today. I was going great and then suddenly I became disconnected and it was all a bit of a difficult day". Whilst climbing in a seemingly okay thermal, when the cloud above inexplicably breaks up it is worth moving straight upwind if you need to continue the climb.

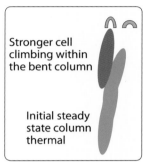

Fig 10.8 The death of a column thermal.

Another *column killer* is, of course, when the column passes over a significant cold area. The key aspect to column thermals is the relative temperature of the descending air to the temperature of the air in the immediate environment. Thus cold air descending into warm air reinforces the structure, but if the cold air is descending into cold or colder air then it will cease to perpetuate the instability.

Reinforced thermals

When a thermal bubble hits the updraft of a wave bar it will go up faster relative to the earth but it does not go up any faster relative to the air it is moving up within. As it drifts into the wave bar it will distort briefly but, relatively quickly, it will return to the classic vortex but not a narrow one. The real indication for us is that the thermal increases for no apparent reason and becomes amazingly smooth. It is easy to become confused as later the normal sink areas of the thermal are simply areas of reduced climb. There will be no column thermals in such environmental conditions.

Yet another form of continual thermal reinforcement is depicted in *Fig 10.9*. The descending air from the evaporated cloud and the cloud shadow reinforce the overall sinking of the air. As a result, the downwind air mass, that is over the sunny ground, generates a rotary flow. In fact the wind vector can be in either direction and the continuation of the process largely depends on the strength of the wind and how it changes with height versus the strength of the thermal, effectively blowing the top off the thermal. The mechanism encourages a large area of rising air within which will be a number of bubble or column thermals.

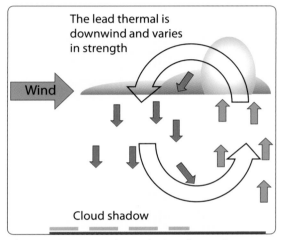

Fig 10.9 Downwind wandering thermals.

Elongated thermals

So far the thermals have been described as circular when viewed from above. Basic physics would only support this shape but from experience we know that there are opportunities for thermals to take on a somewhat elongated shape. These thermals are often frustrating to centre upon but useful on the glide. When we do experience them they are usually in the top half of the sky and more often close to cloud base. On these occasions the force of buoyancy has essentially reduced and the vortex slows, stutters and fans out before breaking. The bubbles are banging up against each other causing a traffic jam. The structure becomes disjointed, breaks apart and the continued rise of warm air is simply a weaker shimmer. In this way some smaller isolated lumps of warm air manage to rise a little faster and the cloud loses its distinct dark centre and round shape, looking larger yet weaker than we would normally expect.

There is not a normal structure of a vortex but an exploration might yield a short improvement to be able to climb higher. When we transit under a large elongated cloud we often find that it appears as though the thermal is also elongated, usually aligned with the wind. Attacking from the downwind side we encounter a large area of sink which is to be avoided by entering from the side. Further penetration yields a confused picture with varying amounts of lift and very little sink, until we eventually find a surge strong enough for us to turn, use and identify as a form of thermal, but not always. It all comes down to the physical properties of the rising air and the air it is climbing through.

Gravity waves and shear wave

ANALOGY **Wave action.** Looking at the sea, the water and the air are two immiscible layers and we know that the wind blowing over the sea generates waves. We can see these waves from above or, if we go under the water and look up, we will see the same wave action.

Just as in the analogy of looking at the sea, an inversion in our air can produce the same situation of two immiscible fluids. This occurs when air is unable to climb into warmer or less dense air above. The wind above the inversion can, through thermic, thunderstorm, frontal activity or hills upwind, start the ball rolling and produce waves in the atmosphere in a similar way to the generation of waves on the sea. It is thought that this action radiates away from a large thunderstorm, rather like dropping a pebble into water and generating ripples outwards called *gravity waves*. If we use time-lapse photography we are able to see the cloud base bouncing when gravity waves occur.

A similar effect, but caused by quite a different action, is *shear wave*. The difference in higher wind speeds just above the inversion causes waves which have very little vertical extension but we can run along them. The benefit to what we call shear wave often appears running in the blue after leaving the top as high as we can go and quite suddenly for no apparent reason the line is amazing and feels just like weak wave. For lateral thinkers, I am not aware of any tidal effects in the air.

Blue days

Blue days are different because they don't have the descending cold air from cloud evaporation to reinforce the core so it is always a bubble day. Dry air is heavier than humid air. The thermal mass is heavier and therefore tends to offer stronger, punchier rates of climb. All hotspots give an uninterrupted flow of bubbles streaming downwind and often generate a useful street. All too often the inversion is too low to fly long distances, particularly if alone without clues from other gliders, and it requires a continuous reading of the ground to be successful.

11
Reading the sky

Dave very soon discovered that there were only two positions for the stick—either neutral or fully deflected. As was admirably demonstrated, the waggly bits otherwise appear to do very little. In the back between Dave's legs in front of the stick sat a soft blue cool bag. This served two purposes, the first being to store the tucker. Second though, as I pulled up to catch a thermal from the sort of speed and rate one would adequately use to loop at, his forehead would fall forward and rest calmly there whilst the stick had moved to engage his right or left thigh tightly held in a vice like grip. Despite being unable to look out he did at least know by the thigh lock which way we were turning so the risk of disorientation was nicely reduced!

Before you can begin to read the sky you have to understand what you are seeing. Reading the sky is effectively learning a new language such as Chinese, where the letters are quite different, or learning music notation or even art. It is a language based on physical properties so it can be understood by both arty and theoretical types of people, but it can be taught and it can be learned. Understanding a spoken language fully is often partly to do with the way something is said (tone) in order to imply a nuance of meaning. In the same way there are unseen interpretations of what the clouds are telling us, and even small indications can tell a different story and have a different meaning. Some people are better at this interpretation than others, but practice will definitely improve your ability to read the sky.

A simplification of cloud types

There are only two types of cloud—good cloud and bad cloud. Good cloud indicates that there is rising air around in which we might be able to climb. Bad cloud does not.

Good clouds are lenticular (wave cloud) and cumulus. There are two types of cumulus: those generated from hot ground thermal sources and those generated from middle airspace instability and turbulence which includes spread-out.

Bad cloud can also be divided into two types: that which indicates sinking air and that which offers cloud shadow, killing off or reducing the strength and number of thermals being produced.

Something to bear in mind is that all good cloud sadly becomes bad.

To be able to see the early wisps developing several miles ahead, glasses, sunglasses and the canopy must be absolutely clean. Canopy covers are important too as they keep the dust off from earlier aero-tow launches and do not just keep the cockpit a little cooler but protect it from the occasional *magnifying glass* burning that sometimes occurs on some part of the instrument panel or seating, depending on the angle of the sun.

Also, if the LCD screens become too hot they become unreadable (blank) until they have cooled down. If the air is especially dry and depending on what material you have used for your string indications, static may build up during the early part of a tow so you may have no string indications for the first 30 minutes or so due to the string *sticking* to the canopy.

Cloud formation

KEY POINT Water is a unique molecule often referred to as the *God molecule*. It has a maximum density at +4°C, yet a minimum density at −4°C. Despite freezing at 0°C it can remain as water at temperatures as low as −22°C and is capable of desublimation, that is, change of state from a gas directly to a solid and vice versa (sublimation), all occurring in the natural world.

Cloud is formed by one of three mechanisms:

- Humid air rising by thermal activity and cooling to its dew point—for example, cumulus, thunderstorms, middle airspace instability and fronts. This mechanism is easily seen and predicted. Clouds on sunny days tend not to hang around too long and often if the sky over-develops the cloud cycles through.
- Mechanical turbulence generates orographic cloud, low and middle-level stratus and lenticulars. At the middle and high heights this cloud lingers because the water droplets are frozen and because the wind at height is often much stronger, it quickly whistles in and the shadow can damp down a large thermic area.
- Contrails are the killjoy of late afternoon summer good days. In the summer mornings the sky is blue and clear because there is little airliner traffic and the sky has had a chance to clear overnight. As air travel increases during the morning the amount of contrails rapidly increase, with the water vapour freezing at temperatures of around −56°C at altitudes near the tropopause. Light winds in summer at these heights reduce the dispersal and on some days a complete high altitude overcast sky can develop which will not clear until after dark. The day is not as good as the forecast predicted.

How to read the sky

Rather like feeling the air, reading the sky is a great concept but what are you actually looking for? For us the day starts with noting just how much cloud there is in the forecast. A lot of cloud such as sunny intervals or broken cloud is not good as it reduces the amount of sun warming the ground and overnight it will have reduced the surface ground and air cooling. Next is to look outside and see if the real weather is close to the prediction and that as time passes, changes truly reflect the forecast. Differences from the forecast imply that the weather window has changed, the day has the potential to be better or won't develop at all.

Once airborne we have to briefly scan the way ahead for key features that will influence our progress. All cloud, including contrails, makes a shadow and reduces the thermal activity. It is quite common for high cirrus to move at 100kts so despite it being 30 miles away and *on the horizon* it will be generating a shadow umbrella effect within about 20 minutes, perhaps at the time you will be trying to connect with your next climb. Mid-level cloud generates a *thick* shadow and is often slow to move away due to lighter winds.

Photo 11.1 Cirrus cloud influencing thermal development.

Finally, assess the cumulus clouds—what types are there and where is the lift and sink likely to be? There are two key aspects that we are looking for. Firstly is the cloud growing? Secondly, as we get closer is there still some rotation anywhere. If there is still rotation then the vortex is still cycling around and we should be able to connect and climb.

The sharp edge of a developing cumulus displays the boundary between the rising air within the cloud and the downwash generated by the descending air around it.

The scraggy edges of a cloud is sinking air produced by the evaporation of the water droplets. Scraggy means dying or dead! Of course you can't see all around a cloud so you have to look at adjacent clouds from different angles to determine what might be happening. Looking at these finer details will help you to interpret what might be happening with respect to rising and sinking air.

Klasification cloud cumulos

> **ANALOGY** **Proof-reading.** There were a couple of spelling mistakes and a muddled word sequence in the title above. There's no surprise if you spotted these errors but that is the point—how did you notice them? Because you looked and not just saw a word, which sounds the same but recognised the detail of the individual letters, because only then would you fully understand the word. Equally you noticed the clumsy word structure.

As in the analogy above, if I present you with a picture of the sky with various cumulus, no doubt you will see cumulus yet notice little else in the detail. Even in the real dynamic world unless you study the picture and how it changes using little clues that help, you only see a snapshot without understanding all that it is telling you, but usually you think no more about it. To read the sky you have to understand what is making it the way it looks, ideally in a series of mental time-lapsed snapshots.

In the books that the Met-men produce the diagrams of clouds are simplistic; there is no detailed information in the structure of the rising or sinking air that form clouds. For us the vertical air current structure under a cloud is critical. The different shapes of cumulus cloud are determined by the various mechanics of the rising and falling air, both underneath and above cloud base. Just how many types of cumulus cloud are there then?

I have named the different types of cumulus as an aid to recognizing the flow pattern underneath. It is important to understand the dynamics of the cloud that you are flying towards to best guess where you might connect with the thermals feeding it.

> **KEY POINT** Until you become more experienced in reading the sky, you should maximise your chances of connecting with the column or the bubble. So, if you are flying into-wind then put yourself into a position to transit

directly under the cloud so that you can connect with either the column, or perhaps later, the bubble. If you are flying downwind, fly to the upwind side of the cloud to catch the bubble and if this fails, continue to fly downwind towards the cloud to hit the column.

Firstly, we have to bear in mind the *ideal* and reality. For example, it is largely assumed that a stream of bubbles from a source will follow the same flight path, whereas this is not so. When we watch bubbles stream from a bubble-making machine we can clearly see that despite the *same trigger* they can advance in significantly different directions. If you watch the launch at a hot air balloon rally, very quickly the balloons go their separate ways. In the same way then, bubbles might follow a similar track from a particular source, but often they won't.

Single bubble cumulus

This is the most common thermal you see when the sky first turns thermic and is a simple bubble where the cloud has little vertical or horizontal extent. The bubble rises and forms a short lived cumulus cloud, as shown in *Fig 11.1*. The cloud will be relatively small and drift downwind as it decays and disappears. After a while it might be replaced with another small cloud in the same spot as the original cloud, starting all over again. These thermals have limited depth so flying *under* the cloud, even under another climbing glider, will probably give no lift. You may connect with the next bubble, possibly before it has developed a cloud, by flying directly upwind.

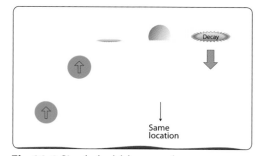

Fig 11.1 Single bubble cumulus.

Streaming cumulus

Here a steady thermal source generates a stream of bubbles, as shown in *Fig 11.2*. The cloud formed is larger and made up of many bubbles but it never grows to be particularly big. Importantly, it displays properties a little like those of a wave cloud. It forms at the front upwind edge and decays at the back. It is important to note that this cumulus does not drift downwind. A typical thermal source for streaming cumulus is a sunny facing slope with a wind blowing up the slope. If the wind is increasing above cloud base this can give the cloud the appearance of leaning downwind, presenting *leaning streaming cumulus*.

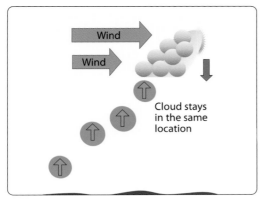

Fig 11.2 Leaning streaming cumulus.

> **KEY POINT** If you join a climbing glider that is at a significantly greater height than you, you may find that you are displaced upwind relative to that glider.

Standard column cumulus

In these column thermals the instability below cloud base drives the mechanism to sustain the thermal as it drifts downwind. Because of this, gliders will climb vertically under one another despite the fact that there may be a breeze blowing.

> **KEY POINT** The fact that there is a column means that you can connect with the thermal at quite low altitudes.

Consider the *standard column cumulus* as shown in *Fig 11.3*. The width of the column containing individual cells can be quite wide.

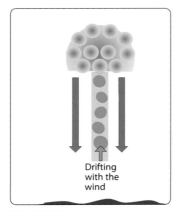

Fig 11.3 Standard column cumulus.

Tall column cumulus

If there is continued instability well above cloud base a tall column cumulus will develop. There will be considerable cloud suck and the thermal core will accelerate and narrow near cloud base, as shown in *Fig 11.4*.

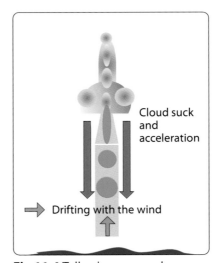

Fig 11.4 Tall column cumulus.

> **KEY POINT** Look for the highest point of the cloud and head for it before you venture underneath.

Broad column cumulus

If the air above cloud base is not particularly unstable, the rising column cannot go upwards so it has to go outwards, so we'll call this the *broad column cumulus* as shown in *Fig 11.5*. This produces a broad based cumulus but bear in mind that the thermal is not broad, it is just the cloud.

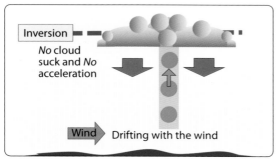

Fig 11.5 Broad column cumulus and broad bubble cumulus above.

Forward tumbling cumulus

If the wind speed increases somewhere in the band above cloud base but before cloud tops the top of the cloud is blown forwards, generating sinking air ahead of the advancing thermal, as shown in *Fig 11.6* (and *Photo 11.2 on page 122*). This rejuvenates the ground trigger actions and stokes up the original thermal. The cloud can become large and broad in a cross-wind direction and the strongest lift is on the upwind side of the cloud.

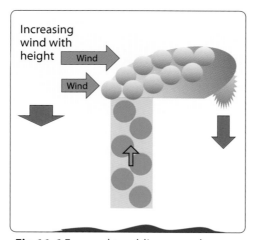

Fig 11.6 Forward tumbling cumulus.

KEY POINT If you can identify this type of cloud avoid routing via the down-wind side.

Backward tumbling cumulus

If the wind speed decreases somewhere in the band above cloud base but before the cloud tops the top of the cloud is dragged backwards, generating sinking air behind the advancing thermal, as shown in *Fig 11.7*. The sinking air is usually marked with mammatus cloud (upside down cumulus). The cloud will become large and broad and the strongest lift is on the downwind side of the cloud.

KEY POINT If you can identify this type of cloud avoid running through the upwind side.

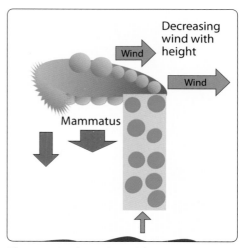

Fig 11.7 Backward tumbling cumulus.

Reverse thermal cumulus

This kind of cumulus is caused by the downwash of extensive sink, most obvious around a rain or snow shower, including thunderstorms. You can experience powerful climbs around the edge, as shown in *Fig 11.8*.

KEY POINT Very powerful climbs will be found all around the edge, often in the edge of the precipitation, but don't count on connecting too low down.

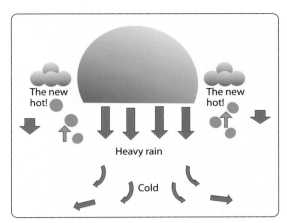

Fig 11.8 Reverse thermal cumulus.

Wave triggered cumulus

The downwash from wave often traps rising air until the moment of wave reversal, the point at which the wave air is now going up. As a result a string of generally cross-wind thermals, aligned to the wave motion (not the wind), cause cumulus to appear and disappear very quickly. They form in the same place or can resemble a streaming thermal, forming on the upwind edge and decaying at the downwind side without moving. They may develop into a street. They also form indicating the upwind edge of rotor at quite low heights, with cloud base below the level of the upwind ridge.

Rolling cumulus

At low levels the rotor which develops under wave motions generates a cross-wind line of cumulus. These are mainly seen in the lee of hills but, sometimes the rotor will cease to be ground anchored and bore off downwind.

> **KEY POINT** Don't get caught on the downwind side of rolling cumulus as the turbo won't save you from landing in a field!

Hill convergence cumulus

On the downwind side of a hill high spot the hill can generate wind convergence behind it. A cumulus will consistently appear at the same spot and can cause short or extensive streeting.

Elongated cumulus

This can be a particularly strong thermal often because of the higher humidity that it carries. It will generate its own little, very local, streeting effect producing an elongated cumulus. The downwind side will have a large area of sink as shown in *Fig 11.9*, so this area is to be avoided. If you want to track upwind then attack this cloud at around the mid-point. It is often difficult to predict just where the next cell is when passing under such a large cloud. Leaving the thermal and tracking upwind is no problem but there is likely to be no lead cell.

If you wish to fly on a downwind track, then attack the cloud at the upwind end and make sure that you consider leaving the cloud by the mid-point, to avoid the sink. In any case, review your options before departure and make sure to get the speed up.

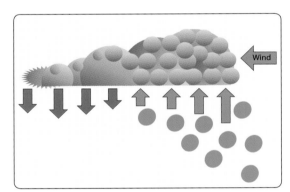

Fig 11.9 Elongated cumulus.

> **KEY POINT** With elongated cumulus the downwind half of the cloud will probably have extensive sink, so avoid this area.

Streeting cumulus

After the initial trigger, streeting cumulus can self-perpetuate. This is wonderful if you have planned to go that way. It is important to note that it can drift cross-wind, rotate or collapse along its full length. It can collapse in a couple of minutes if the air below has warmed sufficiently to break the inversion.

Entrainment cumulus

Entrainment cumulus is usually associated with a small convergence line. This cumulus is often attached to a very large cumulus and has a significantly higher cloud base. It enables you to climb much higher but at a slower rate than the main cells which will give you the ability to transit large void areas. The action of cloud suck drawing air from above cloud base is indicated by the higher abeam cloud base.

Photo 11.2 Large forward tumbling cumulus showing the increase of wind with height.

False cumulus

These are found around a column thermal being generated *only* by the downwash and do not extend to the lower levels. They are not ground generated and do not have all the classic characteristics of a thermal, in particular the gust. This thermal is found next to large active clouds. Often the adjacent strong sink of the large cloud will be encountered but the thermals under these false cumulus are considerably weaker than anticipated. The clouds are small and short lived.

In *Photo 11.3* a number of false thermals have been generated producing small weak scrappy cumulus around the main cells. Often the evaporation of the remnants of a previously strong but now dying cumulus will generate a confused

Photo 11.3 False thermals around two solid columns.

dispersion of lift under it, even after the cloud has fully dispersed.

Vortex cumulus

This standalone cell, shown in *Fig 11.11*, is usually seen as an after-effect rather than planned exploitation. It resembles a jelly fish (not to be confused with virga clouds) with the cloud decaying at and above the local cloud base whilst a strong single-celled cumulus advances upwards with a base of its own travelling up with the cell.

The weak vortex can break apart before cloud base and spread out forming a ring of very weak scrappy cumulus, as shown in *Photo 11.4* and *Fig 11.12*.

The cloud structure of a broken vortex shown in *Photo 11.5* is not unusual. The weak vortex has broken just below cloud base and started to scatter.

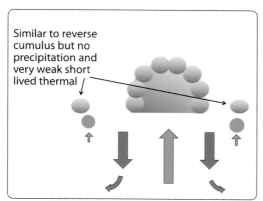

Similar to reverse cumulus but no precipitation and very weak short lived thermal

Fig 11.10 False cumulus.

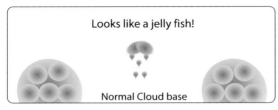

Fig 11.11 Vortex cumulus.

Photo 11.4 Vortex cloud.

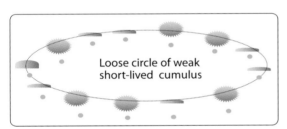

Fig 11.12 Weak vortex cumulus.

Photo 11.5 Weak broken vortex.

Scraggy cumulus

During the development of stratus from a clear sky an extensive area of small promising looking cumulus can develop. This is typically seen during the winter months but whilst this cumulus looks promising it quickly shows signs of decay. Large areas may develop over several square miles in a few minutes and be blue elsewhere. There is no structure to the sky because the thermals are not connected to the ground in any way. You can see from *Fig 11.13* that there is no vertical extent to these clouds. This is just a narrow band of mechanical turbulence and may develop into a layer of stratus.

Fig 11.13 Scraggy cumulus.

Survival

So much for the good cloud, all other cloud therefore is bad! When in doubt, if the cloud looks good, it might be. If it looks bad, then it will be bad. Survival is not about getting low and wondering what to do but recognising the potential for a bad run and reacting immediately. I have been doing 95kts at 1,200ft confident that we were about to climb, yet on another occasion I have been climbing at 1kt in weak wave at 6,200ft, knowing that a field landing was inevitable. It was—47km later!

Survival is about ensuring that we stay airborne and with that in mind reading the bad sky ahead is just as important as recognizing good cloud, perhaps even more so. Showers kill off surprisingly large areas and a very local light 5 minute shower will mean that it will take about 30 minutes for the thermic sky to recover. If you happen to need to go in that direction then there may be a need to loiter, which may seem like a waste of time. Alternatively, a detour may be required to stay safe and this will also help you to feel that you are doing something productive. Climbing in a weak thermal at 3,000ft is so much less dramatic than at 1,000ft and also gives you more options.

Bearing in mind the complexity of the weather currents that we use it is rare for us to romp around a 300km route without there being some requirement to change our flying routines. In fact, more commonly, 50km down track the sky usually demands that we change gear.

Just occasionally we encounter and fly through a light shower of rain. This produces another issue. The glider's rate of descent will increase due to the poor performance of the wing and the flight director will indicate for you to fly faster. However, don't do this because it misinterprets the loss of performance as sink. You need to dry the wings off at slower speeds so flying closer to endurance speed *when clear of the rain* would be a better option.

Wet ground will not generate thermals for some time. Less obviously, the downwash of cold air after a heavy shower may extend 10 to 15 miles to the sides as well, killing those areas as well. There will be a requirement to fly a flat glide.

Whilst gliding cross-country we have to make many decisions. The conclusions and actions we take based on each situation are partly dependent on what we have been taught, what we might have learnt and our previous experience of similar situations with good and bad results. Some decisions will be based on technical merit such as assessing a glider turning ahead, others because we know it is the safe option and of course occasionally we will best guess and hope. Although positive decision making is necessary there is no reason why our final action is not formulated through exercising all our knowledge and experience.

Daily cycle

During the day it is normal to find an inversion somewhere between cloud base and towards the top or a little above cloud tops. There may also be other inversions. In the late afternoon or evening, as the thermal activity stops, the cooling ground will cool the air. As there is no longer any vertical mixing with the upper air the surface wind abates and this heavy air pools in the vales and valleys. A new low level inversion will start to develop and the previously buoyant air above will slowly sink. A little after dawn then, this low level inversion will have reached its lowest point. So when you consider it a bit cool at 10°C as you get out of your tent the temperature at 2,000ft could well be a more pleasant 15°C.

The inversion level is important as it prevents the ascent of any warm air above it and separates the calm lower level air with the possibly quite breezy wind above it. As the day warms up this lower level inversion will rise and weaken. As a result thermal activity will also rise higher and the initial cloud base will move up rapidly. Once the surface wind increases and veers you will know that the inversion has been broken as descending air travelling in the breeze will cascade down to ground level. The thermals, previously just bubbles, may develop into columns. The continued development of the thermic structure of the sky will then depend on the environmental lapse rate. It is only when the vertical development has reached its maximum for the day, at around 13:00, that you can be sure the sky might stay in a steady state. But this will be only for a few hours. Prior to and after these times the structure may be different.

The interaction of one motion with another, coupled with upper cloud, contrails, showers and topography make a complex mix but enough for you to best guess by looking at the clouds as to what might be going on.

Many of the diagrams in this book show cloud sideways on. The shapes of actual clouds can be viewed from any angle whilst sat on the ground. Flying near cloud base would initially seem to give you a disadvantage because of the limited field of view. Actually, you get a far better view of the tops of any extended cloud layers and the shadow will give you an accurate shape. Combining these two views will improve your interpretation of what might be going on. Of course if you insist on not looking out until you have climbed to cloud base where your field of view is severely limited, you're leaving yourself no opportunity to read ahead, plan and make decisions. Remember that shadows will indicate shape but they will not show you whether the clouds are active or dying.

Time lapse

Following the sun. A time-lapse video of a flower shows it bending and tracking the sun as the day progresses, but if you sit in the garden you will not notice this.

Similar to the analogy above, if we analyse a time-lapse video of the sky we see things that we would not notice in real time. Bear in mind that on different days there are many similar looking clouds being formed by different processes. There is usually more than one process operating on any particular day. Any variation of cloud tops is important.

The key whilst gliding is to time-lapse the clouds ahead as you analyse them down track. It is easy to identify which thermal was the strongest by the highest cloud tops, but that was history. All is not lost though, as the cloud which is growing the fastest is the strongest thermal and we can only identify that by time-lapsing the sky. Perhaps in the future some high technology piece of equipment will do this for us. Consider, for example, scanning three adjacent clouds and comparing their development. One may be dying whilst one has reached maturity and the third, which looks similar to the first, the one that you probably should now be heading for, is still in adolescence.

Photo 11.6 Initial photograph (time-lapse).

You have just set off. In *Photo 11.6* the central cloud appears to have three cells. The central and right cell look promising. A useful technique to keep track of the development is to relate the clouds to each other.

Photo 11.7 Second photograph (time-lapse).

Photo 11.7 was taken 90 seconds later. Did you miss the embryonic one on the left of the lead cloud in the previous photograph? The central cell has peaked and the one on the right is dying.

Photo 11.8 Third photograph (time-lapse).`

Photo 11.8 was taken after another 90 seconds and the cloud on the right has effectively vanished and the left cloud is the best one.

Whilst climbing in your thermal then, scan the sky once around each turn (every 20–30 seconds) and then continue routinely checking the clouds and options as you track towards them. Sometimes care is needed when the sky is quite dry and most of the clouds look fairly small.

Consider a boiling kettle. It produces a small cloud but it is continually being fed by hot air and the *cloud* is continually evaporating. A strong thermal source may be working hard at maintaining that small cloud which is continuously cycling through. It can be quite difficult to identify this continually fed small cloud when compared to the temporary cloud being generated by individual bubbles. When you first try this you may get the occasional failure. It does take practice but with experience you will improve your success rate and you will soon be launching off with a little more confidence.

Whilst scanning the clouds you will notice that they are not all the same shade of white. The usual simple reasoning for this is that the lower part of the cloud is in shadow, but this is not the full story. The bright white cloud indicates very small droplets of water, whereas the darker areas indicate larger droplets. Hence, the darker areas indicate greater air activity and may eventually develop into precipitation. Also, the cloud that is still growing will not only maintain a firm cauliflower shape with sharp edges on top but the bottom will remain flat and will also be darkening at its central base.

As you approach clouds you should look for the tallest structure to ensure that you will pass under the most active areas. Once underneath the clouds you should refer to dark areas at the bottom of the clouds, as these will indicate the greatest activity.

Spread-out

Spread-out is caused by over-development of cumulus in a moist atmosphere and a relatively low inversion. This situation is either an irritation or a challenge depending on your point of view. It can form over a huge area in *the blink of an eye* and it might or might not clear.

When there are strong thermals this situation changes more quickly for the worse, to the extent that survival may become the game. When the sky becomes overcast the thermal generation from the ground may subside sufficiently for the thermal activity to stop.

The time of day for this event is very important. If it occurs early in the thermic day then it is truly doom-worthy because the spread-out is likely to

remain for the rest of the day. If it is later in the afternoon the cloud acts as a blanket, although normal hotspots will continue to produce good thermals because there is so much heat radiating despite the considerable overcast sky. The ground acts like a storage heater. In this case a good eye for ground features helps to identify possible sources and the darkest areas of clouds will point to activity at cloud base. The majority of the cloud may disperse and the cycle will start strongly again as the sun is able to heat the ground once more.

So, later in the day there can be two extremes: The overcast spread-out situation and the stunning active sky! The first may become simply a survival situation and the second will suggest that you could push on with confidence.

There are also occasions when there is sufficient heating and humidity so that the spread-out is continually resupplied. The spread-out does not clear and generally only weak thermals will be encountered.

One final point about spread-out is that it reduces the deep heat soak of the area and this will mean that the evening cut-off will occur earlier.

As an example of the requirement to change gear, I have climbed at over 9kts when starting in a competition at Bicester yet had to accept a 1.2kt thermal 45 minutes later due to spread-out, which remained for the rest of the day. You can only cruise as fast as the strength of the *next* thermal. If it does all go wrong, landing out should not be a drama. In fact it often leads to some new adventures, war stories and meeting some new people!

12
Cruising

Whilst standing with my crew watching the late finishers, someone in their first competition made a very well judged final glide to stop shortly after the piano keys on the runway threshold, possibly to shorten his retrieve back to his picket site. Unfortunately the finish line was by the Harrier ski jump, which was about one third of the way down the runway, and he had not crossed it. Having been informed of his error, the assembled audience fell about laughing as the pilot dragged his machine as fast as he could across the line. Regrettably, unlike motor racing, crossing the line in this fashion does not count. He felt a little better when a subsequent finisher came in at high speed, eased up over the airfield boundary and completed a text book circuit but also landed without crossing the line.

For any first long and challenging flight it is important to have the right mindset a couple of weeks before the event. Be positive that you can be successful whilst still flying within your competency. Be motivated and start thinking about cross-country flying and the possible decisions that you are going to have to make. To a large extent the majority of decisions are often made during the cruise, which includes what speed you are flying at and whether you are still going in the best direction. Although there is a mountain of information about the best speed to fly, it should be obvious that flying in the wrong direction at the right speed is not at all productive! This chapter does include information about the speed to fly but also covers effective decision making and aspects of routing, the latter perhaps being the most important.

Preparation for long distance flying

Have you *really* cleaned your glider to get full performance? That means polishing all areas of the glider just as much as the top surface of the wings. After rigging, have you taped as cleanly as possible and if you don't need the winch hook is that nicely taped over too. It will improve performance and usually make the cockpit quieter. Consider a glider that has a 60:1 glide angle. Lift equals weight so this is a 60:1 weight to drag ratio. So the total drag at best glide is as little as $\frac{1}{60}$th of the mass. The total drag of a glider massing 500kg is only 8.33kg. At 750kg it is still only 12.5kg. Go back out and polish again then!

There is a chance of landing out if you, the club task-setter or the Met-man gets it wrong. So learn (practise) self-tasking on any day and see if other cross-country pilots at your club or on the BGA club ladder were successful flying a similar task in a glider of similar performance to your own. You should now understand how to read the sky and have practised this routinely at club level. Part of your preparation needs to be focused on understanding the maps, airspace and useful safe land-out airfields close to your route.

Make sure that the glider, declaration sheet, land-out actions sheet, parachute, batteries, chargers and trailer are ready and your crew know what you expect of them and your spouse understands that you might be late getting home. So in other words, make a full list of all the things you need to have right, before you get airborne.

If the weather permits and it is safe to leave your glider out overnight, then rig your glider the evening before. This will ensure that you have got everything and will take some pressure off you on the day. Consider the following decisions that you must make:

- ► Have you practised the techniques to go a little faster?
- ► How much water should you carry?
- ► When will you dump the water?
- ► When will you get airborne?
- ► Will you wait for someone else to start the task before you go?
- ► Where should the centre of gravity of your glider be?

- How will you achieve a good start?
- What speeds are you going to fly?
- When are you going to slow down?
- When do you do 'S' turns?

Try not to worry about what others might perceive as a failure. Remember, at least you are trying and the real failure is those who don't try. If you prepare properly and stay confidently within your flying ability you will be surprised just how successful you can be.

Speed choices

Consider the simple question of what speed you are going to fly? Here are some speeds that you might consider that are appropriate at the time:

- Minimum Sink Speed—Sat on a ridge in weak lift, in wave, or drying the wings off.
- Best Glide Speed—The day has died and you need maximum distance.
- MacCready—The theoretical ideal for efficiency.
- Anti-MacCready—Strong lift on a street near cloud base.
- Faster than MacCready—Final glide on a good run or street, getting more energy than needed.
- Slower than MacCready—Caution required, need time to decide what to do.
- Block Speed—The simplest speed based on the best guess of the conditions to the next thermal.
- Slower than ideal Block Speed—Caution required getting to the next strong thermal or a need to conserve energy.
- Faster than Block Speed—A short period of better energy, usually on a street.
- Dolphin—Milking the system.

So which speed would you like? There may be an excuse for using any of these!

Block speed

I am not aware of any definition for the term *block speed* and in my previous lecture notes I refer to it as *target speed*. Simplistically, it is the *target*

single speed that you will maintain until your next thermal. In reality it is made up of many considerations including getting to that next thermal at a height that you are comfortable with, which is probably your first priority. Therefore, my own interpretation of the term, and what I teach, is to optimise the fastest glide to the next point or climb. This incorporates consideration for any detour.

Firstly, consider MacCready. The assumption is made that one will encounter an equal amount of sink and lift whereas the line you take may well run along a line of sink or beneficial lift. Using MacCready in a dynamic sense gives us the dolphin technique. This gives us the instantaneous speed to fly on modern instruments and is just that—what you should be flying now.

Despite climbing at 6kts, to reach the next climb might require a much slower glide because the next thermal is so far away. Perhaps, as an example, you anticipate that the route will be influenced by downwards wave. Accelerating in increasing sink is very inefficient so it might be better to use a block speed. Although this is a target speed it makes *very little difference* if it varies by a few knots either side of this target. Flying a few knots slower or a little faster is not overall performance critical, although you may be slower by just a few seconds. In fact, you will gain far more performance by looking ahead for the best route.

Block speed will vary due to the glider's polar curve, weight, headwind or tailwind, height band being used, distance to the next thermal (you have to get to it) and bug factor. This is then modified by the experience of the last glide, anticipated sink en route and the ability to read the sky correctly. Indicators of sink or poor air that must be anticipated include decaying clouds, mammatus cloud, blue sky, wave rotor, poor land mass such as damp areas or a large area of very green wet flat land. It also includes the final glide, being as high as possible at a downwind TP or as low as possible on an upwind TP or the next thermal. As a result, block speed may vary on each and every cruise. Flying any speed in lift is beneficial but flying slow in sink is punishing. Just like a broke gambler, it is the losses that matter most. A common error is to only concentrate on areas of lift but you must also identify the structure of sink in the atmosphere.

The benefit band

Fig 12.1 shows the penalty of brushing past a thermal through a line of continuous sink rather than making the effort to fly through the core and making some subsequent gain of energy by flying through the lift. The accumulative losses incurred passing abeam a number of thermals can become quite significant.

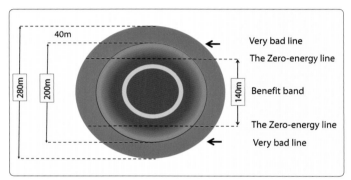

Fig 12.1 The benefit band.

Whilst cruising you must make every effort to hit thermals within the benefit band. The various gains and losses during a cruise through a thermal are slightly complicated to calculate and the result can only be used as a guide. Bear in mind that the only energy we can gain is that given to us by the thermal.

Let us assume that the structure of a thermal has a 200m column of rising air surrounded by an outer sinking ring which is 40m wide. A transit through the centre of the thermal will give us a total of 80m transit through sink and 200m of good air, effectively giving us 120m of gain. The slower we transit the thermal the greater the net gain of height but time will be lost.

Consider a 6kt thermal which gives 10ft/s. A glider cruising at 60kts (30m/s) will take 4 seconds to travel 120m and will therefore gain 40ft.
A glider cruising at 90kts (45m/s) will take 3 seconds to travel 120m and will therefore gain 30ft.

However, whilst these gains appear small, consider more significant losses incurred cruising on a bad line through the sink. A glider cruising at 60kts (30m/s) will take about 6 seconds to travel 190m and lose 60ft. A glider cruising at 90kts (45m/s) will take about 4 seconds to travel 190m and lose 40ft.

> **KEY POINT** Making no effort to route via thermal cores will give an inefficient cruise.

Easily overlooked losses

Apart from the time lost trying to centre on a thermal an aspect often missed is the height *lost* when thermalling. As you endeavour to find and centre in a thermal during the first turn you may encounter some part of the surrounding sink. After-flight analysis will tell you just how much height you lost and the accumulated quantity over a longer task can be considerable and easily more than a 1,000ft. Finding this information will depend on the software program you use to analyse the flight. Another considerable contribution to slow progress is the thermal attempts where you tried to find a thermal but it was illusive or you considered it too weak and moved on. Both of these failures at climbing are relatively costly.

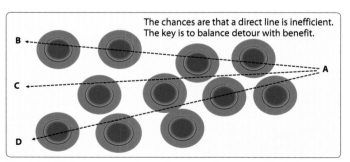

Fig 12.2 Flying any random direct path means likely losses.

Looking at *Fig 12.2* along with the figures used earlier for gains and losses passing straight through a thermal we see that routing is more important than dolphining on track.

Tracking A–B we pass directly through the central area of each thermal.

> Cruising at 60kts we gain 4 × 4ft = +16ft
> Cruising at 90kts we lose 4 × −8ft = −36ft
> Dolphin at 60−90kts we gain 4 × 10ft = +40ft

Tracking A–C we miss all lift associated with each thermal.

> Cruising at 60kts we lose 4 × −82ft = −328ft
> Cruising at 90kts we lose 4 × −80ft = −320ft
> There is no opportunity to dolphin.

Tracking A–D we hit/miss a collection of thermals.

> Cruising at 60kts we gain 2 × 4ft = +8ft and lose 3 × −82ft = −238ft
> Cruising at 90kts we lose 2 × −8ft = −16ft and lose 3 × −80ft = −256ft
> Dolphin at 60−90kts we gain 2 × 4ft = +8ft and lose 3 × −80ft = −232ft

It should be clear that whilst there is a small benefit if we dolphin on track, considerably more height can be retained by efficient routing. An important aspect, the most important aspect missed in dolphin discussions, is the sense to deviate from the straight pull up, float and push down. In other words the 'S' turn, which in effect combines dolphin and beneficial routing.

During the pull-up it is important to note the string deflection and respond to any significant indication promptly. The benefit of doing this downwind is significant because at least you will maintain some track progress whilst climbing. The disadvantage of doing a full 'S' turn into-wind and engaging a weak thermal simply costs time. Whatever manoeuvre you do though costs energy. You only gain energy by what is provided by the air you are passing through.

Variometer instrument lag

Variometer instrument lag is an important issue and needs to be fully understood. *Both the vario and ASI have almost no lag!* They receive inputs via the pitot and static sources which are often located towards the rear of the glider for greater accuracy. At 60kts the source pressure is almost half a second rearwards from the front of the glider. The air pressure change has to move along the small tubes but as it is only transmitting a contained pressure there is insignificant lag here, so in all you have lost about half a second in time between the air that you (and your wing) are in and the indications you see. This aspect is particularly important when you consider a rear mounted static source and a nose mounted pitot tube, measuring dynamic pressure, as shown in *Fig 12.3*. Both the static and pitot feed to the vario in an attempt to give a total energy indication yet they sample different air, which is therefore passed to the instruments at different times. Of course large pitch changes also will give false indications if the static source is on the tail.

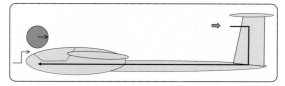

Fig 12.3 Instrument error and lag.

The static system on the fin has dynamic errors as the glider pitches. We readily accept the information that the vario averager gives us with changes of climb or descent at 0.1kt accuracy, updated almost every second. This is 2 inches per second. Pulling up into a thermal, as shown in *Fig 12.4*, the vario initially under-reads as the tail will go down as the fuselage rotates. Whilst pushing the nose down the vario initially over-reads, giving the misleading information that you have just hit a sharp edge to the thermal before the sink. Modern glider designs endeavour to minimize these errors by installing four static holes, two forward and two an equal distance behind the glider's centre of gravity.

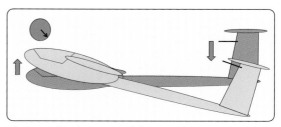

Fig 12.4 Pitch errors of the vario.

Flying block speed and entering a column thermal

Of course, flying at around 90kts instead of 60kts will mean that all of the indications of flying through a thermal happen faster. If you want to thermal you will need to prevent the glider from flying through to the sink on the other side. You have to pull hard to remain in the benefit band, as shown in *Fig 12.5*, and the normal *feel* is usually suppressed during this manoeuvre. Look for the string deflection for which way to turn (Atkinson's string theory).

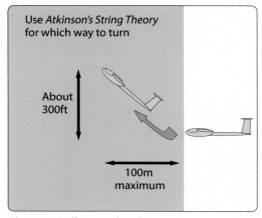

Fig 12.5 Pulling up hard to centre on a column thermal at 90kts.

So if you have flown through the heavy sink and the airspeed and feel indicates an appropriate gust (the vario will also see this as an increase in total energy) start pulling. You are quite likely to achieve around 2.5g, particularly if you do this whilst hitting the middle gust of the strong thermal core. As you pull at speed and increase the AoA the wing will have an increased efficiency so be positive or you will pay the price of flying through the thermal into the sink. Remember that pulling hard into a column thermal is not an issue as you are able to join the core at any height.

Flying block speed and entering a bubble thermal

If you hit a bubble thermal at speed and pull up hard you may well climb above the top of the thermal, as shown in *Fig 12.6*. Joining a glider

that is thermalling a few hundred feet above you will prevent this and you will be unaware of the potential for this otherwise costly mistake.

So, if you are on your own and the thermal is a bubble you might sometimes feel that you have pulled up, turned and lost the thermal. It may, after one turn, appear significantly weaker than you were led to believe. In a bubble thermal you can run the risk of flying out of the top if you just happen to hit it near the top. Even a strong 6kt bubble will take 30 seconds to climb 300ft and catch you up. During this time you will have been busy wondering just where that thermal has gone. Be cautious not to wander off looking for the core if you do indeed need this thermal. It may take a couple of frustrating turns for the bubble to reach you but as long as the air essentially is significantly turbulent and you are not losing excessive height it will be worth the wait. Despite the frustration that this sometimes presents, it is best to try to analyse and learn, recognize the situation and remember it for future occasions. Of course, if you are not charging about quite so fast the situation rarely presents itself, hence the suggestion to use a slower block speed for bubble thermals.

KEY POINT Fly a slower block speed if you recognize that you are amongst bubble thermals.

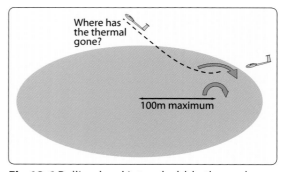

Fig 12.6 Pulling hard into a bubble thermal.

It is important that you enter the correct ballast value into any electronic total energy driven instrument. You will have to make a further adjustment so that the vario reacts correctly for the rate at which you normally pull up for a thermal. During the pull-up you may generate

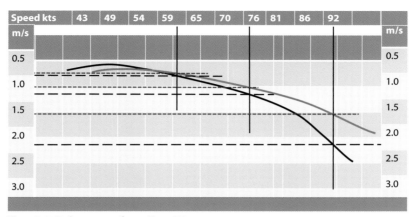

Fig 12.7 Polar curve for a *Duo Discus*.

dynamic lift with the vario increasing excitedly. The vario indication will fall when the glider gets a gust from the core (tail gust). The indications will suggest that you missed the thermal or have turned the wrong way. Sometimes patience is the key and of course occasionally it just does not work, but with experience you will improve your technique and learn to understand what is actually happening in the air.

Block speed and height

When column thermals are well established and control the structure of the sky charging about within a height band is quite easy. On weaker days, or more specifically lower down on good days, when the column mechanism may not be carried to ground level, you will be encountering bubble thermals and need to change gear. This means that even on good days you may need to accept a slower block speed below a certain height as the structure will be disrupted from the dominant column thermals. As you route further afield over the tiny island of the UK, which has an amazing ability to change the local weather, you will need to routinely review the conditions and your strategy.

> **KEY POINT** Identify whether you are in a column or a bubble height band and adjust your block speed to suit.

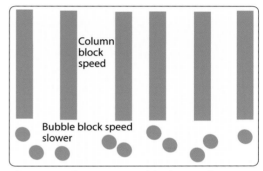

Fig 12.8 Adjusting your block speed.

As shown in *Fig 12.8* it is not unreasonable to find that the column thermals only extend within an upper height band.

Glide performance flying through sinking air

Consider as an example the polar curve shown in *Fig 12.7* for the *Duo*. (You can do the same with the polar curve of your own glider.) First extract the rates of descent at 60/75/90/100kts both at heavy and light weights and deduce the glide angles in still air.

Consider the four green shaded ares in *Table 12.1 on page 134*. At *light* weights with a 50% increase in speed the glider becomes very inefficient. When *heavy* the rate of descent at 60kts is 1.4kts and yet at 90kts it is 2.8kts. This is a 50% increase in speed for a 100% increase in rate of descent in flat air. There are no surprises with this but what if we fly these speeds through sink of 2/4/6kts.

Flat performance of a *Duo* in still air				
Speed (kts)	RoD (kts) Heavy	L/D	RoD (kts) Light	L/D
60	1.4	42.8	1.45	41.4
75	1.9	41.4	2.3	32.6
90	2.8	32.1	4.0	22.5
100	3.5	28.6	5.5	18.2

Table 12.1

Adding the still air rate of descent of our glider to the environmental sink and calculating the glide angle by dividing the speed by the total rate of descent, we get *Table 12.2* and *Table 12.3*:

Flat performance of a *Duo* in descending air (heavy—with water)						
Speed (kts)	RoD-2 down	L/D	RoD-4 down	L/D	RoD-6 down	L/D
60	3.4	17.6	5.4	11.1	7.4	8.1
75	3.9	19.2	5.9	12.7	7.9	9.5
90	4.8	18.7	6.8	13.2	8.8	10.2
100	5.5	18.2	7.5	13.3	9.5	10.5

Table 12.2

Flat performance of a *Duo* in descending air (light—without water)						
Speed (kts)	RoD-2 down	L/D	RoD-4 down	L/D	RoD-6 down	L/D
60	3.5	17.4	5.5	11	7.5	8.1
75	4.3	19.2	6.3	11.9	8.3	9.0
90	6.0	15	8.0	11.2	10.0	9.0
100	7.5	13.3	9.5	10.5	11.5	8.7

Table 12.3

We can see that when flying in sink of 2 down at 75kts (green shading) rather than the poor speed of 60kts (red shading) we get an improved glide performance and are flying 25% faster, whether heavy or light.

Consider the two yellow shaded cells in *Table 12.2*. With typical sink on a good day of 4 down, heavy at 90kts you get a better glide angle (over 20% better) despite flying 50% faster.

You can see that when the glider is light there is no loss in glide performance when flying at this speed. If the glider is flown through air which is sinking at 6kts we find the numbers change even more in favour of the heavier glider. This means that there is no benefit in flying slowly through sink. In fact I consider it a crime to fly slowly through sink and it is why you must accelerate quickly in the lift whilst leaving a thermal.

Dolphin

Dolphin is good if your machine is light, slow and one which possess a disastrous performance at speed. You may simply respond to fluctuations on the vario. In modern machinery though, following the MacCready religiously is potentially efficient but slow, in a similar way that driving a formula one car at best mpg would be fuel efficient but would not win races. Chasing the little ups and downs theoretically is all rather nice but all these little climbs are at nearly half cruise speed. If any accelerations are late then it is a case of accelerating in sink, a huge mistake. The gains by dolphin are in reality very small.

Consider the following:

If you wish to achieve an average speed of 100kph on a 300km task (3 hours) and you were to never spend any time climbing you would need to maintain a cruise speed of 100kph (57kts). However, in reality you do need to stop and climb around 27,000ft.

If you climb 27,000ft at 4kts it will take 67.5 minutes leaving 112.5 minutes for cruising. Your average cruise speed between thermals must therefore be 160kph (86.4kts).

Climbing at 4.5kts means that your average cruise speed must be 150kph (81kts) and climbing at 5kts means that your average cruise speed must be 143kph (77kts).

This shows us two things: Firstly, climb rate is hugely important. We cannot outclimb rising air so you have to pick the strongest thermals and fly good techniques. The entry to the climb must be sharp and the departure on track must be equally efficient to avoid crippling losses. Secondly, we know there is only a small penalty if we are not quite at the correct speed but the much slower speeds whilst flying dolphin means that if you do not achieve significant climb rates you will have to fly faster at some other time. Routing, rather than slowing to dolphin is the key!

KEY POINT Efficient routing should take priority over slowing to dolphin.

Of course it is not unknown for our top pilots, flying in exceptionally good weather, to achieve speeds in excess of 120kph in the UK. To achieve this, even climbing at 6kts, the average cruise speed becomes 171kph (92kts).

Vario configuration

It is worth mentioning the cruise configuration of the cruise/climb option on the vario. Older vario systems have a speed ring which can be rotated on the outside face of the instrument and it acts as a circular slide rule with speed marked and calibrated for a particular glider's performance and average weight. You set the neutral datum at the achieved average rate of climb. During the cruise, as the vario needle indicates changes in rates of descent, the outer scale on the ring indicates what speed you should be doing for the most efficient cruise. In this way you don't have to remember what the different best speeds to fly are whilst passing through various rates of sinking air. A major drawback of this system is that you have to keep looking in to see what you should be doing.

Photo 12.1 Vario showing a speed ring.

As modern gliders can carry significant ballast, then you would need another ring for heavy weights. You would also need some form of bug factor compensation. (The loss in performance on old wooden gliders due to bugs is not likely to be noticeable!) Modern vario systems incorporate an audio system for cruising so that we don't have to look in. We still call the switch position on the vario the cruise position or speed command. These words can be misleading.

In the cruise position the vario needle will indicate zero when you are flying at the correct speed for the sinking or rising air and this is coupled to the audio system. This is adjusted by entering the average achieved rate of climb, weight of the ballasted glider and a bug factor. Tones are used to indicate whether to speed up or slow down to achieve the theoretically perfect performance. To avoid pilots pulling and pushing for every little bump, which would be inefficient due to the drag caused by manoeuvre, a silent band is incorporated. As I have repeatedly stated, small errors in flying the correct speed only impart a small loss in overall performance. When the vario does give a tone some pilots use this as an indication of the need to change speed and dolphin. But can we use this indication better?

What the vario is actually telling you is that you are in better or worse air. A fly slower tone usually comes on when there is a reduction in sink of about 1kt from what the glider should be achieving in still air at that speed. In other words, if you were to slow down now to minimum sink speed you would stay level or better. It is telling you what the air is doing. A fly faster tone is telling you that you are in poor air, sink. Rather than worry about getting the nose down, look around. Is the sink associated with the thermal ahead or are you giving a thermal a glancing blow meaning that you need to turn right or left to connect if you need the climb?

In the cruise position remember that the indications, errors and lag of the vario are still very valid. Modern instruments indicate both climb and cruise at the same time by using two needles, or a needle and a moving dot/graphic. Many very good pilots don't use the cruise selection at all.

If you must dolphin whilst travelling at high speed, simply use the lifting surge much as a gymnast uses a spring board. Make a gentle short pull and bounce to reduce your cruise speed by no more than 10kts. Never do this in a thermal which is weaker than one that you would perhaps have stopped to climb in.

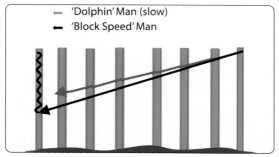

Fig 12.9 Dolphin, a concept for efficiency but not necessarily for speed.

> **ANALOGY** **Motorway driving.** When driving down the motorway and slowing down from 70mph to 30mph at regular intervals for lane closures it is amazing how much time is lost.

So, only dolphin when you are flying at survival speeds. Heavy and fast in a modern glass glider jeopardizes the efficiency of dolphin as the delay between the glider hitting rising air and the vario response is so late that the glider has already transited the lift. Considerable energy is lost in the manoeuvre compared to the minimal gain possibly achieved. Pick a high speed in proportion to the climb rates and simply go for it, looking ahead at the weather.

> **KEY POINT** Only dolphin when you are flying at survival speeds.

Speed to fly

Firstly, how accurate is your ASI? The certification requirement for it to fly requires it to be within 3kts but is this good enough and can you really fly that accurately? Flying too fast or too slow can cause problems.

Flying too fast
Consider setting off at 80kts from 3,600ft expecting to make it because you started with 400ft spare. Because drag is proportional to the square of the speed, that 10% safety height is blown away simply by flying at 84kts.

> $80 \times 80 = 6,400$ total energy required (units not important)
> $\times 1.1$ (10%) $= 7,040$ total energy available
> $83.9 \times 83.9 = 7,040$ used flying 4kts faster

Flying cautiously
It is very common for most successful and competent cross-country pilots to plan on a simple glide of 1km per 100ft (only a 30:1 glide ratio) because the numbers are easy to monitor. When flying high performance gliders at speed this closely equates to the expected performance.

Flying too slow
If you hit unexpected sink you will make a huge loss on the performance. So, if you anticipate a bad line you must not fly too slowly.

Flying in turbulence
Consider the drag curves as shown in *Fig 12.10*. Total drag is made up of zero lift drag (ZLD) which increases markedly with speed and lift-dependent drag (LDD) which reduces as speed is increased. This latter drag relies on the wing being flown efficiently but in turbulence this drag is further significantly increased.

> Assume that at 60kts the total drag is 10kg and at 90kts it is 20kg.
> This is made up of:
> 7kg of ZLD and 3kg of LDD at 60kts,
> 18kg of ZLD and 2kg of LDD at 90kts.

If we assume that in turbulence at 60kts the LDD increases by 1kg whilst at 90kts the increase in LDD is only ½kg. So, the loss of efficiency is much less at higher speeds! In terms of L/D then for a 600kg glider:

> In clean air at 60kts = 60/1 and at 90kts = 30/1
> In turbulence at 60kts = 55/1 and at 90kts = 29/1

This gives about a 90% efficiency at 60 kts but 97% efficiency at 90 kts.

An important aspect to this analysis is that the effects of flying too slow in thermic conditions (turbulence) means that a higher performance glider has a greater loss of performance.

Fig 12.10 also shows the increase in LDD due to turbulence (red curve) and a new total drag curve (dashed line). The new total drag curve clearly shows that at slower speeds the turbulence has much more of an effect on performance.

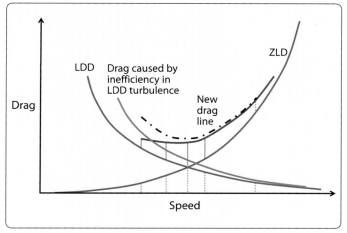

Fig 12.10 The change of drag with speed.

Advantages of flying slowly in weak conditions

You will recall that there is a fine balance between climbing and cruising when the thermals are weak. We tend to spend the same amount of time climbing regardless of thermal strength, up to a point. In weak conditions though, the thermals are closer together. This is important as the cruise speed is less and the sink associated with thermals is also less. In these weak conditions the benefits of dolphin techniques, milking the sky, and detour are more significant and it is important to change gear.

Another point to note is the aspect ratio of your wing. Dolphin flying encompasses significant changes in angle of attack so not only is form drag increased during any pull-up but so is vortex drag and interference drag. Wings with a high aspect ratio are therefore more efficient at benefitting from the dolphin technique whilst those with

a large chord and low aspect ratio generate a considerable increase in drag for a possible small height gain.

Searching for thermals

Consider how you search for thermals. Do you slow down? If so, what speed do you choose? What is the perceived benefit of slowing down? The slower you go means that you will probably lose more height and it will take you longer to get to the next thermal. Bear in mind that the track searching for a thermal is likely to be similar whether you fly at 50 kts or 80 kts. We have seen that we lose more height by flying slowly in sink so if your block speed is 80 kts, search at 80 kts until you are clearly in lift!

Required speed to fly

Consider that the current thermal could be a stubble fire, a power station, the edge of a rain shower (you need to dry the wings and probably run a long way), a thermal supported by wave, a magic late evening 6 kt thermal which will now just put you on final glide if you set 2 kts on the MacCready. The achieved climb rate in all of these situations is not relevant to your new block speed. Your next speed depends on what you need to do with the height that you have just gained.

Operating bands

There is often talk about operating in the ideal or good band. In countries such as Spain, USA, Australia, or South Africa with a cloud base exceeding 12,000 ft, that is fine. In the UK with a cloud base often down to 3,500 ft or less, the ideal band is one where you can make the next 3 thermals (from the top of the band) so keep in the top half of the sky. Bear in mind that 50 km down track the weather in the UK will have changed and the operating heights and block speeds may need to change significantly. So, height bands make more sense when the cloud base is up at 10,000 ft rather than the average cloud base in the UK.

More about dolphin

To some extent, dolphin may be considered a short term, straight line thermalling technique. However for some clarity it is perhaps better to reserve the word *thermalling* for situations when we are circling and *routing* when we are making progress down track, which includes the art of dolphin. Whilst thermalling in circles in zero lift achieves nothing, flying on track in zero lift is a clear benefit because we are making progress along track with no height loss. On the other hand, flying through the same rising air fast is still a benefit due to a reduced rate of descent.

In the same way that we reject thermals that are too weak, is there a thermal strength that we consider too weak to dolphin? One might conclude that there is no benefit to dolphin through any thermal that is weaker than ones we are using on the day to climb in, if we feel certain that we can reach that next strong thermal. Any manoeuvre costs us energy and, no matter what manoeuvre we do, we can only pick up additional energy from the thermal that we pass through.

The decision to dolphin is a balance between the risks of getting it wrong, versus the reward. When transiting through any thermal there is a benefit in flying slower at a better glide speed (reduced RoD) and lingering in the rising air thus climbing higher than if we were to have just maintained our original speed. Slowing to transit a thermal for a few extra seconds gains us some height. The downside is that we will use energy in the manoeuvre. Theoretically, there is the potential to make an additional gain if we hit the middle of the thermal and this also assumes that we have flown the manoeuvre perfectly, which is more difficult flying heavy fast gliders which require faster reaction times by the pilot. Whilst some loss of energy will occur due to the manoeuvre, the real potential loss will be due to accelerating late in the associated sink. Here, you can lose all the height, or more, gained earlier. Also, you are now late, or worse still, have pulled the manoeuvre in a *non-thermal*.

As a means to go faster in dolphin the average pilot appears to make more losses than gains. When the opportunity arises, a lesson that I usually teach in regional competitions is getting my student to follow on the same track at block speed and catch an enthusiastic *dolphineer* in a higher handicapped glider ahead.

There are occasions, however, when there is a line of lift similar to a mini street. Flying slower and feeling our way gently in such circumstances can give us a huge benefit, especially in weak conditions. So a *sustained* straight climb, albeit even in weak lift over a long period, will be beneficial.

As a final point, we already recognize that there is some lag between the rising air and the vario indications. By responding smoothly to the vario means that we will be slowing in the weaker areas of the thermal. If on the other hand we can respond immediately to what we feel and even anticipate it by a couple of seconds then we will get much greater benefit. To reuse the gymnast analogy, to apply a positive push down (jump) at any other time other than whilst on the spring board, is of no benefit.

Detour

We will now consider five types of detour:

▶ Vertical detour.
▶ Horizontal detour.
▶ Necessary detour.
▶ Useless detour.
▶ Short detour.

Vertical detour

Whilst the distance of vertical detour is relatively small, it is the slowing down, dolphin technique at slower speeds than block speed which effectively cause a large time loss.

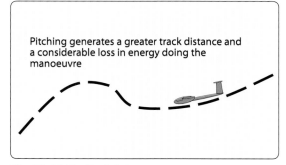

Fig 12.11 Vertical detour.

Horizontal detour

This involves relatively small changes of heading routing off track, ideally less than 30° to one side or the other. The additional distance is more than made up for by the better glide through good air or climbing in stronger thermals. When routing outbound you have a degree of freedom but only up to the mid-point on the leg. After that point you have to ensure that you route to a closure or a significant detour penalty will start to accumulate.

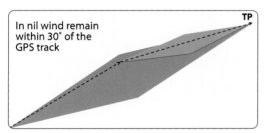

Fig 12.12 Horizontal detour.

Necessary detour

If to stay within 30° of track means a difficult struggle or possible land-out then to avoid any prolonged slow climb and frustration it will be sensible or even necessary to divert as much as 45° off track. It could be just a difficult patch or a cycling of the weather but, rather like loitering high when the going becomes questionable, it makes sense to go where the weather is good and still make reasonable relative down track progress. It is rather like taking the ring road around a town, avoiding the traffic jams. Of course you may need to detour just to stay airborne because of a broad heavy rain shower blocking your path. Don't forget to consider how the change

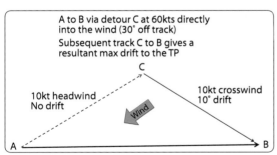

Fig 12.13 Necessary detour and how the wind affects the track.

in cross-wind value will affect your new track to the turn point as shown in *Fig 12.13*.

Useless detour

To fly more than 60° off track means that you are actually flying farther away from your goal. Chasing the *better* weather way off track is probably the commonest error, particularly if you have already started to detour and you have ignored the required track to your TP. Weaker options on track might feel slow but

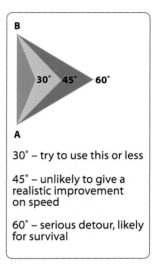

30° – try to use this or less

45° – unlikely to give a realistic improvement on speed

60° – serious detour, likely for survival

Fig 12.14 Different angles of detour.

it is at least progress. The only point of deviating more than 60° is to either ride out poor weather that you know will clear or to abort the task and try to get home.

Short detour

When considering the previous types of detour we assumed *large* detour legs. It is important to note that *short* detours through large angles in order to position onto a good line are usually well worth the extra mileage. For example, it can be perfectly reasonable to do a short 60° detour to link to a worthwhile line. In *Fig 12.15* a short detour to take a line through the thermals will enable a better

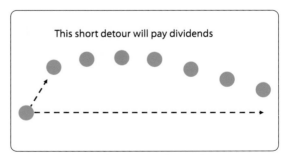

Fig 12.15 Short detour to a better line.

cruise or reduce the time climbing, more than balancing the additional distance travelled.

Accumulative errors with detours

We note and remember big issues and mistakes but as with many things the cumulative errors can build up and become deceptively punishing. If you were to fly a task in the UK from Strathaven to Swindon the direct track distance is 481km. The route essentially follows the motorway structure and if you tracked the motorway the route would not appear to have any significant detour. If, however, you drive the route in your car, the distance covered by gently swathing down through the country via the motorways is 560km. This is an extra 79km and amounts to a 16% additional distance to be flown and depending on your glider's performance, will require an extra 6,000–10,000ft to be climbed.

So how much time do we lose during a detour bearing in mind that routing via the detour means we lose less height which means less climbing time subsequently? Consider a normal day when we might achieve a consistent 2.5kt climb. If we fly a distance of 120km we need 12,000ft to achieve this. If we consistently detour by 30° we need about 15% more height. (13,800ft) and by 45° we need about 30% more height (15,600ft). To consider a realistic single detour, let's look at a tenth of the overall distance, a small 12km glide requiring 1,200ft.

For an effective detour of 30°:

Our detour will achieve a height loss of 1,200 + 180 (15%) = 1,380ft to position abeam the original track position.
This requires 43 seconds of extra climb (180ft at 250ft/min).
The total additional time is therefore about 2 minutes for one detour, made up of 1 minute additional cruise and 1 minute extra climb.
We must, for a worthwhile detour, climb 1,380ft in less than (1,200 at 2.5kts = 4.8 minutes) = 2.9kts.

For an effective detour of 45°:

Our detour will achieve a height loss of 1,200 + 360 (30%) = 1,560ft to position abeam the original track position.
This requires 1.44 minutes of extra climb (360ft at 250ft/min).
The total additional time is about 5 minutes for one detour, made up of 3.5 minutes additional cruise and 1.5 minutes extra climb.
We must, for a worthwhile detour, climb 1,560ft in less than (1,200 at 2.5kts = 4.8 minutes) = 3.2kts.

So, don't detour unless there is a clear advantage to do so, or of course you need to do so to survive.

Occasional extreme detours

As a final point, occasionally it is necessary to make an extreme detour as shown in *Fig 12.16*. The best route is obvious from this view, but would you see the cloud formations?

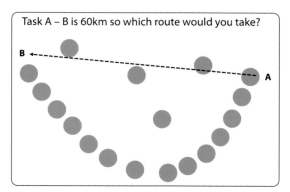

Fig 12.16 A choice of routes.

13
Decision making

W e had been hanging around the start zone longer than intended and the rain showers were heavier and cycling through too fast. We made a break for it and ran a line which gave a clear run downwind to the first TP but turning around meant the inevitable dancing around the rain. The first shower was ok but the next heavy one was becoming a complication. The rain was starting to wash too much performance off and the tension in the back induced a personal need for my P2. There was some noise as the starch bag disappeared out of the DV panel. Shortly after the ASI stuck and the TE was talking a degree of gobbledygook. Yes, the package had planted itself with the handles wrapped around the TE probe whilst the rest of the bag was wrapped around the pitot probe. What are the chances?

I magine that you are flying at minimum sink speed and therefore at the optimum angle of attack, searching for thermals. Is this a good decision? This chapter is all about making some of these decisions to get the best performance out of your glider.

Angles of attack

If flying at *minimum sink speed/optimum AoA* and we then hit lift the AoA increases to a less efficient angle, as shown in *Fig 13.1*, and the initial benefit is lost. Indeed the feel would also be reduced and might be strong enough to induce a stall. So there is little benefit in thermalling or looking for a thermal at too slow a speed and this includes banked attitudes. Flying faster means that when entering rising air the wing becomes more efficient and will produce beneficial lift.

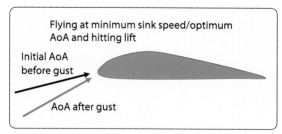

Fig 13.1 Change of AoA hitting lift.

Imagine if we were cruising at *best glide* and encounter sink. The AoA will decrease to a less efficient angle and the glider will immediately sink as shown in *Fig 13.2*, not just because it has

hit sink but again the wing has lost efficiency. There will be a requirement to accelerate up to the ideal speed to transit through the sink to improve performance. So there is no benefit in cruising at too slow a speed when searching for thermals. Flying faster than best glide speed means that entering sinking air the effective change in AoA will be reduced. Therefore the loss of lift will be reduced and you will be flying at a more appropriate speed to transit through the sink.

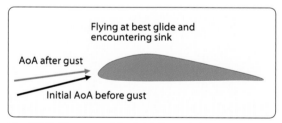

Fig 13.2 Change of AoA hitting sink.

Span or mass?

Now we will consider the pros and cons of different gliders. The aim of the handicap system is so that the winner in a competition is the best pilot.

Discus versus *LS8*

Firstly consider the standard class gliders that are highlighted in *Table 13.1*. The *LS8* in 15m mode does have an edge over the *Discus b* but mainly at the slow speed, best glide end (weak days). At speed on a strong racing day there is little difference.

Performance comparison between *Discus b* and *LS8* in 15m mode									
Glider	Span (m)	Wing area (m²)	Wing loading (Kg/m²)	Water ballast (litres)	Ref weight (kg)	Max glide (kts)	Best L/D kph (kts)	Speed for 2m/s sink kph (kts)	Handi-cap
K21	17	17.95	31.75	0	570	33	90 (45)	157 (78)	85
Discus b	15	10.58	30.72	184	325	42	100 (50)	170 (85)	98
LS8	18	11.5	32.2	180	370	48	90 (45)	170 (85)	106
Discus 2c	18	11.39	33.1	200	377	48	108 (54)	170 (85)	106
LS8	15	10.5	34.29	180	366	44	112 (56)	172 (86)	100
Duo	20	16.4	38.29	201	628	45	128 (64)	181 (90)	101

Table 13.1

LS8 15m versus 18m

Consider the performance of the *LS8* in 15m versus 18m mode, highlighted in *Table 13.2*. There is only an advantage in the glide angle in 18m mode at slower speeds but to achieve this you must fly 11kts slower and get a 6% handicap for the privilege. As a result, when penetrating breezy into-wind legs when glide angle over the ground is important, we see almost no benefit. The 18m should climb more quickly though.

LS8 18m versus *Duo* 20m

Consider the performance of the *LS8* in 18m mode against the *Duo*, highlighted in *Table 13.3 on page 144*. The wing loading benefits the *Duo*, so although it may climb slower and has a reduced glide angle it achieves best glide 19kts faster. At high speed the *Duo* outperforms the *LS8* and then has a 5% handicap advantage. It just so happens

that at 90kts the *Duo* is on a sweet spot on its polar curve.

Duo versus *ASG 29* versus *ASH 25*

Consider the performance comparison of the three gliders highlighted in *Table 13.4 on page 144*. At slow speed, whilst the glide angle increases, the speed at which they achieve this reduces with the *ASH 25* flying 22kts slower than the *Duo*. At high speed the figures appear more balanced but again you must consider the handicap. Bearing in mind the various handling aspects then the handicap system works very well, particularly in the UK with very variable weather. It is very unlikely that you will be beaten simply because someone has a *better* glider.

Performance comparison between *LS8* in 15m and 18m mode									
Glider	Span (m)	Wing area (m²)	Wing loading (Kg/m²)	Water ballast (litres)	Ref weight (kg)	Max glide (kts)	Best L/D kph (kts)	Speed for 2m/s sink kph (kts)	Handi-cap
K21	17	17.95	31.75	0	570	33	90 (45)	157 (78)	85
Discus b	15	10.58	30.72	184	325	42	100 (50)	170 (85)	98
LS8	18	11.5	32.2	180	370	48	90 (45)	170 (85)	106
Discus 2c	18	11.39	33.1	200	377	48	108 (54)	170 (85)	106
LS8	15	10.5	34.29	180	366	44	112 (56)	172 (86)	100
Duo	20	16.4	38.29	201	628	45	128 (64)	181 (90)	101

Table 13.2

Performance comparison between *LS8* in 18m mode and *Duo*									
Glider	Span (m)	Wing area (m²)	Wing loading (Kg/m²)	Water ballast (litres)	Ref weight (kg)	Max glide (kts)	Best L/D kph (kts)	Speed for 2m/s sink kph (kts)	Handi-cap
Discus b	15	10.58	30.72	184	325	42	100 (50)	170 (85)	98
LS8	18	11.5	32.2	180	370	48	90 (45)	170 (85)	106
Discus 2c	18	11.39	33.1	200	377	48	108 (54)	170 (85)	106
LS8	15	10.5	34.29	180	366	44	112 (56)	172 (86)	100
Duo	20	16.4	38.29	201	628	45	128 (64)	181 (90)	101
ASG 29	18	10.5	33	195	388	52	105 (53)	183 (91)	111
ASH 25	25	16.31	42.49	120	693	57	85 (42)	194 (97)	114

Table 13.3

Performance comparison between *Duo*, *ASG 29* and *ASH 25*									
Glider	Span (m)	Wing area (m²)	Wing loading (Kg/m²)	Water ballast (litres)	Ref weight (kg)	Max glide (kts)	Best L/D kph (kts)	Speed for 2m/s sink kph (kts)	Handi-cap
LS8	18	11.5	32.2	180	370	48	90 (45)	170 (85)	106
Discus 2c	18	11.39	33.1	200	377	48	108 (54)	170 (85)	106
Duo	20	16.4	38.29	201	628	45	128 (64)	181 (90)	101
ASG 29	18	10.5	33	195	388	52	105 (53)	183 (91)	111
ASH 25	25	16.31	42.49	120	693	57	85 (42)	194 (97)	114

Table 13.4

The effect of big wings

If you inspect the polar curves for the *LS8* the most striking thing to hit you should be that at 60kts at max weight the 15m curve intercepts the 18m line. Above this speed the 15m easily out-runs the 18m. So, on any racing day when you think that you are going to maintain a high cruise speed you obviously need 15m. So what about the *ETA*, *EB28* and the *ASH 25/30*? It is the same deal. At higher speeds all the gliders effectively achieve a very similar glide angle simply because the lift-dependent drag is minimal and the real deal is in the zero lift drag of surface friction, interference and profile drag. From the front all gliders have the same profile and present around the same area, except for the wings. The wings can't be made any thinner and the fuselage can't be any smaller but if you increase the wingspan, you increase the zero lift drag components. In simple terms you are dragging more wing through the air. This is why the current design trend is towards finding an optimum wingspan, which is about 23m.

Of course light wing loadings to allow slow speed and low sink rates during thermalling are equally desirable and require larger wing surface areas, so as you lose the span, chord lengths increase and the aspect ratio goes down giving greater vortex drag for the same surface friction areas again at lower speeds. This is being overcome by radical modern wing section design which concentrates on reducing drag and is why the very modern 13.5m gliders perform so well.

However, just before you start to believe big wings are not good, you can achieve some outstanding cross countries with big wings in weak conditions. At light weights an *ASH 25* will fall at around 0.4m/sec minimum sink rate whereas the 15m *LS8* will fall at 0.7m/sec. If the thermal air is 1m/sec the rate of climb of the *ASH* is therefore twice as fast (0.6 / 0.3). So it is only on soft days that the big wings enjoy a greater margin in performance, cruising at around 50–60kts. It is worth comparing the cross-countries achieved by the various gliders on strong and weak days, by looking at the national ladder.

Handicapping and a look at different gliders

For competition purposes gliders are handicapped as fairly as possible. A key part of the handicap system is the factory declared performance of the glider on a 2.5kt thermal day. In simple terms then, a higher handicap glider (>100) has an advantage on days when thermals are weak, whilst the lower handicap glider (<100) has an advantage on strong days. But this is a simplistic approach and the handicap system is more complex in an effort to allow the best pilot to win in competition. The handicap system does allow you to have a good indication as to how good a glider really is. However, after saying all this the inconsistent UK weather and general lack of fantastic racing days brings me to the personal conclusion that buying the highest performance glider that you can will give you greater opportunities to fly quality cross-country by *scratching* in straight lines.

The greater wingspan of the higher aspect ratio gliders has other implications, in particular during routing and dolphin flying. Brushing past the edge of a thermal the wing inside the thermal will lift causing the glider to roll away from the better air. Bigger wingspans usually give better feel simply because they reach farther. The normal response is to casually roll back to wings level but this is usually only accomplished after the glider has travelled beyond the effective area of the rising air and now whilst the glider is in sinking or in less beneficial air. If, on the other hand, you respond immediately with full aileron towards the lifting wing the glider will actually climb, using the rising air as though climbing up a step. The bigger the span, the bigger the step. The crux is that you must do this whilst the glider is still on the edge of the thermal. Birds routinely demonstrate this technique, despite their lack of span.

Finally, the additional drag caused during the motions of pitching up and down during dolphin techniques are largely lift-dependent drag. Higher aspect wing designs reduce this therefore gliders like an *ASH* will be able to get more benefit from the manoeuvres than machines with a larger chord and lower aspect ratio shaped wings.

Time lost

Three aspects slow us down:

► Pottering around and flying without purpose.
► Poor and slow decision making.
► A negative attitude.

Consider specifically why we might be slow around a task? We assume it is obvious where we *think* we lost time, but look more closely at all the factors and it becomes clearer. Some of the contributors are:

► Poor start (slow, low, not at max weight, poor line).
► Poor time to start (too early or too late).
► Flying too cautiously (slow cruise speeds).
► Climbing in any weak thermals unnecessarily.
► Dithering at making decisions (wasting time).
► Flying slowly when you should be fast.
► Flying fast when you should be slow.
► Flying light when you should be at max weight.
► Holding water when the conditions are too weak.
► Struggling to centre (tired, distracted, poor techniques).
► Poor flying in thermals (fast, shoddy sideslip).

- ▶ Poor thermalling (not in it).
- ▶ Poor link lines (not detouring and linking the thermals).
- ▶ Over-dolphin (slow technique).
- ▶ Poor discipline at turning points (flying farther than the task).
- ▶ High at into-wind turn points.
- ▶ Low at downwind TPs.
- ▶ Various detours.
- ▶ An overly cautious final glide.
- ▶ Pressing on when you actually need to survive.
- ▶ Giving up.

Flying with water

There are clear advantages of flying with additional ballast on strong and windy days. Surprisingly, an increase in weight has no effect on the best glide angle as shown in *Fig 13.3*, but as weight increases the speed to achieve the best glide increases. This is really useful when flying into-wind. We simply fly faster to achieve the same best L/D ratio.

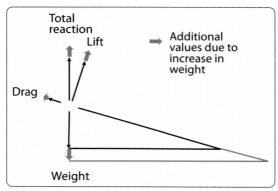

Fig 13.3 The effect of increasing weight on the glide.

Whilst there are mathematical solutions as to how much speed needs to be increased for increases of weight, this is only good for still air and gliders have sophisticated variometers to help us get the best performance in both good and bad air. It is more important to know just how heavy we are, if there is a bug factor or degradation of performance due to rain or ice on the wings and to input this information into the onboard computer.

It is very useful to know the speed required for the weight and thermal strength. A review of the polar curves for your glider can be used as a guide to ensure that the vario information is correct. At a particular high speed a glider will *fall off the curve* and the subsequent drag increase with any further increase in speed will result in a very inefficient glide. This means the performance degrades quite sharply. It is worth noting the speed at which this happens and ensuring that you always cruise comfortably below this, especially if you are feeling overconfident on final glide a long way out.

When heavy, the glider will go just as far but at a higher speed and this is particularly useful whilst flying on any significant into-wind legs. The difference between the best speeds to fly at maximum weight compared to those at minimum weight may be as much as 15kts. Any opportunity to fly just as far at a higher speed, for example on a street, will make a further considerable improvement on average speed.

Of course there is always a penalty and that is simply a slower climb rate in the chosen thermals. Other speeds will change, notably the stall speed. All thermalling has to be conducted at a higher speed and gives a larger radius of turn. The cut-off in simple terms is usually about 3.5kts in order to carry full water but if your start height is limited by cloud base or local airspace there will be an advantage on the first glide out even in weaker conditions, especially if the task first leg is downwind. Just bear in mind that you need to cross the start with as much height, speed and weight as possible.

Other issues are that the whole feel of the glider will undoubtedly change and your usual sense of what the glider is telling you about what the air is doing will be different. If you do go full, when do you dump it and how much do you dump? Is it dumping equally on both sides and does this mean you have now lost your all-important tail water. Many gliders have a way of preventing the fin water being lost if it means the centre of gravity remains within the glider's limits. A compromise might be to takeoff half full, or the common expression *a barrel a side*, but then that means any sustained out of balance flying (for example thermalling at slow speed) will generate a lateral out of balance which may require full aileron to prevent a wing from dropping at slower speeds. This produces a lot of additional drag and further reduces manoeuvrability.

Perhaps future gliders will have a better design with two separate tanks in each wing holding one third in the front section and two thirds behind it, such that you can dump the required amount by emptying one tank whilst leaving the other full.

Equally, with half a load of water the aero-tow itself may become difficult on takeoff if there is a crosswind and the wing runner lacks fast legs. To help you to maintain the wings level on the initial run of an aero-tow, it is common to see pilots have the airbrakes out and for flapped gliders to also start with full negative flap. The common suggestion that it makes the ailerons more effective is inaccurate. The problem of being unable to hold the wings level is the considerable difference in the lift produced by the two wings. As the prop wash rushes back the rotation of the air and any crosswind favours the air flow to one wing causing a significant difference in the lift produced, generating roll. Even if there is no wind or a light wind down the strip the airflow influencing each wing is different. Full negative flap and airbrake both reduce the lift being produced, but more so on the up going wing, which allows the ailerons to have sufficient authority for you to control the glider and maintain wings level. As an aside here, if the glider is tending to weathercock away from the centre line, a brief application of the wheel brake will help the tug, by pulling on the glider's nose hook, to drag you back in line.

Of course you must never consider climbing up through the freezing level with water ballast, unless you really want to seriously change the shape of your wings and fin! Whilst it is very common for water ballast to be used to maintain an advantageous centre of gravity, flying in the icing levels will ruin your day as the fin box splits open.

If the tug pilot tows you at too slow a speed you may find that your glider feels a bit sloppy as though it is near to the stall and the nose often appears to be at a higher attitude than you might otherwise be used to. That is because it is both of these things! Firstly the stall speed of the glider is

higher than when flying without water yet the tug is likely to be towing you at the normal 60–65kts, which is relatively slow for the tug so it too will be at a higher angle of attack. The tug wash, which is a combination of wing wash and prop wash, will generate sinking air for the glider. The glider has to climb against this downwash to stay level. The tug wash will also generate an additional local headwind to the glider, giving an inflated indication of airspeed. All of these effects are most noticeable shortly after takeoff. Additionally, the turbulent air behind the tug generated by the propeller means that the glider wing will be inefficient. Some parts of the wing will be affected by the tug wash, which will generate varying AoA along the wing. Those parts of the wing in clear air (wing tips) will be at a very high angle of attack, if not actually at the full stall.

KEY POINT The tug pilot must be told that you are heavy.

The varying AoA is presented in *Fig 13.4*. You can see how there is a need to increase the angle of attack of the glider to stay up with the tug and how the tips can quickly become stalled in free air.

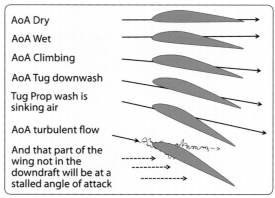

Fig 13.4 Dangerous changes of AoA when heavy and being aero-towed slow.

In summary, for aero-tows at heavy weight, consider the following:

▶ Enough lift must be produced to counter the extra weight.
▶ The attitude will be high to counter the

glider's normal rate of descent and achieve a rate of climb.

► The downwards flow (sink) of the tug wash must be countered.
► The downwards AoA vector of the tug wash must be countered.
► The wing is inefficient.

Compare a simple 100km route, climbing at 3 or 4kts and cruising at the correct and slightly incorrect MacCready speeds. Theoretically the cut-off to carry water is around 3.5kts of climb, however, I fill to full almost every time. *Table 13.5* emphasizes the need to climb in only the best thermals en route. The advantage of additional ballast is firstly that less height gain is needed to complete the 100km glide and secondly, we benefit from a faster glide speed. But this all depends on achieving the same climb rate and in reality climb rates will be less when heavy.

Training

Whenever a cross-country flight beyond gliding distance of your home airfield is not available, there is still a perfect opportunity to learn the skills and benefits of flying with water. This will allow you to become familiar with how the system works by flying a local training triangle such as a 48km triangle. Set off at maximum weight and an appropriate speed for the thermal strength. After a lap or two heavy, dump the water and continue to go around dry and compare this with the feel of flying heavy.

For a club only operating at weekends 70% of good days in a year are lost. The remaining period, weekends, still means that often the UK weather prevents us wandering too far from home so any opportunity to teach, learn or practise any technique must be made. A simple triangular course as shown in *Fig 13.5* with TPs just 9km away from home offers a good chance do this. Further adjustments to the task due to local restrictions can easily be made whilst satisfying the aims, although short out and returns do not because you are passing through a known good or bad line. Adjustment for the weather can be made and never being more than 9km away means that field landings can be avoided as 10km needs only about 1,200ft.

Practise starting with a confident plan that looks like success should be achieved. Look ahead for a good line. Put yourself in an efficient start

Theoretical task speeds at various climb rates and cruise speeds					
Cruise at MacC Dry	Actual Climb	Cruise Time (mins)	Climb mins (ft)	Total Time	Average Speed
3 (65kts)	3	50	34.3 (10,295)	84.3	71.2kph
4 (70kts)	3	46.5	38.1 (11,444)	84.6	70.1kph
3 (65kts)	4	50	25.7 (10,295)	75.7	79.2kph
4 (70kts)	4	46.5	28.6(11,444)	75	80kph

Cruise at MacC Wet	Actual Climb	Cruise Time (mins)	Climb mins (ft)	Total Time	Average Speed
3 (65kts)	3	50	31 (9,283)	81	74.1kph
4 (70kts)	3	46.5	33.5 (10,066)	80	75kph
3 (65kts)	4	50	23 (9,283)	73	82.2kph
4 (70kts)	4	46.5	25 (10,066)	71.5	83.9kph

Table 13.5

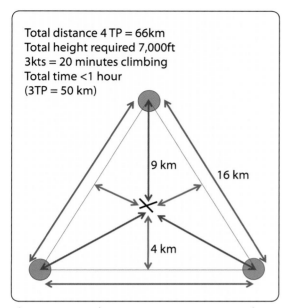

Total distance 4 TP = 66km
Total height required 7,000ft
3kts = 20 minutes climbing
Total time <1 hour
(3TP = 50 km)

9 km

16 km

4 km

Fig 13.5 A simple cross-country training task.

position so that you start as high as allowable, with excess speed if possible and with the shortest flight distance to the good line at maximum weight.

You can easily gain a minute just by making a good start. If you are trying to practise a short task at a high speed, the timing of your start becomes much more critical than on a long task.

Skills that you can learn or practise from this fixed course exercise include:

► Maintaining a thermal core.
► Feel throughout the flight envelope.
► Vario response to thermal gusts.
► Slower rate of roll with full aileron.
► Potential of slower climb rates.
► Technique for accelerating for a good start.
► Use of higher block speeds.
► String deflections at different speeds.
► Pulling up harder to achieve thermal core.

Centre of gravity

Consider the centre of gravity of a glider in the cruise. A simplistic view is that if the elevator is in an up position it is pulling the tail down to maintain the balance of forces. The glider is also producing trim drag (generating lift) and additional profile drag. Worse than this is the fact

that the tailplane is generating lift *downwards* as shown in *Fig 13.6*. If on the other hand, by putting weight in the fin the elevator is neutral or even fractionally down, then the whole tail plane is producing a lift vector upwards and you have just relieved the wings from an unnecessary additional load. Most importantly though, the additional leverage that you have with a more effective up elevator allows you the ability to turn tighter, without running out of elevator authority on the up stop. Of course the potential to stall will now occur at a lesser elevator deflection. So moving the centre of gravity backwards gives greater elevator authority.

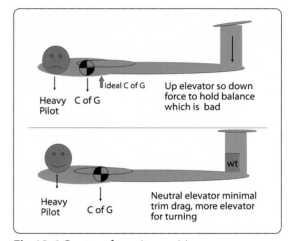

Fig 13.6 Centre of gravity positions.

Speed versus AoB

Table 13.6 on page 150 gives the turn radius achieved for a given speed and angle of bank. The radius of turn (R) can be computed using a simple formula and is equal to the velocity squared (V^2) divided by 37, times the tangent of the bank angle.

Radius = $V^2 \div 37 \times$ tangent of bank angle
Radius at 50kts and a 45°AoB (tan 45° = 1)
R = (50 × 50) ÷ (37 × 1)
R = 67.5m

This could be put in a graph to be more accurate but there is no point in chasing such accuracy as we need to fly by feel rather than with our eyes glued to the ASI. The shaded cells show a turn radius of around 55m, therefore a diameter of 110m, which is the maximum that we would wish to fly for effective thermalling in modern gliders. You can see that all of these shaded numbers have the same AoB as speed.

KEY POINT An easy rule to remember is to match the speed to the angle of bank (45°AoB at 45kts, 60°AoB at 60kts).

Having got the target numbers then we need to be practical and see if we can do better in the real world and relate to the air currents within a thermal.

Turn radius (m) using various speeds and AoB

	40kts	45kts	50kts	55kts	60kts	65kts
35	61.7	78.1	96.4	116.6	138.8	162.9
40	51.5	65.2	80.4	97.3	115.8	136.0
45	43.2	54.7	67.5	81.7	97.2	114.1
50	36.3	45.9	56.6	68.5	81.6	95.7
55	30.2	38.3	47.3	57.2	68.1	79.9
60	24.9	31.6	39.0	47.2	56.1	65.9

Table 13.6

Basic aerodynamics

There is a clear need to clarify some basic aerodynamics, which in many publications is misleading. The rudder does turn the glider and don't believe anyone who thinks differently. This is one reason why most powered aircraft have a rudder trim to counter yaw, so that straight flight with the wings level remains straight. The lateral angle of attack of the fuselage generated by flying out of balance produces a sideways force (lift) and the glider or aircraft continues to turn, albeit slowly. It's how you steer bombs. If you are still not convinced consider this. In gliders, whenever we deliberately sideslip, the turning caused by the wings being banked is countered by applying rudder in the opposite direction. Lift generated by the fuselage also generates drag which at first glance might appear to be a bad thing for us.

Our turn radius is controlled by our angle of bank and speed. Unlike a jet aircraft, however, which has an abundance of power, if we increase the AoB to reduce the turn radius we increase our rate of descent. Flying as slowly as possible will give us minimum turn radius but there is a limit. As we increase our bank we have to increase speed to increase the lift on the wings by pulling back and we get to a point on most gliders where we simply can't turn any tighter because the elevator is being held fully up or we are encountering the stall.

It is worth pointing out that any aircraft will stall when the wing reaches its critical angle of attack; this is achieved by pulling the stick back. Because we can pull the stick back at any speed and any attitude, we can therefore stall (and spin for that matter) at any speed and at any attitude, if the elevator is sufficiently powerful.

Another important aspect as to why we need to keep the turn radius tight is because of the effect of the outflow of air from the centre of the thermal core, as shown in *Fig 13.7*, which in turn makes our turn radius larger and into a weaker track of lift than it would otherwise be. This is a permanent drift outwards, if you will. It is significant because the central core, where we are trying to stay, is the strongest part of any thermal.

There are other aerodynamic considerations. Lateral stability is built into the design by a combination of dihedral, chord profile and

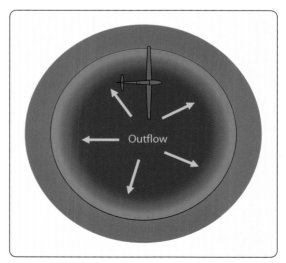

Fig 13.7 Outflow from the core.

sweep at the tips. When a glider sideslips the AoA of the inboard wing increases whilst that of the trailing one decreases. Sweep means that the inboard wing meets the airflow more directly whilst at the trailing wing the sweep is increased. These changes in the lift produced can result in a rolling motion towards level flight. The designer will try to ensure that in balanced flight we feel turbulence on the elevator (pre-stall buffet) as we approach the stall. Also, the centre section will approach the stall before the rest of the wing, reducing the risk of wing drop at the stall. In any turn the inside wing will always be at a higher angle of attack and flying slower than your ASI suggests. The inside wing AoA will increase further in any strong thermal upward gust. In a significant sideslip the pre-stall buffet might occur at the same time as the tip stalls, resulting in minimal warning of an impending stall and perhaps if ignored, a spin.

Consider a 26m wingspan glider turning at 45°AoB with an indicated speed of 50kts. The inside wing will be tracking a turn radius of 9.2m less than the fuselage, the outside wing similarly farther. The fuselage will track a radius of 67.5m and the inside wing tip 58.3m. The speed of the inside wing tip is 43kts and getting close to the stall because of the additional AoA that it has, not just because of the speed.

Wasted opportunity whilst climbing

Imagine climbing in your thermal with 45°AoB and 45–55kts in perfect balanced flight. Will this really give you the best rate of climb? Well the answer is categorically *no!* In a turn keeping the string straight actually has the rest of the glider in a small sideslip which is producing lift off the fuselage, downwards. This in itself is a bad thing. If our turn radius is around 60m the distance from the string to the centre of pressure on the wing is about 2m. The 1 in 60 rule means that our sideslip is currently 2°. This is initially so small as to be unimportant. To be a purist, we therefore need the string to be pointing to the high wing by 2°, but can we do better?

On a normal 300km day we need about 30,000ft of climb. If we climb just 5% faster, so 4kts becomes 4.2kts on every thermal, then we

save 1,500ft of climbing time. This results in completing the task about 4 minutes faster (or 12km farther down track in the same time). Before we can look at how we can climb faster it is worth considering the various aerofoil sections and how they have changed.

The first section is typical of what we would normally consider to be a classic aerofoil

Fig 13.8 Conventional Bernoulli section.

wing section.

A more efficient chord profile is called *super critical*. The point of maximum thickness has been moved back to delay and reduce the area of

Fig 13.9 Super critical section.

turbulent flow, thus reducing drag.

Finally we see the latest section used on modern high speed racing gliders. The bottom of the wing section has been made as flat as possible to achieve as much flat plate lift (Newton's law), minimising the Venturi effect (Bernoulli) yet

Fig 13.10 Modern Newton section.

keeping the point of maximum thickness towards the trailing edge.

Of course in all the good text books regarding flying aircraft and gliders there is considerable emphasis on flying in balanced flight, and if we only consider the lift produced by the wing in still air this does give best performance. Gliding in a thermal, however, requires a new look at the way we can optimise the energy available because the strongest energy is in the middle of the thermal and therefore requires a minimum radius turn. This means a slow speed and high angle of bank, but with excessive bank angles we lose lift in the vertical plane.

Use of flaps

Firstly, consider the purpose of flap settings. There are usually 6 settings for flaps on gliders:

▶ High speed (> 90kts).
▶ Moderate speeds (70–90kts).
▶ Best glide speed (also a thermalling setting).
▶ Thermalling.
▶ Tighter thermalling/heavier/higher.
▶ Land (drag).

As we progressively increase the flap the maximum glide performance reduces and the rate of descent increases. The point is that when using positive flap the speed that the glider can be flown at reduces. Although there is a loss of pure performance, the ability to turn with a significantly tighter radius allows us to use the stronger core and ultimately climb faster.

In the guide shown in *Fig 13.11* there are 3 thermal flap settings:

Flap setting	Glide angle	RoD
1 – Best glide speed	55 : 1 at 50kts	0.9kt
2 – Thermalling	45 : 1 at 45kts	1.0kt
3 – Tighter thermalling	36 : 1 at 40kts	1.1kt

Best speed to fly at 45° AoB is 1.2 x straight flight	45kts	50kts	55kts	60kts
	54.7	67.5	81.7	97.3

45kts x 1.2 = 54kts
40kts x 1.2 = 48kts

Fig 13.11 Some details and a guide showing the change in Performance using Flaps.

So far so good, but just consider the aerofoil sections in *Fig 13.12*. Where do they come from? Have you seen them before anywhere? You may be surprised to know that the bottom shape is the approximate horizontal profile of a *Janus, Duo Discus* or *Arcus* fuselage at 45° AoB.

No doubt you will have seen aircraft fly past on a knife edge either at an air show or the Red Bull

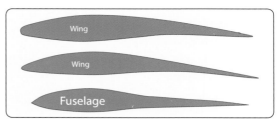

Fig 13.12 Aerofoils.

racers on television flying through the towers. The angle of bank is 90° so what keeps them up? It is quite simply the lift generated from the fuselage. The fuselage is held, using the rudder, at a positive angle of attack to the horizon. Jets have to fly quite fast to ensure adequate control authority and will have a minimum speed at which they can safely fly this manoeuvre whilst propeller aircraft can fly more slowly as they can blow an increased airflow over the rudder.

It is clear that holding the fuselage at a positive angle of attack will produce lift but the real benefit is that it allows you to fly slower in a steep turn. This gives the ability to turn tighter which we must do, otherwise there is no point in doing it due to the increase in drag. In the cockpit this means that the nose attitude will be high and the string will be towards the high wing, as shown in *Fig 13.13* and that the ideal would be achieved with the fuselage close to 15° AoA to the

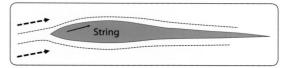

Fig 13.13 The airflow over the fuselage producing lift in the vertical.

horizontal. The stall speed at 45°AoB increases by a factor of 1.19 from the straight and level stall speed, simplistically a 20% increase.

Flying with water is largely beneficial when we are able to climb quickly. Whilst heavier, however, stall speed and thermalling speeds increase, so turn radius increases and climb rates slow. So if we fly a heavy *Duo* in straight flight and the stall speed is 43kts, the stall speed will go up to 52kts in a 45°AoB turn. *Table 13.7* shows the turn radii for flying 50, 55 and 60kts. You can see that there is a huge increase in radius as speed increases. As the AoB is increased the fuselage presents an increased percentage area to the thermal compared to the wings. At 45°AoB the surface area of the wings to the vertical has reduced by about a third and so in simple terms the RoD will increase. If fuselage lift can replace some of the lost wing lift in the vertical plane, the speed required to fly in the turn will reduce and as a consequence turn radius will reduce and

Relationship between turn radius and speed			
	50kts	55kts	60kts
Turn Radius at 45°AoB	67.5m	81.7m	97.2m

Table 13.7

the climb rate will increase. You can see from *Table 13.7* that a 10% increase of speed gives about a 20% increase in turn radius.

So the question is how much slip should we use? This depends on a few things but a simple

Photo 13.1 To be, or not to be in balance?

rule of thumb is the tighter you turn (the fuselage is more on its side) and the stronger the thermal, the greater the benefit.

To find out the amount of sideslip required, on a smooth flat day at a sensible height, simply fly straight and identify the stall speed. Then, keeping the wings level with aileron, monitor the increased rate of descent on the vario averager as you fly more and more out of balance. The point at which significant sideways lift is being produced

by the fuselage will be obvious and it will be the same right or left. Note the string deflection. As slip increases, the RoD will increase and you may even hear the airflow break away from the fuselage. Now practise turning using 45°AoB at slower than normal speeds with the string held towards the top wing, as shown in *Photo 13.1*, but also recognise that if you reduce the slip, the stall symptoms may start to reveal themselves. It is handling on the limits of efficiency that you are practising. Whilst thermalling you are unlikely to be holding this attitude for great periods of time. More likely you will hold it briefly to make a short advantage in the climb. Of course large gusty thermals may present some difficulties in staying centred, which is usually more important

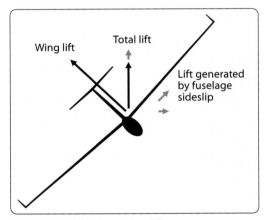

Fig 13.14 Sideslip giving lift.

than optimizing the moment, and you need to be very proficient at doing this before sharing a thermal in close proximity to another glider.

Fig 13.14 shows the additional lift (in red) generated by the fuselage whilst the glider is being held in a sideslip. You can also see in *Fig 13.15 on page 154* how a strong surge hitting the fin and rudder will force the nose down. This can be most efficiently countered by using top rudder as well as elevator. However, it is the rudder that is most useful because you will often find that you are already at full back stick.

So with all this in mind as you enter a thermal, as the speed reduces towards the end of the pull up and you roll, allow the glider to slide out of balance by using too little rudder. Quite often if you roll in using full aileron, full rudder is

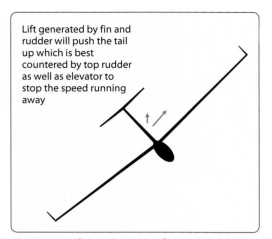

Lift generated by fin and rudder will push the tail up which is best countered by top rudder as well as elevator to stop the speed running away

Fig 13.15 Lift produced by fin and rudder.

insufficient to balance the entry so this happens naturally. This means that you finish entering the turn under-ruddered and then maintain this mild out of balance, even during the initial centring of the core. As long as there is a significant angle of bank the lift generated by the fuselage is beneficial.

However, there is one immediate problem, as indicated in *Fig 13.16*. If you are carrying water in the wings and the tanks are not full then a significant lateral out of balance will occur with a tendency to roll towards the lower wing. As you reduce the speed this effect will become more significant until you may even have full aileron towards the top wing just to maintain a steady bank angle, reducing the wing efficiency. When this situation arises it now becomes up to you to identify the priorities of flying faster, continuing to fly out of balance, flying in balance or whether you still need the water.

Finally, it must be pointed out that to dump water in a thermal on top of other gliders using your thermal is not polite and remember that your registration is clearly visible—you will get shouted at!

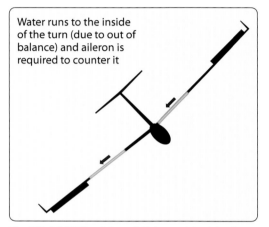

Water runs to the inside of the turn (due to out of balance) and aileron is required to counter it

Fig 13.16 Difficulties of flying with sideslip and half-full of water.

14
Flying the task

For the whole route I had been going cautiously—too cautiously and too slow. Getting behind the required speed when the day is decidedly weak is simply not a good strategy. I had been drifting back in weak thermals, sometimes as high as 1,200 ft, being blown back towards the finish line at Booker, essentially from field to golf course, to field etc. Somewhere around 19:00 near Henley on Thames I called the finish line to pack up as I would be landing out.

The sports fields within the boundary of a large mansion looked fine, and they were. Having vacated the cockpit a huge guy danced down the gentle slope towards me. He was too big for me to question his gait, but as he straddled the fuselage and started shouting "hi ho silver" and started to kick the sides like riding a horse, something had to be said. I made some loud comments after which he ran off. Children of some of the staff who worked there explained that I had in fact landed at the local adult mental hospital and I noticed for the first time the high wire fencing. Understandably this was not at all what I had been expecting. I played rounders for a while with the children who then guarded my shiny machine, a deal brokered by them. I then went off to find a phone.

"Hi Booker control, it is me and I am at some hospital".

"Gosh are you all right?"

"Ah yes, sorry—not that kind of hospital!"

With no mentor perhaps the first two decisions you have to make when setting your task is where to go and how far. Always task for the weather window and, when flying, be prepared to cut the task short if the weather forecast was unduly optimistic. There is no issue planning to go twice around the same or similar triangle if for any reason you don't wish to venture too far from home. However, you must always plan your route via the best weather areas on the day and not just fly on a route which you believe will be easier simply because you have flown it before. Additionally, far more will be learned from flying a 100km in a variety of weather than a 300km in simple weather.

Work cycle management

A very effective method of decision making is to plan the next event (thermal, TP) and look as far as you can reasonably see ahead to make decisions on climbing, pressing on or landing. To glide cross-country the period of the soarable window is always the absolute limitation and so the art of work cycle management is a skill which must be learnt, as it allows you to cope with everything in a managed way.

ANALOGY **A game of chess.** With chess we can see and anticipate several moves ahead, perhaps with a view to defending our position or maybe with an aggressive, attacking plan in mind. But then when our opponent makes their next move our plan often has to be modified in the light of the new position.

As with the chess analogy, it is a case of identifying what the priorities are at any one time and recognizing that these priorities can change quite rapidly. This should not interfere with your own gliding performance or stress you out. For example, flying from your local site with a 1,200 ft winch launch leaves you with 400 ft to do whatever you like, still ensuring to get back to high key at 800 ft for a safe landing. If you take an aero-tow to 2,000 ft you have 1,200 ft to play with but still plan to get to high key at the required height quite calmly. Once you connect with a thermal your attention to getting home is ignored, whilst you can now concentrate on the climb. Whilst climbing on your own you can spend more time devoted to any activity, even having a drink, whereas if you are climbing adjacent to another glider, spacing assumes a high degree of priority.

Decision making in gliding essentially can be split into two distinct types. The need for a fast decision and immediate action (measure once and cut) versus the carefully considered decision for the best (continuously re-measure the situation many times and then when you are certain about the decision, cut).

Immediate decisions

There are very few immediate decisions that have to be made whilst flying gliders. One critical decision is "do I climb in this thermal?" Total transit time through the thermal is 6 seconds, after 3 seconds you are in the middle yet it takes 2 seconds to pile on the bank so actually you have about 1 second to decide to use it or lose it. Dithering costs time.

Considered decisions

As you climb up you have several minutes to decide where you are going next and at what speed and on which route. The major decisions will simply relate to where you want to go (navigation), how you are going to get there (your interpretation of the weather ahead) and where you are going to land. Split in this way nothing becomes a surprising crisis because you have already worked out your next three chess moves. However, rather like chess, the weather is a fickle opponent.

Although you are climbing in a strong thermal, you might feel the need to rush off full of enthusiasm. Is this justified and has the day really got better? If you subsequently bounce several safe thermals but as a result have to accept a weak climb, then this decision to press hard was obviously not a good one. The result could be worse as you are now so low that you have run out of all options and perhaps your current thermal is dying. In other words, when the weather appears

solid ahead just make sure that you do not burn your bridges.

Considered decision making involves a plan 'A' but always leaves available an option for plan 'B'. The inevitable exception is the final decision to land rather than to try to stay airborne.

If you are high and the weather is genuinely good ahead, you can then comfortably prioritize on making good speed. A bouncy level of turbulence en route indicates an active sky, which will support your decision. However, if the air becomes smooth, strong conditions are either only local or generally subsiding and there is a need to adjust your strategy.

Pushing for thermals over an area which has a large number of fields good enough to land in is far less stressful than blindly flying to a hilly and rocky area with nowhere to land should you not climb away. A quick glance ahead whilst thermalling maximises your options and enables you to select a route and the best line. Strange as it might first appear, once at height with a long way to go to your next thermal, the decision making process becomes more difficult because there is so much time for things to change before you get to the area that you thought looked good. The number of options available will reduce the farther you decide to glide, and of course the weather has much more time to change. The number of times you will find that you need to actively change your decisions usually increases with increasing cloud base.

There are other decisions which may have to be made when things do not go to plan. For example, having made a decision to stop and turn suppose that you can't find the certain 5kt thermal that you are convinced is there. How long do you continue searching, losing time and height, before you make the decision to press on? How might you have got it wrong? Have you outclimbed the bubble? Did you turn the wrong way? Are you having difficulty because you knocked the TE off? Or, having bounced a strong thermal you decide after only a minute (that's 2 or 3km on) that actually the options ahead are no longer looking good and you do need to turn back and use it?

And then there is the calamity situation where the route on track is decidedly rubbish with a lot of rain and you have to do a massive 90° detour to just survive, or divert to land somewhere known to be safe. Or do you turn back completely?

Generally, a gliding task can be split into three main areas: climbing; cruising; and the field landing or final glide. As daunting as decision making might sound, you may be surprised to find that in general, operating from your home site, this is a routine that you have already learnt and it only needs a small amount of adjusting to cover all other areas of managing your cross-country gliding decision making.

Whilst flying at your home field on a local soaring flight you are maintaining your climb whilst monitoring where you are drifting, where the airfield is and where you will go to connect with your next thermal. At the same time you are ensuring that all of this does not detract from your ability to make the best use of the thermal you are in, whilst also maintaining an adequate lookout. You never realised that you have been doing so much, did you?

Thermalling decisions

In the past simply flying within your comfort zone at home, track was invariably somewhere to get upwind of the field and then identify a thermal to go for. In other words you played the short game. Going cross-country means that you have to think a little farther ahead, but actually you still play a series of short games.

An established thermalling turn takes about 20 seconds within which a number of tasks must be routinely accomplished: maintaining the thermal centre; looking out down track where we want to go; cooperating with other gliders within our own thermal and achieving an adequate awareness of changing situations. As you are turning there is normally no benefit in moving your head excessively in the cockpit. Simply look across to the horizon on the inside of the turn and monitor the areas and tracks of interest and do your own time-lapse of the clouds whilst listening to the audio vario and responding by feel to the thermal core.

It is now time to plan the next short game. Look at not just the next cloud but the string of clouds which are aligned to the general direction in which you want to go. It will also involve looking

at the terrain ahead as either good or poor thermal sources or good landable fields if you can't reach an acceptable airfield.

The climb itself is split into three phases: the entry where time is concentrated on centring; the established climb and, finally, preparation to exit and go.

Thermal entry

As you enter the thermal (plan 'A') you must also consider the exit (plan 'B'). Confirm the visual features which you can use to ensure that if you reject the thermal then you know immediately where to point and where your next climb might be. This might be required after the waffling 'S' turn. Joining other gliders in a thermal makes centring easy whilst the important aspect is to simply slot in. If you are on your own you can concentrate on identifying that the thermal is one that you want to use and centre as you feel necessary because you have total flexibility to manoeuvre.

Established climb

In the established climb the balance is to climb as quickly as you can in the thermal that you are in whilst identifying the track ahead and maintaining a good lookout. The climb is aided by the audio vario, string and feel. The skill of improving your feel is easily practised by covering the vario indication to stop you visually referring to it—small adhesive notepaper is useful for this. The biggest risk is of unseen gliders coming towards you at high speeds whilst you are in fact more interested in where you are going. Another area of concern is if there are powered aircraft around. In these cases, as with the gliders, you must assume they have not seen you. Also, look for thermalling gliders on your planned track. Analyse the cloud and these gliders' progress before setting off. If you have two unique visual features to help you with track orientation, such as a town, lake, large wood or hilltop then it is quite easy to identify your track. Just try to ensure that you don't set off 180° from where you are supposed to be going. It has been done before even with GPS systems installed.

Check the clouds down route using a *time-lapse* process, perhaps identifying two optional routes and notice how the sky is changing with each turn. So in effect you are reviewing the information that you need to know about your next leg every 20 seconds and this will help in making the necessary decisions.

Thermal exit

Just prior to leaving your thermal you will have a good idea of your planned route, with a confidence factor. Lower down in the climb you will be able to see the clouds down track but near cloud base this is not possible and you will have to use the cloud shadows. Use the height of cloud tops relative to the height of the one you are climbing under to help to anticipate the next thermal's strength. Five turns before setting off consider the following points and bear in mind that it takes about 20 seconds to do a turn and if you are climbing at 6kts then this process starts about 1,000ft before you exit the thermal:

▶ 5 turns to go pick 2 ground features for track, one near and one far.
▶ 4 turns to go, using the far ground feature as a reference, pick 2 energy lines which could be taken.
▶ 3 turns to go, identify the best route considering the crosswind and the most number of thermal options.
▶ 2 turns to go, confirm your route using cloud shadows.
▶ 1 turn to go, look for gliders on your chosen route.

Care will be needed to ensure that as you accelerate away that you don't enter cloud unprepared and that you don't cut in front of other gliders who might be on the outside of your turn. Also, you need to make sure to set off on the correct heading and at the correct speed. Once clear of the cloud, check there is no high cirrus or spread-out shadows, which will dampen the instability and make the thermals ahead weaker than anticipated. Settled in the cruise, immediately look for small beneficial detours, perhaps wisps that you did not see before, but essentially stick with the plan. If flying behind another glider consider wandering 100m left or right to avoid their obvious sinking spot, or

towards his line if he is climbing relative to you. If you do consciously detour though, you must complete the detour or you will simply have flown through a bad area of air with no benefit. Although there will often be more than one workable option, it is better to be decisive on a route that is working than be indecisive and keep switching routes.

A blue day

The decisions required to exit a thermal on a blue day are similar to those made on cloudy days. Thermals will always weaken as they approach the inversion (the height of an inversion, just like cloud bases, can vary locally) and they are always bubbles being generated by ground hotspots. Therefore, it is important to search for ground features. However, the very strongest thermals may break the inversion and appear as little wisps, so look for these. The following is a guide to exiting a thermal on a blue day:

▶ 4 turns to go (before the inversion top), pick 2 visual ground features for track, one near and one far.
▶ 3 turns to go, pick 2 energy lines which could be taken to get you to your next thermal source and really look at the wind, possible street lines and ground sources to get you to your next anticipated thermal.
▶ 2 turns to go, pick the best route.
▶ 1 turn to go, look for gliders on your chosen route.

The cruise

So back to that speed thing again! In the early years of gliding there was a simple rule of thumb for the speed to fly. Go down as fast as you go up. So if the vario read 3 up for the majority of the climb, you would fly a speed en route which gave you 3 down. So one would spend an equal amount of time climbing as cruising.

With the development of better gliders and a desire to achieve winning performances MacCready refined this basic rule, with each glider having a bespoke MacCready ring to suit its specific polar curve. Then John Williams went further and invented the JW calculator which also made allowances for headwinds and tailwinds on a final glide circular slide rule. As a result, information was available to the pilot for the perfect solution for wind and cruise speed versus climb rate to achieve the highest possible average speed along a leg.

MacCready and JW made some obvious assumptions: a theoretical uniform sky and a constant achieved rate of climb from joining the thermal to leaving it. There is no allowance for ditherers or the fact that some glider pilots can't sustain an effective rate of climb so for this reason only the gross achieved climb rate can be used.

Consider the following scenario: Pilot A climbs at 2kts, pilot B in an identical glider in the same thermal climbs at 4kts yet pilot C in an identical glider in the same thermal climbs at 6kts. Each pilot will fly the appropriate speed for his own achieved climb rate but the actual thermal strength was 6kts. How or why these climb rates differ is of little significance, the achieved climb rates are different and pilot A has a lot to learn about thermalling. It is of no consequence as to why the climb is slow, other than the fact that pilot A can't call the thermal a 6kt thermal when they only climbed at 2kts.

You have already seen that slightly inaccurate speed control will only give about a 5% loss and is therefore much less important than your routing. Of course the continued logic is that if the actual speed is not too significant, what is the point of chasing dolphin? Speed to fly really is the least important of your decisions.

In the early part of the cruise you should have an opportunity to relax, ideally with three good climbing options ahead. The only flying that has to be done is to keep pointing to the next cloud or thermal or TP at the chosen in-trim block speed. As a result this is an opportunity to review all of your options including the general weather to the side and the cruise to the TP ahead. If your next leg is coming back on yourself in some way then review the sky and cloud development in that direction.

Before turning have a good look down the next leg. The cloud and thermal structure may be just the same but on the new leg they will appear

different simply because of the angle from which you are now looking at them, as shown in *Fig 14.1*.

Fig 14.1 Clouds can look quite different from different angles.

A choice of routes

Consider the three different routes in *Fig 14.2*.

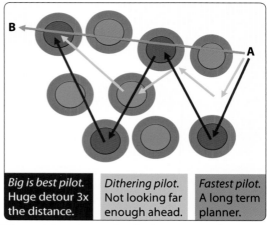

Fig 14.2 Routing A–B, which route to take?

► Dark Blue route—This line only uses the strongest thermals (that is what we have often been told to do). The track is 3 times the direct track and is obviously not the fastest.

► Amber route—Here the pilot sets off for a strong cloud but when closer has a change of mind and heads for a better looking cloud. Again, en route another change of mind and another re-route, eventually having to climb at 2kts simply because this is the first core he hits. The pilot eventually makes it to **B** but has considered it difficult.

► Light Blue route—Having considered the various options there is a plan. Although the first cloud is likely to be a weak thermal it is en route and leads to stronger thermals and it is all on track.

Losses due to flying a poor route can mean your advanced glider achieves the performance of a basic machine. For example, a 15% loss on an *LS4* would mean that the original glide angle of 40:1 becomes 34:1, which is little better than a *K21*.

Cruise decisions

As an aside, adjacent cloud and cloud streets sometimes *look* better than the one you are under, so remember to avoid dithering and flying an amber route as in *Fig 14.2*. Also, the inversion is not necessarily a fixed value and it can change several hundred feet from one climb to the next. Anticipate the inversion top but don't give up too early. It could be that you are returning to a lowering inversion as the day starts to cool down and all subsequent opportunity to climb high will not be available. Alternatively, you might be in one of the few thermals that breaks through the inversion and you might climb a couple of thousand feet higher.

Occasionally on blue days you can get cloud wisps. If you do, it is often worth climbing higher and accepting the lower rate of climb because the visibility at the top improves and you can see the next wisp and therefore the strongest thermals ahead. Once you sink back down into the inversion though, they won't be visible any more so fly accurate GPS tracks.

Remember that to achieve any large distances flying cross-country in the UK's limited soaring window we need to achieve high average speeds and not just fly in a constant survival mode. It is more important to *never fly too slow in sink* than to fly too fast in lift. Street flying allows high average speeds and is really useful when there is a 10–20kts of wind to penetrate, therefore the glider needs to be at maximum weight to optimise any into-wind legs (the glider will fly farther at a high speed if heavy) and ballast must be entered in the vario system for the correct polar curve.

Fly a constant speed to your next anticipated thermal. Flying slower than the block speed limits will incur a reduction in overall cruise speed whilst flying much too fast will be decidedly penalizing. The block speed to be flown can simply be obtained from the polar curves and then converted into a table for reference whilst flying.

With modern instruments, when we dial in the anticipated or achieved average rate of climb they indicate the block speed to be flown. The best speed to fly, however, is dictated by the strength of the next thermal and the current climb may not be an accurate guide. Weaker weather ahead means you must slow down. Equally, whilst the next thermal may well be strong, it may be so far away that you have to cruise slower to reach it. Climb rates must include all parts of searching turns. Wasted turns are exactly that.

Finally, watch out for sea breezes, spread-out, blue gaps, high cirrus and contrails spreading out. These all cool the day and as the sun goes down high cloud 100 miles to the west can soon kill the day early. Keep updating your mental picture of the sky and how the day is developing.

Considerations

Get high and stay high is a commonly held view and advice often given for early cross-country pilots. However, although this might be good advice on a particular day it is not always true and can be unhelpful. For example, the thermals might weaken at height so in this case the technique would be safe, but slow. You must adapt for the conditions on the day.

No doubt you will have heard of the guidance to *set 4kts on the MacCready above 4,000ft, reduce it to 3kts above 3,000ft, 2kts above 2,000ft and zero below 2,000ft*. In my opinion this also makes no sense, especially as at 5,000ft you get a 9% advantage on true airspeed, so 80kts IAS is actually 87kts TAS. Down at 2,000ft 80kts IAS is only 83kts TAS.

Remember that every time you move the stick or rudder you are using energy, either loss of height or loss of speed. The loss of smooth laminar flow decreases wing efficiency and increases interference drag. These effects are rarely considered.

Whilst the LX does give an indication of the wind speed and direction, it does not relate this information to the height required for the task (except on the final glide). The height required to complete the task is therefore only accurate if there is no wind. The LX will only give you the speed to fly as set by the MacCready value in nil wind plus any ballast and bug inputs. Therefore, there might be an advantage to increase block speed when into-wind and fly a little slower downwind.

Often in the UK getting or staying high is not an option and it is more likely a necessity. Good weather usually provides strong thermals and high-speed cruises for at least some of the time. Even then there may be sticky patches which demand a slow down or a change of gear. It is one of the additional challenges of doing the sport in the UK. At times decision making can be simple despite the challenges, with aggressive flying being successful. On the other hand, it can be a constant trial to avoid showers and combat the strong winds.

In weak conditions with a low cloud base the decision to stay as high as possible is easy as we can't go very far before hitting the ground. Fortunately, the thermals will be close together and the key is to keep pushing on with the smoothest touch on the stick at all times, often flying slightly faster than the best glide speed. The advantage of using slightly stronger thermals by detouring is important.

Whenever possible set off with three options to climb ahead. Look for wisps developing and the firmness of the leading edges of clouds. The higher the individual cloud base, the stronger the thermal is, or was, underneath. Bigger gaps between stronger thermals, controlled by the sinking air, means the thermal might die before you get there and it could be a long way to the next one.

Detours

Routing far off track will incur time penalties. Provided we remain within 30° of planned track the penalties are manageable. For a detour of 45° to take a single thermal, the thermal strength needs to be about twice as strong as one on track. Whenever possible we must smooth off the detours so that the benefit of re-routing through good air is maximised. Always check your flying track with the required track.

During cross-wind legs it is always worth searching for thermals that are *upwind* so that if you find a thermal you will drift back towards

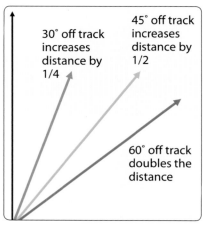

Fig 14.3 Off track penalties (nil wind).

track as you climb. For example, with 15kts of crosswind and cruising at 90kts you could lay off around 10° into-wind and search for thermals within 30° of this new track (not heading), as shown in *Fig 14.4*. If you are cruising slower, say at 60kts, then lay off slightly more.

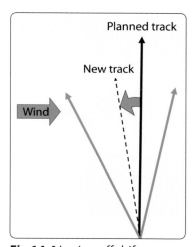

Fig 14.4 Laying off drift.

Significant single detours or a series of individual detours can often cost more than remaining on track. On every occasion it is worthwhile making the effort to have a long term planned route which gives the smoothest detour angles as far as possible as shown in *Fig 14.5*. Look well ahead, ideally as far as the TP to plan the best line.

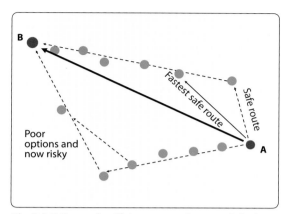

Fig 14.5 Smooth off detour angles to minimise lost time.

Turn points

There is a simple rule that states you should turn high at downwind TPs and low at into-wind TPs but this is often not fully understood. Before reading on, can you answer the following questions:

▶ When would you reject a 5kt thermal for a 3kt thermal on planned track?
▶ When would you stay with a 3kt thermal when you know that there is a 5kt thermal that you can reach ahead on planned track?

To answer these questions we need to consider how the wind will affect our progress. Flying at 60kts, for every 6kts of headwind you must climb 10% higher to achieve the same glide over the ground. Similarly if you are cruising downwind you need to climb 10% less. In total there is a 20% difference in the height required, and this will be more if the wind is stronger.

If the wind is 6kts then a 5kt thermal into-wind is as effective as a 4kt thermal downwind.
If the wind is 12kts then a 5kt thermal into-wind is as effective as a 3kt thermal downwind.
If the wind is 18kts then a 5kt thermal into-wind is as effective as a 2kt thermal downwind.

Of course in these simple examples no allowance has been made for the fact that as you climb you also drift, meaning that the situation is even more in favour of the downwind case and

that there is a bigger penalty when flying into-wind. This means for the 20% difference in height required the wind will be closer to 5kts, rather than 6kts!

So, let's come back to our two questions. If you are flying into a 10kt *headwind* and have the opportunity to use a 5kt thermal but there is a 3kt thermal on your next downwind leg, it might be more efficient to push on and bounce the 5kt thermal. Alternatively, if you are able to use a 3kt thermal drifting towards your *downwind* TP then it might also make sense to stick with it, until you are as high as possible. Using the same analysis, a weaker thermal drifting downwind towards a TP will be more effective than a similar thermal on a *cross-wind* leg.

Table 14.1 shows a brief summary of how downwind thermals compare to upwind ones. In summary, the strongest thermals might not be the strongest *effective* thermals.

The effective value of upwind and downwind thermals		
Wind strength	Upwind thermals	Equivalent downwind thermals
5	5	4
10	5	3
15	5	2
20	5	1

Table 14.1

KEY POINT Thermals on downwind legs do not need to be as strong as those on upwind legs.

Downwind turn points

For downwind TPs make sure that you are as high as you can be if your next track is upwind or cross-wind. Ideally, climb so that as you drift into the TP you reach the maximum height that you can (cloud base or airspace permitting) before setting off on the next leg. If you have reached your maximum height *before* the TP, you can bounce the same thermal (by briefly reversing track) before then accelerating onto the next track.

In *Fig 14.6*, although the first TP has a downwind component the second one has a bigger one so it is fine to go around the first one low. It is the furthest downwind TP where you need to be as high as possible.

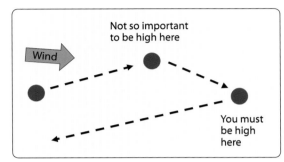

Fig 14.6 Downwind TPs.

Upwind turn points

The obvious theoretical solution is to be as low as possible at the turn so that the minimum amount of time is not wasted on the slower into-wind leg. Perhaps equally important is the speed you fly along the into-wind leg to get to the TP. I fly it as a final glide with the intention to hit the TP at a particular height. In *task mode* the LX does not make any correction for the winds but shows you the calculated wind separately, only showing the height required for the remainder of the task with the set MacCready (plus bug and weight) speed to fly. You can set *turn point mode* in the TP screen so that the LX will now calculate the effect of the wind. For this you must set the MacCready for the *speed* you wish to fly. Remember though, if you do this there is no account for the ½ km circle to indicate that you have now achieved the TP and no audio that you have entered the barrel.

Why is speed rather than thermal strength more important? In part because the thermal strength after the turn is so much more effective on the downwind leg. Secondly, because height lost flying faster will be easily offset by the time saved and possibly because less height will be lost regardless. The following is an *exaggerated* example for an into-wind TP:

Consider a wind of 45kts and just 2nm (4km) to go to the TP. (I have flown a standard class nationals with a 45kts wind at 5,000ft.) Best glide (zero MacCready) is about 50kts but that

gives a 5kts groundspeed, therefore it would take 24 minutes to reach the TP, *giving a height loss of about 2,400ft.*

At 55kts (groundspeed now 10kts) it takes 12 minutes.
At 60kts (groundspeed now 15kts) it takes 8 minutes.
At 65kts (groundspeed now 20kts) it takes 6 minutes.
At 70kts (groundspeed now 25kts) it takes 5 minutes.
At 75kts (groundspeed now 30kts) it takes 4 minutes.

So, at 75kts there is a height loss of only 800ft!

Now consider a more normal wind of 20kts with 6nm (12km) to go to the TP. Best glide might be 50kts but that gives a 30kts groundspeed which would take 12 minutes to reach the TP. *That is a height loss of about 1,200ft.*

At 55kts (groundspeed now 35kts) it takes 10:30 minutes.
At 60kts (groundspeed now 40kts) it takes 9 minutes.
At 65kts (groundspeed now 45kts) it takes 8 minutes.
At 70kts (groundspeed now 50kts) it takes 7 minutes.
At 80kts (groundspeed now 60kts) it takes 6 minutes.

So, at 80kts there is a height loss of about 850ft.

So you can see that speed is good. The stronger the wind and the weaker the thermals then the more important it is to get this right. Remember too that the wind is usually stronger and may veer with height.

KEY POINT When into-wind consider increasing your speed.

Finally, on into-wind legs when streeting is present the streets can often be run with no height loss turning close to abeam the TP. This means that the wind is not so much of a problem. A generally safe height running the street is not lower than about halfway between cloud base and the ground. So a 3,000ft cloud base will mean flying no lower than 1,500ft.

Turning at a turn point

It is common for glider pilots to break their routine of making decisions as they approach a TP. A number of different distractions cause this:

▶ Over-concentration on the TP and flying through the same bad air outbound as inbound.
▶ Poor track selection causing a loss in height.
▶ Failing to have a continued strategy of 3 options to climb.
▶ Frustration leading to impatience, especially being able to see the TP for so long on an into-wind leg and trying to make a dash for it.
▶ Delaying the plan about staying airborne until after the TP.
▶ Thinking that as the next leg is downwind you will some how run into more thermals. (You won't, you will just have a greater selection of fields to pick from because your groundspeed is so much higher.)

Getting near to the TP at 80kts requires your full attention. You must be efficient by hitting the 0.5km circle head-on and not at a tangent, as shown in *Fig 14.7*. Why fly farther than you are required to? Align your track as accurately as possible and pick a visual feature well beyond the TP so that you are not continually looking inside. You will soon be departing on quite a different track and the sky needs to be investigated and a plan made. It is amazingly common for people to

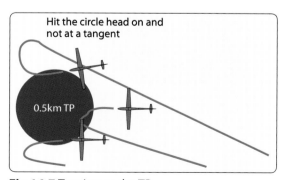

Fig 14.7 Turning at the TP.

land out shortly beyond the TP, largely because they failed to make a plan and an adequate decision. Remember that your first priority is to stay airborne.

You can start turning before you actually enter the *beer can* type TP and if you are coming back on yourself a good guide is to start at 0.7km to go.

Fig 14.8 shows the effect of turning at different speeds. A turn using 45°AoB at 60kts (30m/sec) will have about a 50m radius. Turning at 90kts gives a rather large turn radius (200m) and is inefficient so it is better when 0.7km away to pull up to slow down and *then* turn. (At 60kts in nil wind you are 6 seconds from the barrel and it takes a *Duo* nearly 3 seconds just to get the bank on). This gives a much smaller radius turn and uses less height. You might consider using high angles of bank for this manoeuvre.

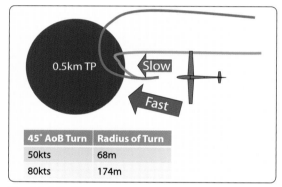

45° AoB Turn	Radius of Turn
50kts	68m
80kts	174m

Fig 14.8 Pulling up to turn.

On windy days it is worth making an allowance for the wind. At height TAS will be faster and the turn radius larger. Delay the turn to 0.6km or even less when into a strong upwind TP but you *should* be flying fast so a pull up to correctly slow for the next leg to then search for thermals will work well.

On a downwind TP ideally you will be climbing near the max height allowed. If cruising you are likely to be slightly slower but still turn at 0.7km and accelerate after the turn is almost complete. Whatever you do though, you can't afford to miss the TP and have to go around again so practise at a local TP. You can even practise this on a flat day along with techniques such as starting and the final glide; this will give you confidence in your final-glide computer.

Gliding to a landing

As the weather deteriorates there is always a chance of a land-out. The basic rule of three continues (always have three options), so 3 thermal sources become 2 thermal sources plus a land-out area. Then 1 thermal source and 2 land-out areas with one specific promising field and finally 2 good fields with 1 reserve. As further height is lost and clarity of the chosen landing area is made using the 6 S's of *Size, Shape, Slope, Surface, Stock and Surrounds,* a field will be approached with success. A safe field landing is never a failure, always a total success.

Lead and follow

One of the biggest problems about lead and follow is that the decision making is taken away from the student who spends the majority of their time staring so as not to lose the leader. There is little opportunity without conversation to absorb why things are being done in a particular way and there is always the tendency for the student to fall back. In consequence then, the leader should always have a glider with a lesser performance.

Lead and push

In the case of lead and push the instructor might be relieved to hear that it is better to have the higher performance glider. As shown in *Photo 14.2*, the *students* ahead are free to make the decisions, whilst the follower is available to offer short, sound advice.

Photo 14.1 A classic lead and follow.

Photo 14.2 A classic lead and push.

15
Final glide & planning

- ► The final glide
- ► Glider performance
- ► Altimeter settings
- ► Marking and understanding your map
- ► Final glide to a diversion
- ► Practising the final glide
- ► After-flight analysis
- ► An attitude of mind

A junior had entered his first regionals and in true family support his mother had volunteered to be his crew for the midweek period. Unfortunately, quite late in the day on one final glide, we stood and watched as he sank below the required glide to make it back to the airfield. Sometime later he walked into control to report that he had landed out and went off with mother and trailer for the retrieve. Nearly two hours later they appeared safely back at the airfield with the trailer but without his glider, because they couldn't find it. The situation was resolved by launching the motor glider to search, find and return with a latitude and longitude of the lost glider. Eventually with this important information and a little more help than just his mother, they returned to fight another day.

You are in a steady final glide and the equipment says you can make it home. Fantastic, well done. Or, perhaps it is time to wake up and smell the *danger*. You are likely to be tired, pleased, relieved and overly relaxed. You must not stop the routines of thoughtful flying which has got you to this point.

The final glide

Whilst cruising we set off at a speed, best guessing the thermal strength of the next thermal that we have to get to. Similarly, on a final glide we set off at a known height after making a best guess as to the glide performance but this can be just as easily wrong as guessing how strong the next thermal is likely to be.

Just because you can top up on the last thermal and then set off on track does not mean that the anticipated sink that will be encountered is necessarily correlated to that last thermal. There can be a considerable number of reasons why the numbers are wrong. It has already been explained why flying a direct route through thermic air can be punishing. 200ft may seem quite a lot of spare height but encounter strong sink, albeit briefly, and things look less comfortable. Also, regardless of how clean you think the wings look, there will be bugs and dust.

It is worth remembering that 10% of height is lost flying 84kts rather than 80kts and also remember the possible ±3kts in accuracy of your ASI. Also, the wind value will change during the descent to the ground. Flying into a strong wind means that flying slower will reduce your achieved distance over the ground.

There comes a point of no return, the marginal final glide that won't ever make it home. That is when you are too low to safely continue and too low to wander off and find a thermal to save the day. Occasionally I have seen pilots hoping for those extra 200ft on the final glide, which then did not materialize. Hope will not generate thermals.

Bearing in mind the height of the cloud base, anticipate where the final glide might begin. This gives you a target to aim for, helps in your en route planning and later in the flight when you are likely to be tired it will help you to feel confident about the final glide when you get to that point. You must establish a safe final glide without any chance of having a late field selection and landing short. The FAI certificates require a satisfactory landing to be completed. If you aspire to enter a competition a likely finish score of less than 900 points becomes a land-out score of more than 600 points.

Dial in the expected MacCready to indicate the height that you have available, never less, plus a safety margin on top, and then drive in. This planned speed must be faster than the best speed to fly against any anticipated headwind. In this way a slight slowdown will improve the glide and should you encounter an area of increased sink, you will already be flying through it at best speed to fly.

If gaining on the glide dial up a higher MacCready (or block speed). Whilst passing through the good air do not pull up. You have already identified that you can make it, now you just want to get back a little quicker.

Failing to maintain the planned glide can be serious if you have no idea why it is happening. If you know that you are about to pass through a thermal core and the increased sink is associated with it, fine. If, however, you cannot identify the cause, it could be serious. As you have been flying faster than best glide for the conditions, you do have the option to reduce the MacCready setting (or drop the block speed) to *hold* the safety margin. If this fails to hold the safety margin then it is safest to assume that you have to climb again. This climb should be done at the very next thermal that you encounter to recoup the safety margin. In this case it usually only means as little as two turns.

The perfect finish is a *slight* acceleration for the last few miles, burning off some of the safety margin for a straight-in approach. *To prevent landing wheels up and damaging your glider it is essential to check that the landing gear is down and locked.* An acronym that might be usefully modified is WULF, normally Water, Undercarriage, Loose Articles, Flaps (becoming Wheel, Undercarriage, Locked, Flaps).

On a normal day for a *Duo* a safe final glide works out at about 100ft/km, (70kts dry/80kts wet) plus a safety margin. This 100ft per km works for most 98+ handicap glass gliders and it is very easy to monitor and it is just the block speed which will change depending on the performance of each particular glider.

The safety margin depends on how high and far away you are from your airfield and the prospective good or bad conditions for the home run into the wind. So 40km out needs 4,000ft plus perhaps a 400ft margin.

We have to look more closely at the losses missing thermals on a straight final glide because this time it is inevitable that we are going to hit the ground—somewhere. Our attention often becomes fixated on finding our destination airfield, sometimes being distracted by other gliders around us, yet we must still ensure that our routing is efficient. The computer assumes that you are going to pass along a line where you will achieve gains to counter the associated losses as you pass through thermals, not just brushing

past them. In *Fig 15.1* we can see the sort of losses we might expect if we become target fixated. On final glide you must still pick the best route.

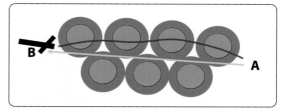

Fig 15.1 Direct line final glide losses.

If you are following others, watch the gliders ahead and see if they pull up to show good areas. Perhaps you can get an idea of a good area by seeing a bird thermalling. Do not just blindly fly on track but deviate if there is an obvious advantage to do so. Also, if gliders ahead start climbing in weak lift then make a more efficient glide early. Whenever possible, stick with your own safe and confident plan and adjust as your experience increases.

Fig 15.2 shows a nil wind example using 6kt thermals. We can estimate the gains and losses flying directly home at high speed and indirect routing via thermal cores.

Routing direct from A to B on a final glide at 90 knots we lose $6 \times 40\text{ft} = 240\text{ft}$. Alternatively, routing indirectly from A to B on a final glide at 60 knots we gain $6 \times 20\text{ft} = 120\text{ft}$. It would only take 1 minute of climb at 4kts to make up the difference. Also, the indirect routing has an air track that is 50% longer, therefore at least 50% slower. This should only be done if you need the height, not the speed.

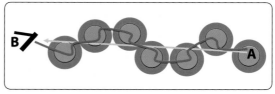

Fig 15.2 Direct line losses on final glide can eat up your safety height.

There are other dangers in the final glide. One such danger is the discrepancy between what the LX is telling you and reality. The LX is simply a computer and you must understand the shortfalls. It assumes that you have entered the current QNH, correct weight, that the air ahead will follow a standard thermic model and that the glider is really polished. The LX tries to give you a realistic compensation for the wind on the final glide. However, it is only a simple calculator and it can not give you the full picture in terms of height needed to get in. Look out of the canopy and bring back the John Willy!

How accurate is the altimeter at height and how much lag do you get on the run in? The QNH might have changed by a couple of millibars (or more), which is 60ft. A slight tap of the sticky altimeter can make an okay looking final glide look immediately marginal, with the loss of most of your safety height in a blur. This is a part of knowing your glider. The altimeter is likely to continue sticking during the final glide, possibly giving you the wrong kind of reassurance.

Another danger is the fact that the LX can not predict any wind change on the final glide as you descend. It might still be working on the 3,000ft wind and a subsequent increase in headwind as you descend, such as a sea breeze, will have a big influence on the height required. To simply set a lower MacCready, at height, and slow down so the numbers appear to work may not be good enough.

Fig 15.3 shows a final glide in different conditions. Having the height to make it back safely means that speed may be increased. However, a confident start to the final glide is a must. Whilst this diagram holds good for a final glide, it would be logical to assume that it must therefore hold good for achieving higher speeds on a street running to an into-wind turn point. The red line shows a glider flying through flat air. The blue line shows a glider which cruises through a thermal and follows the dolphin

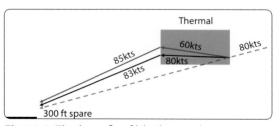

Fig 15.3 The benefit of block speed.

technique, slowing down, losing a considerable amount of time climbing, when additional height is not required. The black line shows a glider that cruises through the same thermal at block speed.

There was a period when pilots would make a mark on the canopy and monitor progress in a number of ways to help judge how things were going. Flying a modern glider with a fantastic performance means that the ability of the pilot to judge whether he can just make it home is almost impossible.

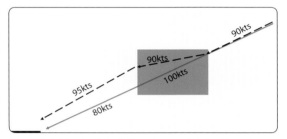

Fig 15.4 Final glide following anti MacCready.

On many navigation displays there is an indication of required glide angle (R) and current glide angle (E). This is an accurate tool for us to use as an aid in assessing how the final glide is progressing, because high performance flat glides are so difficult to judge visually. It is useful and gives you an indication of the loss of performance as you are passing through sink. Bear in mind that it is giving you a glide angle, not a safety height. The current glide angle should be slowly improving as you get nearer, not staying the same, or you are losing out.

Fig 15.4 shows two gliders, one flying block speed (black line) and the other flying a constant glide angle anti-MacCready (red line). The red line follows and simply maintains a constant glide angle which means slowing down in the sink and speeding up in the rising air (anti-dolphin). This is inefficient and even risky. The glider following the black line glides at the planned block speed in lift and accelerates afterwards, which is a much safer and more efficient technique.

If you require a glide angle of 30:1 and you are achieving 30:1 the proportion of safety height with distance to go will remain the same but the actual height will reduce as you run in. You will cross the boundary fence at zero ft.

Duo glide angles (dry) into various headwinds (zero on the MacCready for final glide)						
IAS	RoD	No wind	10kts	15kts	20kts	25kts
50	1.2	41.6	33.3	29.1	25.0	20.8
53	1.3	40.7	33.0	29.2	25.4	21.5
55	1.4	39.3	32.0	28.6	25.0	21.4
60	1.7	35.3	29.4	26.5	23.5	20.6
65	2.0	32.5	27.5	25.0	22.5	20
70	2.25	31.0	26.6	24.4	22.2	20
75	2.78	27.0	23.4	21.6	19.8	18
80	3.25	24.6	21.5	20.0	18.5	16.9
85	4.25	21.0	20.0	17.6	16.5	15.3

Table 15.1

Duo glide angles (wet) into various headwinds (zero on the MacCready for final glide)						
IAS	RoD	No wind	10kts	15kts	20kts	25kts
50	1.25	40	32	28	24	20
55	1.3	42.3	34.6	30.7	26.9	23
60	1.5	40	33.3	30.0	26.6	23.3
65	1.7	38.2	32.3	29.4	26.4	23.5
70	1.9	36.8	31.6	28.9	26.3	23.7
75	2.2	34	29.5	27.3	25.0	22.7
80	2.5	32	28	26	24	22
85	2.85	29.8	26.3	24.6	22.8	21.1
90	3.3	27.2	24.2	22.7	21.0	19.7
95	4.0	23.8	21.3	20	18.7	17.5

Table 15.2

In *Table 15.1* the theoretical achieved glide angles are tabulated using IAS against various headwinds flying a *Duo* when dry. *Table 15.2* shows similar data when wet. The yellow shaded data indicates the best glide angle, red data indicates flying too slow and green shaded data allows for some safety. If you fly 10kts faster than the best glide speed this gives a significant increase in groundspeed, particularly when the headwind increases. If you subsequently reduce speed it does then give you a better glide. In other words you have a small additional safety factor. If you only fly 5kts faster than best speed to fly it invariably gives almost no benefit if you subsequently slow down. Whilst climbing remember that you will lose height when accelerating to block speed so you will need extra height for this.

KEY POINT In any theoretical discussion about final glides it is worth remembering the simple fact that you have to get back. It is a case of plus whatever and absolutely minus nothing!

Table 15.3

Speed	L/D	Height	Time (mins)
75kts	23.4	3,846ft	14.9
60kts	29.4	3,061ft	19.4
50kts	33.3	2,702ft	24.3

Height required at light weight for final glide (10kt headwind)

Table 15.3 indicates the height required, at light weight, running in on a 30km final glide with a 10kt headwind. The point of this table is to show that *if you take the time to climb you reduce the time to the finish*. Consider the glide at 50kts which takes 24.3 minutes. If you were to climb at just 2kts it would take 6 minutes to climb 1,200ft so you would now be able to run-in at 75kts. This would get you back in 14.9 + 6 = 20.9 minutes as opposed to 24.3 minutes, and this is only after a climb in a weak thermal! Obviously, stronger thermals will make the run-in even quicker. Also, should you only climb for 2 minutes and gain 400ft you could run in at 60kts and be 3 minutes quicker than running in at the slower speed.

Table 15.4

Height required at heavy weight for final glide (10kt headwind)

Speed	L/D	Height	Time (mins)
75kts	29.5	3,050ft	14.9
60kts	33.3	2,702ft	19.4
55kts	34.6	2,601ft	21.6

In *Table 15.4* note that if heavy, if you were to climb at just 2kts you only need about 2.5 minutes to climb 450ft to enable you to run-in at 75kts. This gets you back 4 minutes earlier than running at 55kts without the climb. Of course, when wet we need far less height to get back because of all the water (weight). It is worth mentioning here the disastrous effect of dumping your water too early or worse, not telling the computer that you have dumped it.

In summary, make sure that you take a climb if you need the height for your high speed run-in. Any thermal over 2kts will give an advantage,

making the final glide faster and safer. Thermals stronger than 2kts add to the benefits.

In stronger headwinds it becomes even more important to take a climb so that you can run-in at high speed and penetrate into the wind. Also, it is much more beneficial if you are wet. *Table 15.5* and *Table 15.6* indicate the height required, at light and heavy weights, running in on a 30km final glide with a 20kt headwind.

Table 15.5

Height required at light weight for final glide (20kt headwind)

Speed	L/D	Height	Time (mins)
75kts	19.8	4,054ft	17.6
60kts	23.5	3,829ft	24.3
50kts	25	3,600ft	32.4

Table 15.6

Height required at heavy weight for final glide (20kt headwind)

Speed	L/D	Height	Time (mins)
75kts	25	3,600ft	17.6
60kts	26.6	3,383ft	24.3
55kts	26.9	3,345ft	27.7

You should notice that you need 3,600ft to get home when dry flying at 50kts and the same 3,600ft when heavy flying at 75kts. The latter gives you a small margin to slow down and do better, the former does not.

If you spend just one minute longer climbing (heavy) from 3,600ft to above 3,750ft you would cruise in at 80kts arriving earlier and with added safety.

Glider performance

Many times you will hear that one's glider does not perform as well as the manufacturer suggests. Perhaps on occasions this is true, but are you really giving it a chance?

As a reminder, a glider weighing about 600kg which achieves a glide angle of 60:1 is actually producing only about 10kg of drag. Drag can be split in to two main components, lift induced drag produced purely by the action of producing lift and zero lift drag, which is produced independent of any lift. This zero lift drag is further divided into 3 components. Form drag is simply the frontal shape of the glider and is fixed, with the exception of airbrakes, retractable main wheel (and retractable tail wheel), flap settings and trim drag caused by the elevator displaced from the design neutral. Interference drag is the drag caused by the interfering flows between the fuselage and wings etc. Surface friction drag is on every surface on your glider.

Reducing form drag

Have you correctly balanced the glider so that the centre of gravity is towards the optimum position? If you haven't then the elevator will not only give you trim drag because it is not in line with the airflow but it means that the whole of the tailplane is producing a larger force (and thus drag) to counter the invariably heavy weight in the front cockpit. It also means that you must displace the elevator a long way from neutral to achieve the desired pitching moment and in some cases this limits the angle of bank you can turn at effectively.

Reducing interference drag

There is little we can do here except make sure we tape as perfectly as we can. Do not pull the tape tight and stretch it. Pulling too hard causes a recess or groove and if this was a good thing we'd have lots of grooves all over the wing. The tape will soon split especially in the cold air if you get high. It should be simply laid onto the surface and then pressed to secure.

Of course flying in really smooth air minimises the turbulence over the glider and if you have really cleaned your glider it will normally then perform very close to specification. If you are trying to get the same performance flying through thermic air then it simply won't work as well. This is rather like trying to find how fast your car will go over the grass or how fast you can ski over the moguls.

Reducing surface friction drag

Try making a paper plane out of sandpaper; it does not fly well. So why would you fly a dirty glider? When did you last thoroughly clean and polish every bit of your glider? That means *every* bit including all the bottom surfaces of the wing, fuselage and tailplane. Dirty skid marks behind the main wheel are common drag generators. Failing to clean and polish thoroughly could have just devalued your performance by about £10,000!

Determining your glider's performance

Modern satellite navigation instrumentation give a GPS derived glide angle. It would be sensible that having bought such an expensive piece of hardware that you try it out on a flat day and see what glide angle it says you are achieving. It does not matter what the manufacturer suggests it will do because this is the glider that you are flying. Bear in mind that it will give you a calculated glide angle over the ground, so any wind will affect it. Simply fly out, *upwind* or *downwind*, towards a fix (only until you have a steady reading at a particular speed) and then fly back and take the mean of the two. So if it suggests 40 out and 48 back then the achieved glide angle will be 44.

Of course another modern tool is the logger. Fly a very specific set of speeds in trim, hands and feet off. Try this at different weights and centre of gravity positions and review the results at your leisure. Bear in mind that you really need flat air to get accurate figures and that as your glider is probably laid up for the winter to save on insurance costs, this exercise is best accomplished at the beginning of the season.

Altimeter settings

There are three different pressure settings that you can set your altimeter to and you need to be aware of these before you go cross-country. In a competition one specific pressure setting will be given at briefing which is the one they use at the end of the day for scoring penalties for airspace infringements.

▶ **QFE**—This is what we normally use when we fly from our local airfield. The altimeter will read zero when the glider is on the ground. Military airfield zones in the UK are based on this. Be aware that the pressure can change during the day and may be several millibars different after several hours (3 millibars = 90 ft would not be unusual). If you are on task during this period then you might not be as high as the altimeter indicates.

▶ **QNH**—With this setting the altimeter indicates height above mean sea level (amsl). With a map indicating ground heights you can then estimate your height above the ground by subtracting the height indicated on the map from what your altimeter indicates. Some restricted airspace and danger areas are measured using this setting. Civilian airfields normally use QNH.

▶ **1,013 mb**—Called the Standard Pressure Setting, this is the setting you will need to avoid controlled airspace (airways) as the airliners fly on this setting.

As a word of caution, if whilst on task you ever change away from your routine altimeter setting, make sure you change back to the original setting. If in doubt, call home to get the latest wind and QFE. I've known an occasion when someone simply zeroed the altimeter and took off with it set it 1,000 ft out and only discovered the error on final glide.

Marking and understanding your map

In previous years, with air data computers, maps, a basic compass and cameras, there was a lot to prepare and study on a map to ensure that you had the mental capacity to cope on difficult days, especially in the poor visibility generated by the smoke from stubble fires. Today, with current GPS accuracy and computing power, a lot of the work is done for us as long as you know how to use the various modes of your equipment. There are, however, a number of details which are worth considering before setting off on task. The route needs to be marked on the map, ideally as a thin broken or dotted line that does not then obliterate the one frequency that you require to talk to someone or a key feature which you can see for real but can't find marked on the map. The second item of consideration is the actual TPs so that you will get a general feel of where you are

going as you approach them. Of course work from big feature to small, all of the time. Just because you can see a roundabout on a dual carriageway it does not mean that it is the correct one. Look for other unique large features on each track to help you remain orientated, not just with track but where possible diversions are.

It can be quite amusing to see the occasional pilot climb as hard as they can and then whoosh off in the wrong direction, especially whilst under training in a two-seater. Great positive mental attitude and decision making but we're going in the wrong direction! Knowing the name of the TP is immaterial, but an idea of what it will look like orientated from the direction in which you are approaching or passing by it, is. Identify possible landable diversions where you know that you can concentrate on a weak thermal and not continuously have to consider a perilous approach or landing in a farmer's field.

Airspace is becoming increasingly invasive and the weather often forces us to detour, so look both on and near to your route (within 20km) so that there is no surprise that you now have to stay on one particular side of track or stop climbing or descending. A forecast which anticipates that you should easily stay high does not necessarily come true. On the other hand, having accepted that the forecast says you will never get above 4,000 ft but you find yourself at 6,000 ft infringing the dreaded airspace can be alarming and possibly even dangerous.

Now consider the weather forecast and why you have been set in the direction that you are planning. Consider the higher terrain where your height will be significantly less above the ground, the potential for sea breezes etc. and look for possible energy lines or good thermal areas as well as potentially good landable flat ground.

Final glide to a diversion

One of the comforting aspects of gliding is to have a plan that when executed with full consideration appears to work, and this includes timely and well executed field landings. Judging distance can be difficult unless you work at it but there are a lot of features to help you and many advantages of being able to do so. Whilst no doubt you will be thinking that a final glide is to the planned completed task destination, it can also easily be to a diversion en route when things just happen to go sour. The judgement of distance on a dog-leg to a possible thermal source ahead, which fails, and then off to an airfield is one such example as the instrumentation cannot give you this information. As you climb up you can see the clouds down track clearly so before they disappear at cloud base have a good look to see which ones are good and which are bad. Approaching cloud base you can see the cloud shadows so you can safely set off with the knowledge that you are at least going in the correct direction for the first good cloud. Looking ahead and estimating the distance of each cloud, allowing 100ft per km, you can then estimate just how high you will arrive under each cloud. So if you think the next 3 clouds are about 5, 9 and 13km away, you know that if you set off from 4,000ft you should be at 3,500ft, 3,100ft and 2,700ft respectively. So you can set off confidently knowing that even if you press on for the last cloud you will still have a good altitude. If no thermals were then subsequently encountered then you could easily achieve a glide to a diversion 20km away from this 2,700ft.

Practising the final glide

On a potential 100km task flown at 100kph (60 minutes) the overly cautious final glide could easily lose five minutes and lower the average speed to 92.3kph (65 minutes). Over caution into a headwind can have a greater effect. So, apart from recognizing that it is important to fly an efficient, safe, final glide, you need to practise it many times, particularly before any competition if that is one of your future goals. A competition is not the time to start learning anything new. Set a simple task on a flat day with light winds and pick or invent a TP some 5 or 6km from your site. Ideally this will be a downwind TP which subsequently allows for a straight-in approach to land.

This 10–12km task requires less than 1,100ft in a *Duo* or an *LS8*, a little more in the *Discus*. The additional height gained on the launch is the safety height which can be used to teach or learn how to manage a final glide.

You must ensure that the LX altitude (QNH) is set correctly and that the finish point is the airfield. If you only set the airfield finish point the time required to get to this point should be a small negative value. This negative value assumes that you are not exactly on your finish point and it is indicating the height you need to gain to glide to your chosen spot. If the LX indicates a positive figure, greater than 30ft, then there is a problem. If you now set in the task it should indicate approximately minus 1,100ft.

Off the wire fly this flat glide task with zero set on the MacCready to set a base line for the final glide. You can compare how accurately the set-up of your navigation computer is compared to the actual performance that your glider achieves. Discrepancies can be compensated for by adjusting the weight value and/or the bug factor. Older gliders tend to have minor blemishes on the outer skin, ill-fitting undercarriage doors or rough finishes which prevent a factory predicted perfect performance. It is also worth noting the level of lag in your mechanical altimeter. If you don't carry a logger, note with a stopwatch the actual time it takes to fly the task at best glide speed.

Even if the LX has not calculated the light wind accurately, the gain of performance outbound will essentially be lost inbound. On the first launch (MacCready at zero) you will get an idea of how high you might start and how much spare you have to play with. Now re-fly the mini task with 2, 3 or 4 set, as you are able, in the MacCready and again note instrument accuracy and time taken. Simply wind up the MacCready, remembering to allow for the height lost accelerating up to the block speed, so that the height needed to do the task is a little less than this. Allow a bit for the turn (and a little bit extra if you wish) and start the turn at 0.7km, don't wait until you are in the barrel. This should also improve your TP skills and should give you a small gain as you will cut the corner by almost 1km. You might want to fly the same task with dirty wings; this will definitely encourage you to make sure that your glider is always polished!

You can also fly this task by setting the TP upwind but not the return as a final glide to a straight-in landing, as you will be recovering to the airfield downwind and we don't do downwind landings.

The practice of achieving the turn point efficiently and accurately is extremely beneficial. Fly at the optimum speed to achieve best L/D over the ground to the upwind turn point. Make a positive decision when to pull up and turn to achieve an efficient fix in the barrel. Return slowly at minimum sink speed. In this way you will develop confidence at turning efficiently at upwind TPs. Whatever you decide to try though, you are practising final glides and you must get in safely every time.

These exercises will give you confidence in the computer systems, teach you what a controlled straight-in looks like, which will improve your judgement and improve your cross-country speeds achieved on any task. Again, as an aside, another simple rule of thumb is that each minute slower than the winner in competition will cost you 10 points. In a 9-day competition, losing 3 to 5 minutes on every final glide could mean as much as 300 to 500 points lost.

This exercise can be practised many times and different techniques may be incorporated. It should not be practised on a thermic day. The potential loss flying a bad line at slow speed is potentially too much and this will do nothing for your confidence.

It might be worth keeping a record of all spare height and run times for future reference. Also, don't forget to inform the Duty Instructor what you are doing and don't forget to lower the gear as you will be doing a straight-in from 6km away.

> **KEY POINT** You might be interested that in the *Duo, dry,* the following speeds are flown with the associated MacCready settings: Zero/1 = 55kts+; 2=70kts 3= 75kts; 4=80kts; 5=85kts; 6=90kts.

After-flight analysis

Currently there is a lot of after-flight analysis that can be reviewed. It often suggests that a tortoise might have been faster; however, this analysis can be misleading. Sometimes you have to see the picture and the weather conditions to understand why you made any particular decision. The analysis may suggest that you should have ignored a thermal and pressed on to the strong one 8km farther down track, which you took later to top up, but there is no evidence to indicate that the strong thermal would have been available earlier if you had pushed on. You might have arrived too early and missed it, ending up struggling farther down track. This is the reason that I usually video flights for review afterwards.

In the post-flight analysis reference is often made to the number of left and right turns; this is not important! The direction of turn may already have been established by any thermalling glider that you join. It is more important that you turned the correct way and that you centred immediately. There is no reason why you don't even plan to join to one side of a thermal so that you know which way to turn when you hit the lift.

Loggers do not give total energy indication but a continuous plot of GPS altitude. So during analysis it is difficult to identify correct thermalling gains when the pull-up is recorded as a climb and accelerations mainly recorded as a descent.

An attitude of mind

To be successful you have to want to be successful. The challenge is the weather, nothing else. Theories and rules of science are all well and good but the science of weather forecasting is an imprecise one. You will improve by exploring and not giving up just because it looks a little more difficult. Experience will not defy either physics or aerodynamics. In almost every task there will be an opportunity where you will have to change gear, fly differently or perhaps think *outside of the box*. Situations will often occur which you have not seen before so stay flexible, use effective decision making and always be prepared to change your plan.

16
Self-tasking

During the 1980's I was invited to fly in the back of a beautiful high performance two-seater, equipped with one of those new air data computers that you could use to work most things out for you. On the second leg P1 decided he would call up Cosford to advise them that we were coming over the top and, to sound professional, adjusted his altimeter to QNH, declaring our height on QNH. I flew the third leg and then running home P1 took it for the last leg to demonstrate the final glide. During the glide, as the day was now dying, we had some discussion about the air data computer. I was told that if you look out of the window you could not possibly believe that we could make it home. Well, "No" I said, pausing, "but then I still have QFE on my altimeter" (my 'kit' confirmed my suspicion that we couldn't make it). I swear I could see the look of stunned shock on the back of the head of the man in front. A couple of kilometres later—surprise, surprise—we were climbing in a weak thermal, so it all ended well!

After the FAI Silver Distance qualifying 50km, the next hurdle is the Gold which requires a flight of 300km. This task length means that the flight will likely take more than 3 hours. This challenge needs more than a little bit of luck on a good day and you will have to return against any wind that favoured earlier legs. If there is no club coach available then a way to improve your chances of success is through short self-tasking, whenever the opportunity arises. To stand any chance and to avoid a distant land-out, you will have to learn, if not teach yourself, all the necessary skills to be successful.

Problems to be overcome

Apart from a lack of confidence or lack of ability I have of course heard any number of reasons why members are reluctant to go cross-country and here are some of them:

► Weather not as good as forecast.
► Weather window insufficient.
► Weather only looks good for a small area.
► A lack of fields to land in due to high crops.
► A lack of field landing currency training.
► A desire for the club glider to be back for others (or syndicate partner) to use.
► A promise to be home early.
► Difficulty (hassle) de-rigging a club glider and the expense of the retrieve.

► Car/trailer issues
► Volunteer crew issues
► It's a blue day!

A club's top machine invariably means that the ratio of bums to seats is not good. The high performance machine is often poorly utilised leaving aspiring cross-country pilots on the ground, feeling frustrated. With the flight time often limited it is necessary to learn the most from each flight and to share that knowledge. This can only be achieved by setting a goal to learn or practise some aspect on each flight, and for others to know what that goal is and to be supportive.

The short task

Simple but very useful tasks are the 10km trainers. In these, visual features can be used for gliders without GPS systems, using a minimum height at each TP.

The first of these is simply two turning points making a 40km task. Selecting, for example, a TP 10km east and a TP 10km west of the airfield, gives a 40km task which passes just to the north or south of the downwind leg. This gives the training practice of flying block speeds both to upwind and downwind TPs.

You will know the strength of most thermals, often returning to ones that you have recently left, enabling you to learn to read the sky and refine your block speed. In this way you will achieve a series of TPs and therefore a mini cross-country with little chance of landing out—well no one has yet! It is normal to fly to the downwind TP

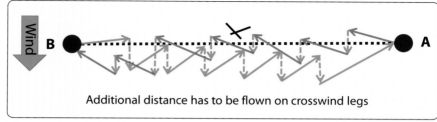

Wind

B A

Additional distance has to be flown on crosswind legs

Fig 16.2 Simple local tasking out and return.

first with sufficient height to always make it back to home in a single glide. If there is a northerly component in the wind streeting is often available.

In a northerly wind, the same run can be used to train for cross-wind tracks, identifying the crippling drift and penalties of picking downwind thermals. In *Fig 16.2* the wind is across the planned task. Flying from left to right, the green lines indicate the tracks when climbing in a thermal and the blue lines indicate the cruise tracks countering the accumulated drift. You should be able to see that on the return leg, from right to left, the situation is just as bad and the red tracks are similarly offset into wind.

The 48km triangle

Having learnt the skills to fly individual legs the next progression is the 48km triangle made up of TPs 9km from base. In this case the pilot is flying a combination of head, tail and cross-wind components and after 48km the sky has usually changed.

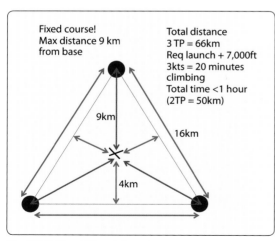

Fixed course!
Max distance 9 km from base

Total distance
3 TP = 66km
Req launch + 7,000ft
3kts = 20 minutes climbing
Total time <1 hour
(2TP = 50km)

9km

16km

4km

Fig 16.1 The 48km triangle.

The 48km triangle enables you to achieve a cross-country task without actually going outside of your home comfort zone. It can be a very effective teaching exercise for pre-solo cross-country students. The key is not the specific distance flown but the solo training value of a task with almost no chance of a land-out. The minimum height around each TP to safely get back home and the height required to complete the triangle will vary depending on the weather conditions (mainly the wind) and glider performance. So what exactly can we learn from this seemingly simple task which could be flown in a two-seater with an instructor? Well, we can learn almost everything to do with flying a successful cross-country, and the following are just some of the learning points:

► Map and route planning.
► Satellite navigation aids.
► Decision making.
► Work cycle management.
► Distance estimation.
► Starting.
► Different wind effects on performance.
► Turning point procedures.
► Final glide.

No doubt you will be aware that the little tasks that I have suggested mean that navigation should not be a challenge because you are routing over only what is likely to be known terrain. But you will be actively turning your back on the airfield with the aim to go specifically to a point rather than just aimlessly wandering around. It means that you can concentrate on the new skills of flying. If you want to go significantly farther it would make sense to use modern technology. By this I mean look up the route using internet satellite maps and see the big features that will make your visual navigation very easy.

The need to train

Often in regional competitions many pilots will recognize that they are either great on survival days and poor on racing days, or vice versa. The point here is that different weather requires different techniques. A *racer* is impatient, flies at maximum weight and charges off at speed even to low levels assuming that there will be no weak thermals and that they will always just make it. The cautious pilots trail slowly behind, but usually get round the tasks.

Meanwhile weak days require a very sensitive approach and patience, meaning often diverging quite far from track. The impatient racers have ignored that last weak bounce and are in trouble, often on the ground watching slower gliders overfly at height. You need to develop both skills and everything in between.

The cat's cradle

For pilots who have gained some experience the next progression is the cat's cradle. The cat's cradle allows pilots to chase after wherever they think the weather is best. A number of turning points are selected around home base and declared but you can only turn at each point once and you pick your route as you see fit, trying to achieve

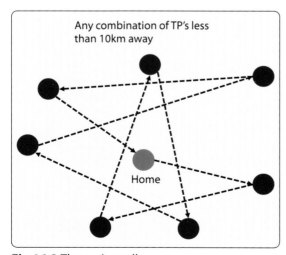

Fig 16.3 The cat's cradle.

the furthest distance or be the fastest around a particular distance. It can be used for very effective training including AATs without being very far from home especially if the weather is only good locally. With modern GPS loggers you can find out exactly how far you had achieved. The BGA TP list does not offer so many turn points within such a small area so you are going to have to invent a few of your own for local use. Of course you can use visual features such as local villages, roundabouts or lakes etc.

The local airfield task

Assuming that you are allowed to thermal as low as 600ft agl at your local airfield, then it would make huge sense to plan and fly a route such that you could always arrive at an appropriate landing site at 600ft, rather than juggle with the open countryside. In this way you can concentrate on gliding and success rather than worrying about picking a farmer's field and the 6 S's. You may even plan to fly this task using a remote start. Tasking a little farther away from home but always having a safe alternative will mean that you can concentrate on gliding, rather than landing.

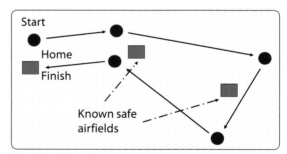

Fig 16.4 Planning a route.

Self-learning

Perhaps by now you are approaching or have achieved that milestone point in your gliding where the view of the local instructors is that you are competent enough for safe solo and require no additional checks. You now need to think how you will gain the knowledge and many complex skills and techniques to progress further. This can be painfully slow, frustrating and an expensive way of learning from your many mistakes. I know this because this is the way that I, and the vast majority of experienced glider pilots, have learnt. Alternatively, if you fly for an hour or so with an experienced instructor, who will teach you some aspects of the content included in this book, then your progress will be accelerated many times over and it will avoid those tedious and frustrating failures.

A comment made by one of my students was that the only similarity between the flying that he had been taught and the flying that I was teaching him was to fly safely, as every other aspect was seemingly completely different.

The sporting code

The FAI sporting code requires you to make a declaration before any FAI attempted task and explains all the requirements (declaration, rules, and evidence required etc.) that must be fulfilled to make a successful flight—a qualifying flight. You need to thoroughly read this document before finding an *Official Observer* at your club who will clarify any parts you don't fully understand. The sporting code also deals with rules concerning records and international competitions. The documents for section 3, which deals with gliding, can be found at: *www.fai.org*.

Planning

From the outset it is better that you plan where you are going to go, even for your first 50km silver distance, so that you can fully comprehend the planning requirements for any subsequent long distance cross-country flight. Consideration includes the basics of navigational features to look out for, airspace restrictions, topography, diversion airfields and the suitability of farmers' fields en route, any requirements regarding operations at the planned destination and of course the predicted weather. This prior planning makes more time available once airborne and the ability to concentrate on staying airborne.

Make sure that you know how the glider de-rigs and secures safely in the trailer with all the tools and fittings. Can you or your crew, ensuring they are insured, drive (and reverse) your car hitched to a glider trailer? Whilst the crew will bring your empty trailer to your landing point it is

Photo 16.1 Planning a task.

traditional that the pilot takes the responsibility of returning the glider and trailer home, usually via a restaurant or pub.

Other things to consider are whether you have a suitable car to pull the glider and trailer through a ploughed field? Have you a tow rope and torch? Is there a satnav in the car and have you a set of phone numbers with the phone fully charged?

Task setting has to start with an aim, invariably to learn, practise or develop new techniques and to do this so that the exercise is accomplished with little anxiety or distraction. Most lessons in cross-country are learnt solo (sadly), so it is important to set off on any task with a specific aspect to learn and afterwards measure the level of that success. With this in mind the chance of a field landing and a subsequent expensive and time consuming long distance retrieve should be minimised. After all, on a good day the weather is generally the same over a large area so there is no point setting a task over difficult terrain 100 miles away. This offers a greater risk but with no real benefit. It makes sense to plan any task such that for at least for some of the time (if not all of the time) known safe landable sites are in easy gliding range and some thought should be made as to just how far from home you need to go. *The challenge is the weather not the route,* so flying the same route 10 times in different weather will contribute to learning. It just means that the visual navigation is easier. Another really useful contribution can be made by flying the same route with somebody else, even mutually supporting each other, but please use the radio sparingly. The frequencies are national ones, not private chat lines.

Photo 16.2 Flying mutual support.

The training tasks

With smaller weather *windows* or smaller good weather *areas* along with airspace restrictions (SPINE is a very useful aid), planning the length and shape of the task needs some thought. To optimise the training need on a given day requires a sensible, flexible approach, particularly when the forecast may be unreliable. Romping around a 50km triangle six times still achieves the aim of a 300km task even though it does not qualify for a FAI badge. The navigation is made easy and any land-out would be close to home so the pilot can concentrate on the job in hand which, invariably in the early days of cross-country, means reading the sky and staying airborne on track, and later achieving faster lap times. Of course if others are doing the same task then the higher performance machine should be finding the thermals first for everyone to follow; all of a sudden advanced gliding becomes a team sport. You should have a good idea of your current ability and glider's performance so each task should just stretch or reinforce your progress so far. It means that you can task yourself later in the season on bigger tasks away from home knowing that you can fly fast enough to be successful.

At the beginning of the season give yourself a large number of goals to achieve. It is particularly important to achieve shorter tasks (100–150km) at improved average speeds in the same conditions so that when the 500km forecast comes around you will be successful. This is done by recognising streeting conditions, holding block speeds confidently and linking good lines of energy rather than using every thermal that you bump in to. The club ladder is a good way of scoring your overall improved cross-country achievements of going farther and faster, even if you only do the scoring for your own benefit. The variability of summer weather does mean that your achieved performance is not necessarily an indication of a lack of progress during some years.

A good task should be completed with the minimum of luck. Programs such as RASP give you an excellent set of tools to identify whether a task is feasible, assuming the forecast weather is correct, with the earliest and latest start times offering a sensible window to go off on task. Even if you are unable to fly midweek, internet tools allow you to *practise* setting a task if the only good weather happens to fall at this time. Consistently *under-setting* your tasks fails to take advantage of the few better days. Consistently *over-setting*, however, results in mental disappointment. If you always romp the planned 250km you would be delighted, yet if you always fail the 300km on the same days you would be disappointed. The balance of self tasking does improve with real experience.

The key to setting a good task is to establish what the meteorology information suggests is the *rough area* where the task should be best set and what the *length* of the soaring day is. Again, programs like RASP offer a good indication of this so 2 or 3 days in advance you can start to look at possible tasks which you might want to complete if the weather window remains as forecast. An example of a simple fixed-course task is shown in *Fig 16.5*.

Enhanced option fixed-course task

For distance cross-country badge claims, a flight can qualify if you complete a task by flying within the sector beyond the TPs or within the barrel.

For training purposes there is no reason why you do not set yourself the option to use the enhanced option TP as in *Fig 16.6*. This type of procedure is used in competitions whenever a degree of shower activity is forecast. The distance

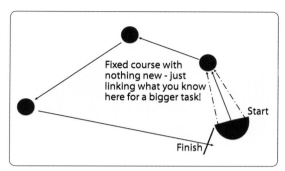

Fig 16.5 Simple fixed-course task.

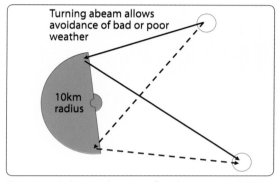

Fig 16.6 Enhanced option fixed course task.

that you fly is no more than 1km farther than flying through the barrel but it can reduce becoming bogged down at a TP simply because there happens to be a bad area of air there (not necessarily showers) which was not anticipated.

Tasking from first principles

The question is whether you do tasking from first principles or use one of the many programs that are available; there are advantages to knowing both. Tasking from first principles allows you to develop a thorough understanding of the atmosphere that you see in front of you as you progress en route. This allows you to recognize that the weather forecast is either correct or significantly inaccurate. Modern programs give outstanding and almost instant mathematical solutions based on a predicted forecast, with almost no room for real time adjustment.

Firstly, we need a rough guess as to what the weather will be. Consider that the air above us today travelling at 20kts is likely to have been about 500 miles away yesterday and about 3,000 miles away a week ago. During the period before its arrival the development of high or low pressures can make a huge difference to the timing of any changes in our weather or a large change in the weather itself. There is a saying that the weather forecast is always essentially correct, it is just the timing or place which is wrong.

Consider our estimate of a good day. A large difference between maximum and minimum temperatures gives us a high cloud base and a strong thermal strength. A wind of 8–15kts reduces the risk of stagnant dominating column thermals and increases the chance of some streeting. A simple comment or picture in a forecast that depicts some cloud is great news as it reduces the chance of a blue day or over-development.

The advantage of these simple deductions allows you to immediately compare the forecast with reality and recognize that the sky is developing as anticipated, or it is better or worse and adjustments to the task need to be made before getting airborne.

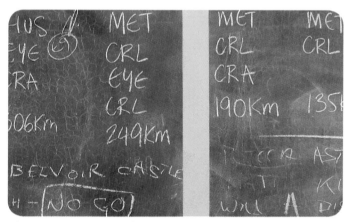

Photo 16.3 Tasking information does not have to be very sophisticated.

Tasking programs

There are a number of software products and fantastic work done by many specialists offering an edge to the black art of tasking which may include some extremely useful self-tasking additional tools. Using RASP, if you enter your task and glider type, then vary your start time, the estimated speed and speeds to fly on your chosen task are displayed for each leg. It will even tell you if the task that you have set is possible with the predicted weather. The thermal strength multiplier is especially useful. On the other hand, despite the huge volume of information that might be available, tasking from first principles is usually good enough.

Duty of care

We owe it to ourselves and to others, whom we might plan for, to ensure that the route is not unnecessarily challenging. We are only too familiar with the difficulty of selecting suitable fields throughout our cross-country season and this is made more difficult during June and July (supposedly our best two weather months of the year) when farmers' crops are especially high. To mitigate against this, setting a task which ensures known landable places are available if we are above a certain height (1,500ft) significantly reduces the tension and allows far greater effort to be used in flying the task successfully. Clearly this is difficult in some areas of the country but at least it allows one to confidently push on without it being essential to remain high and use every thermal that you encounter. Laps of a smaller circuits or short out and returns remain good practice as the thermals and their locations relative to the turn points are likely to be different each time around.

A final word

For me gliding has always been my real passion in flying. In my opinion it is one of the few true, fun, safe, challenging, skilled and personally rewarding things you can do in life. I have written this book in part because people have asked me to, but more because I hear of so many people who do not manage the transition to go

confidently beyond the glide range of home. Most clubs, often for various understandable reasons, find it hard to offer training beyond the cross-country endorsement. To wander farther from base requires considerable knowledge of the lower atmosphere and it is clear that even the professional meteorologists whom I have taken flying are really not aware of just how subtle the air motions are.

When asked where in the world I would most like to fly cross-country, the answer is in the UK. Quite simply this is because it is not a forgone conclusion that any task will be successful without taking appropriate care and it is usually a dynamic game of chess. Every 50km down track requires a quick check that the situation has not changed, yet often it has. Commonly, another reading of the sky is required and a new plan is necessary. In short, you need a full bag of tools. At the end of the day we simply fly in and have to interpret the sky we see ahead. Practical training tasks, often with patience, should result in your progress giving you many adventures and memorable moments. These should be just around the corner and not, as it has been for many of us, years in the making.

Photo 16.4 The author's syndicate partner, Angus Watson, offering congratulations after a 762km, 9 hour 40 minute flight in May 2013.

Glossary

AAT	**A**ssigned **A**rea **T**ask. This is a task around pilot-selected points within prescribed areas, in order. In competitions, a designated time is set which will penalise competitors racing for a shorter period.
agl	**A**bove **G**round **L**evel. Height in feet above ground level.
amsl	**A**bove **M**ean **S**ea **L**evel. Height in feet above mean sea level.
AoA	**A**ngle **of A**ttack. The acute angle between the chord of an aircraft wing or other aerofoil and the direction of the relative wind.
AoB	**A**ngle **of B**ank. The angle at which the glider is banked away from wings level.
ASI	**A**ir **S**peed **I**ndicator. An instrument to indicate the speed at which the glider is travelling through the air.
Benefit band	The area of a thermal which if you transit through you will get a net gain of energy.
BGA	**B**ritish **G**liding **A**ssociation.
CFI	**C**hief **F**lying **I**nstructor-they who must be obeyed.
DHT	**D**istance **H**andicap **T**ask. A task with fixed turning points incorporating variable barrels to allow lower performance gliders to turn short of these turning points, depending on the glider type handicap.
Dolphin	A technique to extract the greatest efficiency from the vertical air movements.
EFIS	Electronic Flight Instrument System. An instrument display system in which the display technology used is electronic rather than electromechanical.
FAI	**F**édération **A**éronautique **I**nternationale.
FLARM®	An electronic collision warning system which uses GPS. The names derives from **F**light A**larm**.
Gas Laws	The physical laws describing the behaviour of gases under various conditions, for example Boyle's Law, Avogadro's Law etc.
IAS	**I**ndicated **A**ir **S**peed. The airspeed read directly from the airspeed indicator on an aircraft, driven by the pitot-static system.
LCD	**L**iquid **C**rystal **D**isplay. This is a flat panel, electronic visual display, or video display that uses the light modulating properties of liquid crystals.
LDD	**L**ift **D**ependant **D**rag. This is a drag force that occurs whenever a moving object redirects the airflow around it to produce lift.

Leech	A glider pilot who achieves good cross country speeds in competitions by following others.
MacCready	Paul MacCready devised the MacCready Theory on the correct speed to fly a glider depending on conditions and based on the glider's rate of sink at different airspeeds. Glider pilots still use the "MacCready speed ring" (fitted around the variometer).
NOTAM	Notice to Airmen. This is a procedure for advising pilots of various restrictions, such as danger areas, airfield opening times etc.
PV/T	Pressure multiplied by Volume divided by Temperature in degrees Kelvin.
QFE	Airfield Surface Pressure. QFE is the barometric altimeter setting that causes an altimeter to read zero when at the reference datum of a particular airfield (in practice, the reference datum is either an airfield centre or a runway threshold).
QNH	Equivalent Mean Sea Level Pressure. QNH is the barometric altimeter setting that causes an altimeter to read airfield elevation above mean sea level when on the airfield.
RASP	**R**egional **A**tmospheric **S**oaring **P**redictor. This weather forecasting was developed by Glendening (Dr Jack), an American atmospheric scientist and glider pilot. The UK version of RASP is run and maintained by Paul Scorer at Leeds Metropolitan University.
RoD	**R**ate **o**f **D**escent. The rate of decrease in altitude or height is referred to as the rate of descent or sink rate. In gliders it is commonly measured in knots or metres per second.
SC	**S**peed **C**ommand. A setting on a variometer which gives fly faster or fly slower indications.
SPINE	**S**oaring **P**ilot's **I**ntelligent **N**OTAMs **E**ditor. Soaring Pilot Information—a tool to view airspace and NOTAMs on an electronic map.
TAS	**T**rue **A**ir **S**peed. This is the speed of a glider relative to the air mass in which it is flying.
TE	**T**otal **E**nergy. A variometer which indicates the total change in energy experienced by the glider, including both altitude and speed.
TP	**T**urn **P**oint. A specific point on the ground.
VNE	**V**elocity **N**ever **E**xceed. The maximum speed of a glider, never to be exceeded.
WULF	**W**ater/**U**ndercarriage/**L**oose Articles/**F**lap. This is a before landing checks mnemonic.
ZLD	**Z**ero **L**ift **D**rag. This is the drag that is generated due to profile, surface friction and interference drag. These values change with speed, and flying altitude.

Figures

Tables

Acknowledgements

A special note of thanks to the following people:

- ► My long-suffering crewman John McAulay
- ► Tony Cronshaw
- ► Steve Longland
- ► Martin Goodwill
- ► Roger Morgan
- ► Dave Scott
- ► Angus Watson
- ► Miriam Watson
- ► Simon Atack

Index